EUROPE AND THE FRENCH IMPERIUM

1799-1814

harper 🔥 torchbooks

*A reference-list of Harper Torchbooks, classified
by subjects, is printed at the end of this volume.*

THE RISE OF MODERN EUROPE

Edited by WILLIAM L. LANGER
Harvard University

* *In preparation*

EUROPE AND THE FRENCH IMPERIUM

1799-1814

BY GEOFFREY BRUUN

HARPER TORCHBOOKS THE UNIVERSITY LIBRARY

HARPER & ROW, PUBLISHERS , New York

To

GRETL AND OLGA

Arcadians both

EUROPE AND THE FRENCH IMPERIUM

Copyright, 1938, by Harper & Row, Publishers, Incorporated
Printed in the United States of America.

This book was originally published in 1938 by Harper & Brothers in The Rise of Modern Europe series edited by William L. Langer.

First HARPER TORCHBOOK edition published 1963 by Harper & Row, Publishers, Incorporated, New York, Evanston, and London.

Third Printing   December 1965

TABLE OF CONTENTS

CONTENTS

LIST OF ILLUSTRATIONS

The illustrations, grouped in a separate section, will be found following page 144.

MAPS

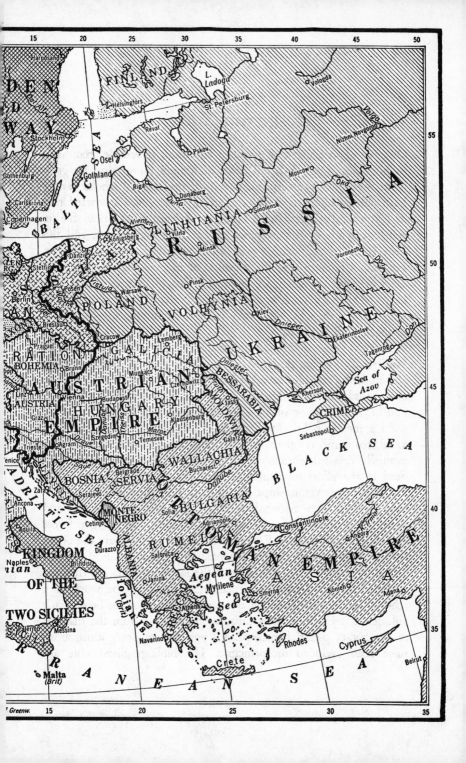

INTRODUCTION

Our age of specialization produces an almost incredible amount of monographic research in all fields of human knowledge. So great is the mass of this material that even the professional scholar cannot keep abreast of the contributions in anything but a restricted part of his general subject. In all branches of learning the need for intelligent synthesis is now more urgent than ever before, and this need is felt by the layman even more acutely than by the scholar. He cannot hope to read the products of microscopic research or to keep up with the changing interpretations of experts, unless new knowledge and new viewpoints are made accessible to him by those who make it their business to be informed and who are competent to speak with authority.

These volumes, published under the general title of *The Rise of Modern Europe* are designed primarily to give the general reader and student a reliable survey of European history written by experts in various branches of that vast subject. In consonance with the current broad conception of the scope of history, they attempt to go beyond a merely political-military narrative, and to lay stress upon social, economic, religious, scientific and artistic developments. The minutely detailed, chronological approach is to some extent sacrificed in the effort to emphasize the dominant factors and to set forth their interrelationships. At the same time the division of European history into national histories has been abandoned and wherever possible attention has been focussed upon larger forces common to the whole of European civilization. These are the broad lines on which this history as a whole has been laid out. The individual volumes are integral parts of the larger scheme, but they are intended also to stand as independent units, each the work of a scholar well qualified to treat the period covered by his book. Each volume contains about fifty illustrations selected from the mass of contemporary pictorial material. All non-contemporary illustrations have been excluded on principle. The bibliographical note appended to each volume is designed to facilitate further study of special aspects touched upon in the text. In general every effort has been made to give the reader a clear idea of the main movements in European history, to embody the monographic contributions of research workers, and to present the material in a forceful and vivid manner.

For more than a century there has been an uninterrupted outpouring of books on Napoleon. His career has fascinated one generation after another and there is as yet no indication of any falling off of general interest. As a man, the great conqueror has been viewed from almost every conceivable angle, admiringly by most writers, critically by many others. But as a rule Napoleon has been approached biographically. There has been rather little study of the actual organization of his régime in France and even less effort to see the French imperium as a phase of general European history. This is exactly what Professor Bruun has attempted to do in the present volume. His clear analysis of the Napoleonic system and its working, his incisive discussion of what it meant to Europe and how Europe reacted to it, and his general estimate of these fifteen years of revolutionary change should be of the greatest interest to any thoughtful person in these days when in many parts of Europe democratic government has been discarded and men have once again entrusted their fate to dictators.

WILLIAM L. LANGER

PREFACE

IF THIS survey of European developments during the period of the French ascendency under Napoleon is to be classified at all it will be found to fall in most readily, I think, with the school of interpretation associated with the name of Albert Sorel. The Napoleonic empire was an anomaly in a continental society already sundered and diversified by nationalist traditions, and the restoration of a balance of power among the nation-states is viewed here as a more or less predictable resolution of an abnormal situation. A secondary thesis which may be traced in the following chapters is the assumption that throughout the revolutionary era political thought and practice were complicated by an unresolved dichotomy. Eighteenth-century critics had stressed the desirability of restricting the powers of the government in the interest of individual liberty, while at the same time they recognized the necessity of regulating the activities of the individual in the interest of more effective government. The first ideal found its most vigorous expression in the destructive and egalitarian legislation of the revolutionary assemblies, the second in the efficient despotism of the Empire. How practical and thoughtful men of that day sought to reconcile the contradictions implicit in these twin ideals is an issue of more than local or temporary significance, and this must serve as an excuse if the problem intrudes itself unduly in the present narrative.

To thank by name the many colleagues upon whose patience and specialized knowledge I have drawn in preparing this volume is not possible in a limited space, and I must also forego the pleasure of acknowledging individually the many courtesies extended to me by officials in the libraries and museums to which I have applied. Every page which follows bears witness to this generous collaboration, and serves to remind me that the only portions of the book in which I have an undivided equity are the failings and the mistakes. These, thanks to the assistance which I enjoyed in the typing of the manuscript, to the vigilance of friends who read various chapters in proof, and particularly to Professor W. L. Langer's unstinted help and inspiring criticism, are of a less frequent and less serious nature than I would otherwise have to blush for. The time-consuming labors of typing, correcting and indexing have been speeded for me by the blithe and tireless coöperation of Margarete Hill Bruun and Phyllis Planta.

GEOFFREY BRUUN

BROOKLYN, N. Y.
February, 1938

Chapter One

PRELUDE TO CÆSARISM

I. INTRODUCTION

ON DECEMBER 25, 1799, when Napoleon Bonaparte assumed his official duties as First Consul of the French Republic, the officer of the day reported to inquire the new password for the consular guard. *"Frédéric II,"* was the brief response, *"et Dugommier."* Observers curious to forecast the guiding principles of the new régime might have found something to ponder in this phrase, which linked the name of the great Frederick, most famous enlightened despot of the eighteenth century, with that of Dugommier, an obscure but valiant general of the French revolutionary armies. The spirit of enlightened autocracy, combined with the spirit of revolutionary zeal, were to be the twin arbiters of a new France. With the histrionic touch characteristic of him, General Bonaparte had coined the watchword, not of a day, but of an epoch.

The major misconception which has distorted the epic of Napoleon is the impression that his advent to power was essentially a dramatic reversal, which turned back the tide of democracy and diverted the predestined course of the revolutionary torrent. That this Corsican liberticide could destroy a republic and substitute an empire, seemingly at will, has been seized upon by posterity as the outstanding proof of his arrogant genius. To reduce his career to logical dimensions, to appreciate how largely it was a fulfillment rather than a miscarriage of the reform program, it is necessary to forget the eighteenth century as the seedtime of political democracy and remember it as the golden era of the princely despots, to recall how persistently the thinkers of that age concerned themselves with the idea of enlightened autocracy and how conscientiously they laid down the intellectual foundations of Cæsarism. Napoleon was, to a degree

I

perhaps undreamed of in their philosophy, the son of the *philosophes*, and it is difficult to read far in the political writings of the time without feeling how clearly the century prefigured him, how ineluctably in Vandal's phrase *l'idée a précédé l'homme*.[1]

All the reforming despots of the eighteenth century pursued, behind a façade of humanitarian pretexts, the same basic program of administrative consolidation. The success achieved by Frederick the Great in raising the military prestige and stimulating the economic development of Prussia provided the most notable illustration of this policy, but the same ideals inspired the precipitate decrees of Joseph II in Austria, the cautious innovations of Charles III of Spain, the paper projects of Catherine the Great of Russia and the complex program pursued by Gustavus III in Sweden. Military preparedness and economic self-sufficiency were the cardinal principles guiding the royal reformers, but they also shared a common desire to substitute a unified system of law for the juristic chaos inherited from earlier centuries, to eliminate the resistance and confusion offered by guilds, corporations, provincial estates and relics of feudatory institutions, and to transform their inchoate possessions into centralized states dominated by despotic governments of unparalleled efficiency and vigor. In crowning the work of the Revolution by organizing a government of this type in France, Napoleon obeyed the most powerful political tradition of the age, a mandate more general, more widely endorsed, and more pressing than the demand for social equality or democratic institutions. Read in this light, the significance of his career is seen to lie, not in the ten years of revolutionary turmoil from which he sprang, but in the whole century which produced him. If Europe in the revolutionary age may be thought of as dominated by one nearly universal mood, that mood was an intense aspiration for order. The privileged and the unprivileged classes, philosophers, peasants, democrats, and despots all paid homage to this ideal. Napoleon lent his name to an epoch because he symbolized reason enthroned, because he was the philosopher-prince who gave to the dominant aspiration of the age its most typical, most resolute, and most triumphant expression.

[1] A. Vandal, *L'Avènement de Bonaparte*, I (Paris, 1911), iii.

II. THE HERITAGE OF PHILOSOPHY

To the student accustomed to think of the eighteenth-century *philosophes* as heralds of the French Revolution, it must always prove a disappointment to realize how ambiguously they announced it. These knights of the pen, from Montesquieu to Turgot, whose criticism helped to dissolve the foundations of the old régime, were themselves no friends of revolution or of democracy. The ideal at which they aimed was a more rational order of society; but their remedy for the evils of despotism was, in general, more despotism, and their solution for the problems of an increasingly dynamic age was to make social institutions more stable and more static. A violent upheaval, factious assemblies, and mob rule had no part in their program, for they were more inclined to put their trust in the wisdom of princes than in the deliberations of parliaments. Because their agitation hastened a revolution which few of them foresaw and fewer would have applauded, they have been extravagantly honored by liberal historians. But these historians have not always felt it necessary to point out that the most logical fulfillment of the *philosophes'* ideals was not the republicanism of the Jacobin commonwealth, but the despotism of the First Empire.

The central clue to the reform program of the philosophers was their faith in natural law. Mankind, they agreed, stood on the threshold of a new and glorious era. All that was needed to unlock the millennium was a supreme legislator, a Euclid of the social sciences, who would discover and formulate the natural principles of social harmony. The mathematical generalizations which formed the ground plan of physics and astronomy had been propounded by a few bold thinkers, and it seemed a reasonable surmise that the fundamental laws of human society would likewise be discovered by some inspired genius rather than by a parliamentary assembly. This optimistic faith that a rational constitution for society might shortly be comprehended and codified was not confined to philosophical circles in France, it was the common property of almost all eighteenth-century thinkers. Even Immanuel Kant gave to the sanguine quest the imprimatur of his cautious approval as early as 1784 in his *Idea of a Universal History on a Cosmo-Political Plan*:

We will see if we can succeed in finding the cipher [to such a universal ground-plan for society] and then leave it to Nature to produce the man who can solve it. So, once, she brought forth a Kepler, who reduced the excentric orbits of the planets to an orderly formula in unexpected fashion, and a Newton who clarified the universal principles governing the natural order.

Once a legislator of outstanding genius had rationalized human institutions, it followed that each man would respect them because they would be in harmony with his reason and his instincts. In yielding obedience he would achieve complete liberty, for he would be responding to a categorical imperative, or, as Rousseau had expressed it, he would be identifying his individual volition with the general will. This concept of perfect liberty as the product of perfect laws was one of the finest flowers of eighteenth-century rationalism, but it is important to note that such laws could be introduced quite as easily by a despot as by a democratic assembly. The prayer attributed to Turgot in 1774, "Give me five years of despotism and France shall be free," expressed a hope which at the time few people considered paradoxical. The demand for liberty in the age of enlightenment did not necessarily imply a demand for popular government, however frequently later writers may have chosen to ignore the distinction.

A second possible misconception against which it is well to guard when considering the arguments of the *philosophes* concerns their use of the term *republic*. It is the modern habit to classify governments by their external form, but the political thinkers of the age of reason were interested in the functions of the ideal state rather than in its structure.[2] A republic, to them, meant nothing much more specific than a well-governed commonwealth, and their use of such phrases as "republican monarchy" and "monarchical democracy" suggests the fluidity of their political terminology. "I give the name *Republic* to every state that is governed by laws," affirmed Rousseau, "no matter what its form of administration may be. . . ."[3] The distinguishing characteristic of a republican society was then considered

---

[2] R. Soltau, *French Political Thought in the Nineteenth Century* (New Haven, 1931), Introd., xvii-xxviii.

[3] J.-J. Rousseau, *The Social Contract*, ed. by G. D. H. Cole (London, 1913), part II, chap. 6.

to be a certain health and good condition of the body politic, not the existence of any specific electoral machinery for assuring the primacy of the popular will. How such imprecision in the use of terms might facilitate the transition to a dictatorship is evident enough. Napoleon was able to insist, without inviting serious contradiction, that with the establishment of the consular régime "the Revolution was grounded upon the principles which had inspired it." Even the constitution of the Empire opened with the propitiatory phrase, "The government of the Republic is confided to an emperor," and the imperial coinage bore for several years the ambiguous superscription *République Française: Napoléon Empereur*.

The heritage of eighteenth-century philosophy thus aided in two respects the realization of Napoleon's projects for personal rule. By stressing the benefits which a genius on a throne might introduce, the political writers had popularized the idea of enlightened despotism. By leaving the ideal form of government undefined they made it possible for Napoleon to unite the republican and monarchical traditions in a workable formula of democratic despotism. It is easy, however, to overemphasize the ideological element in revolutionary politics. Fundamentally and practically Napoleon's popularity rested upon the fact that he rescued France from social demoralization and foreign threats. To the generation which welcomed his advent to power his régime represented the close of a dangerous experiment, a return to order and stability after a decade of perilous opportunism and incertitude.

III. THE REVOLUTIONARY DEVIATION

The first French Republic, proclaimed in 1792, was a stepchild of the Revolution, ushered in, *faute de mieux,* after the collapse of the monarchy. Even its most devoted protagonists could not deny that its birth was inauspicious. For the Revolution had supposedly ended with the establishment of a responsible monarchy under the constitution of 1791, and French public opinion was unprepared for the critical events which followed—for the outbreak of the foreign war in March, 1792, the destruction of the throne in August, the proclamation of a republic in September, and the execution of Louis XVI in January, 1793. From the outset the republican experiment was marked by violence and uncertainty. Frenchmen felt with justice that they had been hurled, against their better judgment, down an unknown road. However resolutely they might seek to persuade themselves that it was the most logical road to that regenerated society of which they dreamed, they were troubled by the knowledge that it was an unintended choice, an unpremeditated deviation. Even revolutionists have their traditions. The French people had been ready, before 1789, to acquiesce in a sharp break with the past, but they expected the reforms to follow a recognizable pattern. By 1793 all but an intoxicated minority were secretly dismayed at the extremities to which they had been driven, the thoroughness with which they had broken up the roads behind them.

Assailed by the armies of the First Coalition, the new republic defended itself in 1793 and 1794 with remarkable energy, and turned a defensive into an offensive war. By 1795 France was able to conclude a favorable peace with Prussia and Spain, and the Austrian armies were hesitating. But military success abroad could not cure disorder at home. The government of France was still vested in the national convention, which had been elected after the fall of the throne in 1792, and the nation was impatient to see this temporary or "revolutionary" government supplanted by a constitutional régime based upon "organic laws." To meet this demand the convention drafted the constitution of the year III (1795) and submitted it to the nation, which, voting on terms that approximated universal manhood suffrage, accepted it by a vote officially announced as 1,057,590 to 49,977. This charter, which was to form the basic law of France for the next four years, marked the beginning of a reaction from the democratic ideals of 1793. It provided for two chambers instead of one, vested the executive power in a committee of five directors, and organized the electoral machinery in such a way that it assured the political supremacy of the bourgeoisie. Although a majority of the voters ignored the plebiscite, and there are some evidences of official coercion, the acceptance of this constitution by a majority of more than 20 to 1 suggests that the French electors were prepared to sacrifice the ideal of democracy for a promise of peace and stability, a truth which the Napoleonic plebiscites demonstrated still more clearly a few years later.[4]

Only a popular and unified administration could have concluded the foreign war advantageously and repaired the internal evils fostered by six years of revolution, and the Directory was neither popular nor unified. Admirers of Bonaparte have found it convenient to stress the corruption and incompetence of the régime which he helped to overthrow in 1799, but the men who governed France under the Directory were more cynical than corrupt, more helpless than incompetent. They represented an oligarchy, of which the ex-members of the national convention formed the core. These administrators, who had saved France and the Revolution by their terrible decrees in the torment of 1793 and 1794, had earned the hatred of a great part of the nation which they had saved, and they feared to lay aside the shield of office and expose themselves to reprisals. Their determination to maintain control of the government led them to insist in 1795 that two-thirds of the deputies chosen for the new chambers (the council of ancients and the council of five hundred) must be ex-members of the convention. They justified this violation of the popular will on the ground that it was necessary in order to safeguard the Republic from a royalist reaction; when the Parisians rose in armed protest, the expiring convention crushed the insurrection with the aid of General Bonaparte's cannon (October 5, 1795). Three weeks after this bloodshed of Vendémiaire the new government of the Directory was installed. The "perpetuals," as the disgusted nation dubbed the 483 *conventionnels* who continued in office, had proved that they were prepared to use political chicanery or military force to keep themselves in power.

The French people were ready to endorse any government which proved that it could assure genuine peace and stability, but the Directory was condemned to betray their hopes. The executive committee, continually at odds with the legislative chambers, followed a policy of trimming, and used its control of the troops to extricate itself from successive crises. All the elections, *coups d'état*, proscriptions, and changes in the directorial personnel during the years 1795-

[4] For an estimate of the work of the Directory (1795-1799) consult the preceding volume in this series, C. Brinton, *A Decade of Revolution* (New York, 1934), 212-245.

1799 failed to solve the administrative deadlock. Although some salutary and constructive reforms were attempted (notably the effort to reëstablish a stable currency), they were never very successful and almost always unpopular. From month to month Frenchmen grew more disillusioned with the Revolution and with the government which it had spawned, more desirous of the restoration of a durable peace and a stable régime at whatever cost.

A victorious peace with Europe would have appeased the nation, but in foreign as in domestic affairs the Directory pursued a contradictory policy. Dependent upon army support, and upon the indemnities levied on conquered provinces (Bonaparte's first Italian campaign alone brought in 80,000,000 livres from the Italian states),[5] the directors hesitated to end the war. When the peace party in the legislature threatened to gain the upper hand, three of the directors, Barras, Rewbell, and La Revellière, carried through a *coup* with military aid and proscribed their opponents. From Italy, Bonaparte congratulated the triumvirs on their stroke and assured them that he had 100,000 soldiers who would compel respect for their decrees.[6] This *coup d'état* of Fructidor 18 (September 4, 1797) marked a triumph for the groups which favored a war of propaganda and annexation beyond the "natural limits" of France, the Rhine, the Alps, and the Pyrenees. Bonaparte, through the fortunes which had enabled him to carve out a proconsulship in Italy, was allied with the party of expansionists. Their resumption of a policy of aggression, at a moment when the French Republic had come to terms with all its adversaries except Great Britain, postponed the hope of a general settlement and revived the apprehensions of the conservative monarchies. The crystallization of the Second Coalition a year later was a logical and predictable result.

In 1798, while Bonaparte led an expedition to Egypt, Austria, Russia, and Great Britain united their energies for a new campaign against France. By the spring of 1799 the French armies had been defeated in the Germanies and all but driven from Italy. At Paris these reverses completed the ruin of the Directory. After antagonizing both the left and the right wing of the legislature by its

[5] A. Meynier, *Les coups d'état du Directoire*, II (Paris, 1928), 178.
[6] *Correspondance de Napoléon Ier Publiée par ordre de l'empereur Napoléon III.* 32 vols. (Paris, 1858-70), III, 289. No. 2188.

coups and proscriptions, the executive committee proceeded to alienate its last and most indispensable allies, the army generals, by an honest but imprudent attempt to curb their exactions. Without their support, backed up by the bayonets of the republican armies, the directors were powerless and vulnerable. Seizing this opportunity to assert the independence of the legislature, the councils reconstructed the executive committee, reduced it to a subordinate position, and proclaimed their intention of saving the Republic. Jacobins in the Five Hundred clamored for a new committee of public safety, levied a forced loan of 100,000,000 livres on the rich, and enacted a law of hostages which struck at counter-revolutionaries through their innocent relatives. But Frenchmen still remembered the first reign of terror too vividly to endure a second. The French armies were already rallying after their first reverses, and the decline of the military threat from without in the summer of 1799 doomed the Jacobin offensive within. A "Party of Order," representing bourgeois republican sentiments, resumed its ascendency, and with the cautious Siéyès at its head cast about for the means to revise the faulty constitution and reconstruct the shattered executive. An army general was indispensable to the "organizers" in the execution of their plan, and Siéyès' choice fell first upon the young and popular Joubert, who was killed at Novi in August. Jacobin schemers, likewise alert to the political drift, plotted to revise the constitution through a leftist *coup*, and sought to enlist Bernadotte as their military figurehead; but he hesitated and let slip the chance.[7] The "organizers" were still looking for a general who would collaborate with them in the task of political reconstruction when Bonaparte, having left his marooned army to waste away in Egypt, landed at Fréjus on October 9, 1799. By the 16th he was in Paris.

IV. THE SEARCH FOR STABILITY

What Frenchmen desired in 1799 was a government strong enough to guard the Republic against a hostile Europe, a legitimate aspiration which had become confused in the popular mind with the

[7] E. Achorn, "Bernadotte or Bonaparte?" *The Journal of Modern History*, I (1929), 378-399.

preservation of French influence in Belgium, Holland, Switzerland, and Italy. They also desired that the new régime should maintain civil equality. Particular groups—soldiers, speculators, emancipated peasants, purchasers of national lands, regicides and others, who had supported the Revolution and might suffer by a royalist reaction—wanted protection and immunity. Because the tradition of a centralized despotism was still strong in France and parliamentary government, as practiced under the Republic, had been discredited by frequent crises, proscriptions, and factional strife, popular sentiment favored the restoration of a strong executive control as the most certain guarantee of peace and security. The moment was ripe for an act of administrative consolidation, and Siéyès and his followers were prepared to profit by the opportunity to perpetuate their ascendency.

The appearance on the scene at this juncture of the most successful and most popular of the republican generals helped to precipitate a decision. Within two weeks Siéyès and Bonaparte, the man of the pen and the man of the sword, had joined forces. Napoleon's brother Lucien, president of the council of five hundred, and Talleyrand, who hoped to regain the portfolio of foreign affairs, acted as intermediaries, and the conspiracy was revealed in varying degree to fifty or sixty associates.[8] From the first conferences, Bonaparte's breadth of view was as surprising as his desire for caution. He insisted that any revision of the constitution must be submitted to the nation for approval, and he advised the lawyers to provide the *coup* with the necessary gloss of constitutionality. As worked out in the first week of November, the plan called for the deliberate precipitation of a political crisis in order to open the way for the "organizers" to take control. On Brumaire 18 (November 9) the council of ancients, where Siéyès had a strong following, was informed that a Jacobin plot had been uncovered in Paris, and was persuaded to exercise its constitutional prerogative and transfer the legislative body to Saint-Cloud for greater security. A second decree introduced by the conspirators named General Bonaparte commander of the armed forces of the capital and of the seventeenth

[8] The number initiated into the secret has been variously estimated. Etienne-Denis, Duc Pasquier, placed it as high as 150. *Memoirs*, trans. by C. E. Roche, 2 vols. (New York, 1893), I, 153.

military district. To compel a reconstruction of the executive committee Siéyès and his henchman, Roger-Ducos, then resigned from
the Directory, and Barras was persuaded to do likewise, leaving
the remaining directors, Gohier and Moulins, powerless. The *coup*
was to be consummated when the two councils met at Saint-Cloud,
by inviting the legislators to appoint a provisional government
under three consuls, Siéyès, Ducos, and Bonaparte, who would collaborate with leading members of the councils in preparing a new
constitution.

At Saint-Cloud, on November 10 (Brumaire 19), the plan very
nearly miscarried. Jacobin republicans in the council of five hundred, suspicious of Bonaparte's ambitions, prepared to declare him
outlawed. The traditional accounts of that dramatic day invariably
stress the manner in which Napoleon and his brother appealed to
the troops, which dispersed the council of five hundred by force, a
measure adopted by the conspirators reluctantly and as a last resort. This show of bayonets has tended to obscure the more significant truth that the *coup d'état* of Brumaire was primarily a moral
revolution. Napoleon stated the issue clearly when he announced
to his soldiers that France was weary of misgovernment. The profound and widespread aspiration for order which had stirred the
French people in 1789[9] still remained unsatisfied, and had, indeed,
been quickened by the pseudo-anarchy of the revolutionary epoch.
Brumaire represented a battle of prestige between the constitutional-
ists, who stood by an inept and discredited government, and the
organizers who wished to remodel that government along more
stable and conservative lines. It was Bonaparte's fortune, as a
symbol of the most efficient and most popular institution of the
nation, the republican army, to carry the day for the organizers.
His clear perception of the issue, and of the decisive rôle which circumstances had forced upon him, encouraged him to claim the
lead in a project undertaken by others, a project in which he had
been expected to remain the instrument and possibly the dupe of
the politicians.

The provisional government established in the evening of Bru-

[9] E. Champion, *La France d'après les cahiers de 1789* (Paris, 1897), 29-31; B. Hyslop,
A Guide to the General Cahiers of 1789 (New York, 1936), 104-105.

maire 19 was illegal, and no editing of the proceedings could disguise this fact. The decrees which entrusted the executive power to Siéyès, Roger-Ducos and Bonaparte, as consuls, and appointed two legislative commissions of twenty-five members each to assist them, were voted by a minority in the council of ancients and by less than thirty members of the council of five hundred.[10] Paris, and France, permitted this small group to usurp the direction of affairs because its spokesmen pledged themselves to complete the Tennis Court Oath of ten years earlier, to found the administration upon organic statutes and give the nation a government of laws, not of men. The provisional government was obligated to submit a permanent constitution to the French people for their approval within three months, but the consuls were empowered to attack without delay the five major problems which had to be solved before France could enjoy tranquillity. If the group which had seized power could, in addition to drafting a satisfactory constitution, end the civil war in the Vendée, reduce the national finances to order, codify the revolutionary legislation, and conclude an honorable peace with Europe, thirty million French citizens were ready to unite in gratitude and loyalty to sustain it. The history of the Consulate in France is, in brief, the resolution of these five problems. To them Bonaparte added a sixth, of which the proclamation of Brumaire 19 and the constitution of the year VIII had made no mention. The settlement of the religious discord, provided by the concordat of 1801 and by the law for the regulation of cults (1802), was to be his most personal and most courageous contribution to the pacification of France.

Bonaparte climbed to office on the shoulders of the oligarchs and made them the pillars of his power, but he never freed himself from his obligation to them. He transformed them, in Nodier's contemptuous phrase, into a "mercenary corps of elevated slaves who reacted with all the weight of their moral degradation upon the inert and servile masses,"[11] but he continued to pay them tribute

[10] P. B. Buchez and P. C. Roux, *Histoire parlementaire de la Révolution française ou journal des assemblées nationales, 1789-1815,* 40 vols. (Paris, 1834-38), XXXVIII, 227-229.

[11] C. Nodier, *Souvenirs, épisodes et portraits,* 2 vols. (Paris, N.D.) 201-203.

and he never bound them to him by anything more idealistic than their hopes and fears. In contrast, the "servile masses," which he bound to himself by no special privileges, but only by the boon of an orderly and vigorous government, offered him in return a genuine gratitude and a patient loyalty. Devotion, like happiness, varies in proportion to humility, and the disinherited classes had never demanded much more from the Revolution than Napoleon was able to give them: a unified, orderly, and efficient administration. His destruction of representative institutions and his perversion of democracy aroused them to no protest, because they were prepared to concede, like loyal Fascists in the making, that effective government is more important than popular representation.[12]

The French people were waiting for a leader of talent and decision, and they had abandoned hope of finding one among the political residue of the revolutionary assemblies. Bonaparte's great advantage in 1799 was his lack of a political past. The politicians who planned to use him for their own ends failed to perceive how great an advantage this could be. The nineteenth Brumaire was for them a day of dupes in which they became the victims of their own vanity. Since the death of Robespierre the revolution had produced no leader of exceptional prestige, and the myopic schemers who believed themselves at the center of things were among the last to recognize the master when he appeared. Pasquier, who became chancellor under the Empire, admits in his memoirs that Bonaparte's dramatic return from Egypt excited no premonitory stir in the official world of Paris:

The effect produced on me by the knowledge of this fact, and on the greater number of those who received it simultaneously with me, was in no way proportional to the consequences which were to follow. . . . I state all this because a number of people, believing that they were adding to their hero's greatness, have since sought to present him as having been ardently and impatiently expected. . . . To my mind, Bonaparte appears far greater when he is thought of as arriving when no one expected him or dreamed of him, when he faced the disadvantages of a return which resembled a flight, when he triumphed

[12] G. de Ruggiero, *The History of European Liberalism*, translated by R. G. Collingwood (London, 1927), 84.

over the prejudices which this return raised against him, and when in the space of a month (*sic*) he laid hand on every form of power.[13]

To the French populace, however, and to more than one foreign observer, Bonaparte's sudden emergence seemed appropriate and logical. Five years earlier Catherine the Great of Russia had predicted that if France survived the agony of revolution the nation would fling itself into the arms of a strong man. The power and popularity of the army made any successful general a probable candidate, and Bonaparte stood out as the one army leader whose political and diplomatic gifts were equal to his military talents. His Italian victories of 1796-1797, and the brochures and prints which advertised them in all the shop windows, had made his odd name and keen, saturnine features familiar to the Parisian crowds. Even in America an account of *The Campaign of General Buonaparte in Italy* found ready subscribers as early as June, 1798, and the fortunes of the Egyptian expedition were followed on both sides of the Atlantic with lively interest.[14] This Corsican youth of obscure origin, who, while still in his twenties, had confounded the most venerable strategists of Europe, outmatched the Vatican in diplomacy, and won election to the Institute as a scientist, stirred the popular imagination in that romantic age. The events of Brumaire turned the white spotlight of fame upon no unknown man. Even his domestic difficulties, which might easily have brought him ridicule, had helped to advertise him without seriously compromising his dignity. His ardent courtship and hasty marriage to Josephine Beauharnais before he left for the Italian campaign, the rumors of her infidelity to him while he was in Egypt, and his magnanimity on his return, provided a sentimental touch which pleased the taste of the time. The public prefers its heroes to reveal an occasional tincture of mortal frailty, and it fitted classical precedent that the darling of Mars should bow to the wiles of Venus.

[13] *Memoirs of Chancellor Pasquier*, trans. by C. E. Roche, 2 vols. (New York, 1893), I, 150-151.
[14] H. M. Jones and D. Aaron, "Notes on the Napoleonic Legend in America," *The Franco-American Review*, II (1937), 11.

Chapter Two

FRANCE AND THE CONSULATE: THE RESTORATION OF ORDER AND AUTHORITY (1799-1804)

I. THE CONSTITUTION OF THE YEAR VIII

IN THE six weeks which followed the *coup d'état* of Brumaire, the "organizers" hammered out a new constitution for France. The debates were often tense and sometimes stormy, for it was no easy matter to effect a compromise between the conflicting aspirations of Siéyès and Bonaparte. As chief of the revolutionary oligarchy, Siéyès was concerned to seek for his followers that security, permanent political office, and adequate income which was the goal of their desires, but a goal few of them could hope to attain through the medium of a popular election. Bonaparte, with a political following smaller and far more nebulous, could best oppose Siéyès by putting himself forward as the spokesman of the nation confronting the spokesman of a faction. His ascendency in the political world was not gained easily; the strain under which he labored during the six weeks of the provisional consulate (November 10-December 25, 1799) almost undermined his health.[1] In the bargain which he sought to drive he used to the full the prestige with which his popularity invested him, for he knew that it rendered him indispensable to the discredited oligarchs. He made it clear to his associates that the price of his coöperation was the highest office they had to offer, and that in return he would allow Siéyès to find them positions of dignity and affluence under the new dispensation. To Bonaparte the power, to Siéyès the patronage.

On December 13th the constitutional debates ended, a draft revised under Bonaparte's direction was adopted, and the session closed with the election of three permanent consuls. The nominees,

---

[1] F. A. Aulard (ed.), *Registre des déliberations du Consulat Provisoire* (Paris, 1894), *passim*, reflects his cautious assumption of leadership.

15

Bonaparte, Cambacérès, and Lebrun, were proposed by Siéyès and endorsed unanimously, a consummation which clearly suggests pre-arrangement.[2] As First Consul, Bonaparte was to have at his right hand the able Cambacérès, an ex-regicide but a moderate-minded man of reputable character, whose legal training fitted him to assist in the codification of the laws. On his left, Bonaparte was to have Lebrun, a man already respected before 1789 for his literary efforts and his upright character. Lebrun's mild constitutional royalism was calculated to win confidence from the forces of the Right, and his knowledge of fiscal problems was to prove useful in reorganizing the insolvent treasury. Both men were well suited to discharge consultative rôles, for neither had the personality or the prestige to dispute the predominance of the First Consul.

That Siéyès and the *Brumairiens* regretted the necessity of confirming the general in power there can be little doubt. They found their consolation, however, in article XXIV of the constitution, which entrusted to Siéyès, Roger-Ducos, Cambacérès and Lebrun the privilege of naming a majority of the new senate.[3] This body, after expanding itself to the number of sixty by coöptation, was then to draw up a list of one hundred notables to form a tribunate, and a list of three hundred to form a legislative body. A senator's salary was to be 25,000 francs a year, a tribune's 15,000, a legislator's 10,000. In substance this placed Siéyès in a position to control the appointment of some 460 functionaries who would touch a combined yearly income of 6,000,000 francs. The oligarchs were in sight of a safe haven at last, but when the personnel of the new chambers was announced publicly, the journals voiced the disgust of the nation at finding over three hundred "perpetuals," ex-members of the council of ancients and the council of five hundred, still in office. Cupidity, combined with the desire for security and influence, was betraying the party of Brumaire into Bonaparte's hands. Siéyès, on the proposal of the provisional consuls, Bonaparte and Ducos, had been offered the estate of Crosne, valued at nearly half a million francs, and compromised himself by accepting this extravagant reward for his services.

---

[2] Vandal, *L'Avènement de Bonaparte*, I (Paris, 1911), 523.
[3] *Archives Parlementaires*, 2ᵉ série, I, 2.

The composition of the legislative bodies rendered them unpopular from the first, and weakened them in their efforts to curb the despotic temper of the First Consul. But the persistent misconception that the constitution of the year VIII consecrated a dictatorship at the outset must be classed with other Bonapartist myths. It perpetuated the division of powers between the executive and the legislature without achieving a stable balance between them. A First Consul, with two advisers, replaced the five directors and gained the important prerogative of initiating legislation. But the projects sponsored by the government had to be approved by the tribunate and then submitted to the legislative body, which decided by secret ballot whether they should become law. If the constitutionality of an act was in doubt, it was to be examined by the senate, which could sustain or abrogate it. As under the Directory, the executive appointed the ministers, but they were deprived of their former immunity, might be denounced by the tribunate, or sent before a special court by decree of the legislative body. The vexatious problem of the national budget was settled by a compromise. The government controlled the income and expenses of the state in accordance with an annual appropriation, and each minister was required to itemize his departmental expenditures. Thus the new constitution undoubtedly strengthened the executive, but it did not assure the First Consul that irresponsible authority which he desired to exercise. He anticipated the opening of the first legislative sessions in January, 1800, with some apprehension, convinced that he could not assure the superiority of the executive power without a struggle.

The national plebiscite, in which the French people approved the constitution by a vote officially announced as 3,011,007 *yeas* to 1,562 *noes*, fortified Bonaparte for the expected contest. For his name was in the charter, and the popular response made him, in a sense, the representative of the nation. The legislators nominated by Siéyès had not dared to risk, and could not have secured, such a vote of confidence. Their mandate from the people had lapsed and had not been specifically renewed. Although the constitution provided that the citizens of each commune should elect one-tenth of their number as a communal list, these notables of the commune to designate one-tenth of their number for a departmental list, and the departmental representatives to elect one-tenth of their body for the national list, there was no time to complete these elections before the new government was formed. In consequence, the members of the senate, tribunate and legislative body were nominated at discretion, and declared to be, by virtue of this nomination, members of the first national list. The whole project for the compilation of popular lists (which were, in point of fact, never completed) was a transparent device designed to preserve universal manhood suffrage in form while nullifying it in practice. The willingness with which the French people acquiesced in the deception confirms the impression, already suggested by the election of 1795, that they were ready to sacrifice democracy for the promise of stability.

In choosing his ministers and composing his council of state Bonaparte vindicated his boast that he "would not be the man of a party." As his minister of police he retained the adroit ex-terrorist, Fouché. Talleyrand accepted the portfolio of foreign affairs. Berthier, a meticulous and tireless organizer, directed the department of war, Gaudin that of finance, Abrial that of justice, and Forfait that of marine and colonies. The department of the interior was transferred to Lucien Bonaparte, completing the list of seven ministers. Significant, too, as an indication of Bonaparte's disregard of political antecedents, was the composition of the council of state. This executive cabinet of thirty members was to be the axis of his government, and to it he invited able men of all political colors from Jacobins to Royalists. General Brune, who had served with him in Italy, Boulay de la Meurthe, who had assisted in the *coup d'état*, the discreet and indefatigable Roederer, the ex-noble Champagny, all rubbed elbows in this workshop where the destinies of France were to be hammered out anew. At its first session (December 25, 1799), the council set an important precedent by restoring the rights of citizenship to the relatives of *émigrés* and to ex-nobles, thus rehabilitating an outcast class on the presumption that the laws against them had lapsed with the introduction of the new constitution. At the same session the council reasserted the complete religious freedom of all citizens, and reinvoked the decree of Prairial 11, of the year III, which left religious edifices at the disposal of the faithful.

In hastening through these decrees before the legislative councils assembled, Bonaparte made a personal bid for the attention and gratitude of the nation. The press, which had enjoyed almost complete freedom since the eighteenth Brumaire, reflected his popularity and urged him openly to override any obstacles set in his path by querulous legislators. When the councils assembled in January, the nucleus of a constitutional opposition speedily formed in the tribunate, and some members of the legislative body permitted themselves the luxury of criticizing the administration in their journals. Bonaparte wisely avoided any definitive test of strength which might, at this stage, have produced a deadlock. But he did not hesitate to silence the newspaper controversy by suppressing all but thirteen Parisian newspapers. In his most important project during these first weeks, the reorganization of local administrative units to bring them into harmony with the authoritarian ideal, he was able to win legislative approval. The law of Pluviôse 28 (February 17, 1800) replaced the elected boards and councils by a prefect for each department, a sub-prefect for each *arrondissement*, and a mayor for each commune. These officials were to be invested with their authority by the First Consul. The original list of prefects was compiled very largely by Lucien Bonaparte as minister of the interior, and the selections reflected the preference of the administration for men who had distinguished themselves by their probity, talent, and moderation. In attacking a second urgent problem, the suppression of the endemic warfare in the western departments, Bonaparte found the legislators equally obliging. Having obtained their permission to suspend constitutional guarantees in the afflicted areas, he was left free to utilize the full resources of the military arm, with results that proved speedy and permanent.

II. THE PACIFICATION OF THE WEST

Three times, during the first decade of the Revolution, civil war had swept like a recurrent fever through the Vendée and Brittany. The outbreak of 1793, which followed upon the downfall of the Girondists, was broken before the close of that year by the murderous methods of repression authorized by the committee of public safety. But hatred of the godless government which had executed their king, persecuted their priests, and conscripted their young men, lived on among the peasantry; and the royalist militia, though dispersed, was not disarmed. In 1795, in the face of new revolts, the convention entrusted the task of pacification to the firm but tactful Hoche, who recommended that the government promise freedom of worship and the abrogation of conscription to the disaffected departments. The *Chouan* chiefs accepted peace on these terms in April, the Vendéeans in May, and the West settled to an uneasy truce by the close of 1795.

In the summer of 1799 the law of hostages and the proclamation of compulsory military service incited the royalists to a new campaign. At least six rebel bands were soon under arms, from Normandy to Poitou, but as before they failed to unite or to maintain adequate discipline. The expiring Directory allowed General Hédouville, commanding the Army of England (as the Army of the West was grandiloquently termed) to treat with the leaders, who accepted an armistice on December 9th. Under the provisional Consulate the period of the armistice was extended to January 21, 1800. After December 25th, however, when Bonaparte assumed added authority as First Consul, the negotiations moved more briskly. He was determined to pacify the West in the shortest possible time, for he wished to free the republican divisions for a spring campaign against Austria. In seven weeks his resolute methods settled a problem which had troubled the Republic for seven years.

The revocation of the law of hostages (November 13th), the restoration of the rights of citizenship to the relatives of *émigrés* and ex-nobles, and the proclamation of religious liberty which the council of state issued December 25th, had softened the grievances of all but the most implacable of the insurgents. When the royalist agents, D'Andigné and Hyde de Neuville, held an interview with Bonaparte on December 27th, the First Consul made it clear that since France now possessed a government which all Frenchmen could trust, he would recognize no excuse for further resistance in the West. On the morrow the *Moniteur*[4] proclaimed a general amnesty for all rebels who surrendered within ten days, but declared

---

[4] *Moniteur,* 7 Nivôse, An VIII (December 28, 1799).

that those who failed to avail themselves of it would be hunted down as outlaws. Bonaparte's fear that Hédouville's temporizing might be mistaken for weakness led him to supersede that tactful negotiator and appoint Brune to command the Army of England. At the expiration of the days of grace, the soldiers of that army were charged in a special order to pursue the bandits without rest and without pity, until the last *Chouan* ally of England and of Austria had expiated his crimes against the fatherland.[5]

Wiser than their followers, and aware that they would be held to a sterner accounting, the insurgent leaders almost without exception advised capitulation. But their submission was delayed and Bonaparte, growing impatient, urged Brune to make a few examples by shooting rebels apprehended with arms in their hands. For another month, however, grace was extended to those fugitives who chose to surrender at discretion, the stubborn Breton, Georges Cadoudal, being one of the last to submit (February 14th). For Louis, Count de Frotté, whose good faith Bonaparte doubted, the story had a more tragic conclusion. At Alençon, whither he had come to treat under a safe conduct, Frotté was seized on February 15th, tried by a court-martial three days later, and shot with six of his companions. Minor conflicts of authority and confusion in the dispatches make it difficult to assign the blame for this breach of faith, but as Bonaparte had demanded some drastic examples and never rebuked the officers immediately responsible for this dishonorable act, history has held him accountable for it. In his defence it may be urged that he considered issues rather than men, that he was determined to make his government feared and respected throughout France, and that his measures were successful in bringing organized rebellion in the West to an end.

III. FISCAL REFORM

The intricate task of restoring the French finances to order had already been half accomplished when Napoleon came into power. The paper money issued by successive decrees of the revolutionary assemblies had fallen by 1796 to less than one-third of one per cent of its face value, while the amount in circulation had risen to

---

[5] E. Gabory, *Napoléon et la Vendée*, 4th ed. (Paris, 1932), 63.

something over forty billion livres. An attempt to achieve partial stabilization by substituting a different paper currency, the *mandats territoriaux*, resulted in further depreciation, and in May, 1797, the Directory reverted to a metallic currency and demonetized all *assignats* and *mandats* still outstanding. This step required courage, for it added to the unpopularity of the directorial régime, but it prepared the way for a restoration of the national credit.[6]

In dealing with its second major obligation, the public debt, the Directory pursued a similar but slightly less drastic policy. A decree of September 30, 1797, provided that owners of government bonds should receive two-thirds of the face value of their investment in the form of drafts payable to the bearer. For the remainder, known as the "Consolidated Third," they were offered new government bonds bearing interest at five per cent. As the drafts, like the currency, depreciated at once until they were almost worthless, this maneuver was equivalent to a repudiation of two-thirds of the public debt, a step which antagonized the *rentier* class and further discredited the government.

Even the "Consolidated Thirds," on which the interest was guaranteed, fell in 1799 to seven per cent of their nominal value on the exchange. Their rapid recovery after Brumaire, which carried them to 44 in 1800, has often been cited as evidence of the confidence which the consular régime inspired in financial circles. It is significant, however, that bankers were almost as reluctant to advance credit to the government of the Consulate, especially during its first months, as they had been to float loans for the bankrupt Directory. Gaudin, who accepted the post of minister of finance a few days after the *coup d'état*, found the treasury empty, and had difficulty raising even three millions for current expenses. So desperate was the situation that he thought of reverting to the foresworn expedient of a paper issue of sixty million livres secured against the unsold national lands.[7]

To obtain funds for the spring campaign of 1800 the government was forced to offer the French bankers five per cent monthly on advances, and to raise six million livres in Genoa and Hamburg.

[6] S. A. Falkner, *Das Papiergeld der französischen Revolution, 1789-1797.* (Munich, 1924). S. E. Harris, *The Assignats* (Cambridge, Mass., 1930).

[7] M. Marion, *Histoire financière de la France depuis 1715,* Vol. IV (Paris, 1921), 177.

Gaudin pressed for the imposition of indirect taxes to augment the revenue, but Bonaparte feared to provoke discontent by reviving imposts reminiscent of the *aides* and *gabelles* of the old régime. Politically as well as financially his administration was in a precarious state during these months of improvisation. The notion that Bonaparte's advent restored immediate order and confidence to French finance requires firm correction. Even in the days of his greatest popularity, after the Peace of Amiens in 1802, French consolidated government bonds which paid five per cent were quoted at 48 to 53, while the British *Consols*, at three per cent, fluctuated between 66 and 79.[8]

Gaudin's first reform, initiated before the close of the provisional Consulate, was to withdraw from local officials the power to apportion or to collect the national taxes, and to entrust this responsibility to agents of the central authority. The remarkable administrative centralization which was to distinguish the new government was thus first introduced in the domain of the treasury. A general director at Paris, deputy directors for each department, and inspectors and assessors in each commune assured the minister of finance undisputed control over the machinery of taxation. The tax rolls were audited and redressed, the rate of assessments regulated, a new land survey undertaken to simplify the task of the assessors, and the collection of rents and other receipts from the public domains entrusted to the national agents. With the functioning of the new system, the national revenue became more predictable and more adequate and the collection of the taxes less arbitrary.

To consolidate the public debt, Gaudin prepared to call in all the paper obligations of the government, the drafts for the two-thirds issued in 1797, outstanding bills of exchequer, warrants, vouchers, and requisitions, to assess them at a sum slightly above their depreciated market value, and to offer creditors in exchange consolidated government bonds at five per cent interest. The completion of this project required several years and resulted in a slight increase in the public debt, although the repurchase by the state of its own securities at a depreciated level was criticized by the creditors as a further partial repudiation. To promote public confidence in the

8 G. Lefebvre, *Napoléon* (Paris, 1935), 119.

consolidated five-per-cents, a *caisse d'amortissement* was established to guarantee the interest and to purchase the bonds on the bourse whenever the quoted value threatened to decline unduly.

During the first year of the Consulate the burden of interest charges and the liquidation of arrears absorbed more than half the national revenue, but by the year X (1801-1802) the budget was balanced at approximately 700,000,000 francs, an achievement rendered possible by the improvements in the tax system and the strict economy exercised in every department of administration. Yet even in this budget, probably the frankest issued during the Napoleonic régime, there were elements of deception and uncertainty. The extraordinary receipts, for instance, were credited as forming five per cent of the national revenue in the year X, but must have amounted to a much larger sum. No audit can now be made of the subsidies levied by the French government on the tributary states in that year, or exacted in the form of war indemnities. Paralleling the official record of receipts and expenditures there was an invisible budget, the condition of which was known only to the trusted advisers of the First Consul. The secrecy which veiled the sources of these private funds, and their arbitrary utilization, fed the inextinguishable distrust with which bankers and financiers viewed all Bonaparte's fiscal operations. In the sober judgment of Stourm, nothing that could be regarded as an exact budget, nothing that may be described as organized public credit, issued from Bonaparte's hands.[9]

To facilitate the payment of annuities and the discounting of government notes, the administration required the services of a banking institution, and this need led to the decree creating the Bank of France (February 13, 1800). The most reputable and successful of the Paris banks, the *Caisse des comptes courants*, was reconstructed, its capitalization increased from 5,000,000 to 30,000,000 francs, and its list of shareholders enlarged to include the First Consul, members of his family, and leading officers of state. Though it remained technically a private institution, the new bank enjoyed special privileges, carried government accounts, and cashed the coupons on treasury bonds. On April 14, 1803, a second reorganiza-

[9] R. Stourm, *Les finances du Consulat* (Paris, 1902), 352.

tion raised the capital stock to 45,000,000 francs and awarded the
bank the exclusive right to issue bank notes in Paris. It proved impossible, however, despite Napoleon's persuasion, to dispel the deep
distrust of paper transactions which prevailed in financial circles,
and French bankers continued to hinder the expansion of trade
by the extreme caution which they showed in discounting commercial paper. Partly to offset this disadvantage, the coinage was
standardized in March, 1803, and a decimal monetary system introduced on a bimetallic basis. The relation of gold to silver was
fixed at 1 to 15.5, but the lack of adequate supplies of specie continued to embarrass commercial operations.[10]

The need to increase the supply of precious metals, the desire to
enlarge the revenue derived from import duties, and the conviction
that a policy of protection would stimulate French manufacture,
combined from these earliest years to direct Bonaparte's thoughts
towards a form of modified mercantilism. His knowledge of political economy, for the most part second-hand and second-rate, was
ripened by the long duel with Great Britain. In the years after
Austerlitz his predilections were to bear their fateful fruit in the
grandiose ramifications of the Continental System.

IV. THE LEGAL CODES

In the reform program of the *philosophes* no point had been
more earnestly stressed than the need of replacing the chaotic mass
of inherited legislation by a simple and unified code. To the revolutionary ideologists the true legislator was a sort of Newton of the
social sciences, whose success was assured because he would not
make laws, but *discover* them. To suppose that Nature, or Nature's
God, could have provided majestic and inflexible regulations to
govern the stars in space, yet have left the affairs of men to chaos
seemed a pessimistic and inconsistent notion. The problem was to
discover by right reason the natural and fundamental axioms upon
which a just society should be based, and then to codify them in a
form so clear and laconic that the wayfaring man, though a fool,
might not err therein.[11] "Every political edict which is not based

---

[10] G. Ramon, *Histoire de la Banque de France* (Paris, 1929), 22-23.
[11] C. Becker, *The Heavenly City of the Eighteenth Century Philosophers* (New Haven,
1932), chap. II.

upon Nature is wrong," declared the doctrinaire Saint-Just in 1793. "I believe," he added, repeating the common revolutionary credo, "that if man be given laws which harmonize with the dictates of Nature and of his heart he will cease to be unhappy and corrupt."[12]

Although the abolition of ancient statutes and outworn institutions in the first years of the Revolution had cleared the ground, the legislative committees of the successive assemblies labored in vain to complete the ideal legal code so hopefully awaited. Slowly the realization spread that (as Edmund Burke was insisting) "the lines of morality are not like the ideal lines of mathematics." In theory it might appear reasonable and just to weaken family ties and parental authority in the sacred name of liberty, to lower the age of majority, decree the equal division of an estate among all the children, and elevate bastards to legal equality with legitimate offspring. In practice, however, such proposals, carried to their individualistic conclusion, threatened to produce a society of uncorrelated atoms, as Napoleon later complained. By 1795 the tide of opinion was deserting the pure philosophic concepts of liberty and equality. Under the Directory the legislators found it advisable to reknit family ties, reinforce parental discipline, and permit a testator to dispose of at least one-fourth of his estate at will. The judicial spirit was regaining its sway, particularly among those "organizers" who felt the need of restoring a greater degree of authority in government and stability in social relations.[13]

With the advent of Bonaparte the reversion towards authoritarianism received a powerful stimulus. In August, 1800, he entrusted the preparation of a civil code to a committee of four, Tronchet, Portalis, Bigot de Préameneu, and Maleville. Their draft, completed by the end of the year, was debated and amended by the council of state, with Bonaparte presiding at about half the sessions. The resulting code was the product of a double compromise, a compromise between doctrinaire aims and legal traditions, and a compromise between the written *droit romain* of the Midi and the Teutonic

[12] Louis Antoine de Saint-Just, *Œuvres complètes*, ed. by C. Vellay, 2 vols. (Paris, 1908), I, 419-420.

[13] P. Sagnac, *La législation civile de la Révolution française, 1789-1804* (Paris, 1898), 349. C. Brinton, *French Revolutionary Legislation on Illegitimacy* (Cambridge, Mass., 1936), offers a brief but brilliant analysis of the conflict between theory and practice on one aspect of revolutionary law.

droit coutumier of the northern provinces. In four important particulars the new code preserved the social aims of the Revolution, for it affirmed the equality of all citizens before the law, the right of the individual to choose his profession, the supremacy of the lay state, and the freedom of the individual conscience. But the concern which had been manifested earlier in the Revolution for the rights and liberties of minors and dependents was notably diminished. The wife was subordinated to the husband's authority and even her property was at his disposal. The father of a family regained the power to place an adolescent in confinement for a period not exceeding six months, and a testator could dispose at will of one-half or less of his estate, depending on the number of his children. Bastards were denied a claim to any part of their parents' inheritance unless they had been legally acknowledged, and even then their share was less than that of legitimate children. The retention of divorce by mutual consent, and of the practice of legal adoption, both of which Bonaparte advocated, have been cited as evidence that he sometimes yielded to private reasons in his decisions, but no proof that his personal marital problems influenced him at this juncture can be definitely adduced.

The civil code protected the interests of the new society, dominated by the propertied classes, which had risen to supremacy through the Revolution. As land was still the most important form of wealth, the regulations governing mortgages and liens, and the transfer or inheritance of landed estates, were traced in detail, but the sections covering the newer forms of industrial wealth were inadequate, and the attempt to fix a legal rate of interest reflected Napoleon's hostility towards the financiers. To the disinherited classes, the wage-earners and those without possessions, the code offered little save the guarantee of civil liberty. The commiseration so often expressed by the legislators of '93 for the "indigent patriots" had yielded to a callous indifference. The state assumed no responsibility towards the unemployed; workers were forbidden to organize for collective bargaining (law of April 12, 1803); the testimony of the employer was preferred to that of the worker in wage disputes. With the introduction of police regulations compelling each employee to carry a card relating his vocational vicis-

situdes, and the official comments thereon, the subjugation of the
working classes was assured.

Legislative opposition to the civil code delayed its promulgation
until 1804, and the supplementary compilations, begun during the
Consulate, were completed under the Empire. The code of civil
procedure (1806) revived in substance the court methods of the
old régime, but retained the provision, dear to the revolutionary
idealists with their faith in right reason, that litigants must make
a final effort at conciliation before the case opened. The code of
criminal procedure and the penal law (1810) buttressed the growing
despotism of the imperial government by augmenting the penalties
for crimes against persons and property, and particularly for political offenses. Where the spirit of revolutionary penology had favored
the defendant, the revised procedure fortified the prosecution. The
accused was still permitted public trial by jury, but the jurors were
to be selected by the prefect, and a simple majority vote sufficed
for a verdict. The ball and chain, branding, and the barbarous
custom of striking off a parricide's hand before execution were
reintroduced, and some lighter forms of judicial torture condoned.
The commercial code, issued in 1807, was the most incomplete and
ill-organized of all, though it included much that was excellent
from the ordinances of the monarchy. Napoleon's attitude of suspicion towards promissory notes and his dislike of usury were
again evident in the restrictions imposed on the hypothecation of
real property and the severe penalties enforced against the fraudu-
lent bankrupt.

In their totality the codes well represent that compromise settlement which Napoleon imposed upon France. They recognized
and embodied, in principle at least, the leading demands of the
revolutionary program, the profound aspiration for order, for a
unified national system of secular legislation, for civil equality,
religious liberty, and a soil freed from feudal encumbrances. They
recognized no privileges of birth, opened all careers to men of industry and talent, promoted the distribution of property and discouraged the accumulation of large landed estates. In this sense
they were a summary of the Revolution, and were so regarded in
neighboring states which attacked or adopted them.

The abuses of the old régime had engendered among its critics a spirit of hostility towards all constituted authority. The work of demolition carried through in the first years of the Revolution was inspired by a deep conviction that it was necessary to limit the powers of the government in the interests of individual liberty. Resistance against oppression was listed as one of the natural and imprescriptible rights of man, orators assured insurgent multitudes that "the voice of reason and the voice of the people are the same thing," and mob violence was dignified as "the sacred right of insurrection." For such anarchical postulates and their sanguinary conclusions Napoleon had a soldier's contempt. The spirit of his codes is the antithesis of the liberal philosophy, for they are dedicated, not to the principle that government must be restricted in the interests of liberty, but that liberty must be restricted in the interests of government. In this sense the Napoleonic laws were a prefiguration of the mood which was to dominate the European courts after 1815. In this sense they were reactionary.

V. THE CONCORDAT

No complete or durable peace within France was possible so long as the religious issue remained unsettled. The Revolution had created a schism in the Gallican church which reached into every diocese and every parish. The constitutional clergy, disowned by the Pope and distrusted by the revolutionary government to which they had rallied, were a disorganized minority numbering according to some estimates no more than seven or eight thousand.[14] The legitimate clergy, more numerous and rendered more dignified by their sufferings, were for the most part in exile or in hiding, but they continued to exert considerable counter-revolutionary influence. This, to Bonaparte, was the critical factor. The rebels of the West, so recently disarmed, were still disaffected. They might be persuaded to forget their legitimate king, but they would never abandon their legitimate priests. It was imperative, therefore, to persuade the refractory priests themselves to support the consular régime, and for this conversion the assistance of the Pope was essential.

[14] A. Boulay de la Meurthe, *Histoire de la négociation du concordat de 1801* (Tours, 1920), 7.

It is significant that Bonaparte opened his negotiations with the newly elected pontiff, Pius VII, in June, 1800, immediately after his victory at Marengo had restored French domination in Italy. Throughout the discussions the papal court was not permitted to forget for a moment that the republican armies might enlarge or diminish the temporal domains of the Papacy at a word from Paris. Eager to consummate a project upon which he had set his mind, Bonaparte soon grew impatient at the procrastinating tactics of the papal envoys. He rightly guessed that delays were introduced because the congregation for ecclesiastical affairs at Rome doubted the stability of his régime and wished to await the final outcome of the war before risking the enmity of Austria and of the Bourbons by concluding an arrangement with republican France.[15] When the battle of Hohenlinden (December 3, 1800) had been followed by the Peace of Lunéville (February 9, 1801), and the French ascendency was confirmed, Rome prepared to come to terms, only to discover that the First Consul had shifted his position and stiffened his demands.

The state of public opinion in France convinced Bonaparte that it would be prudent to keep his conversations with the Vatican secret. Though half the French population was still Catholic in sentiment, it was the less vocal and less influential half; in intellectual circles, in the world of politics, and in the army, irreligion was the order of the day, and millions in the lower ranks of society could best be described as indifferent. Attempts to introduce a substitute for Christianity, a worship of the Goddess of Reason, a religion of the Supreme Being, a cult of Theophilanthropy, had all failed, and the group of constitutional clergy, disowned at Rome, was disintegrating despite the efforts of Grégoire, Archbishop of Blois, to unify it. The first papal negotiator, Monsignor Spina, who reached Paris in September, 1800, recognized at once that Bonaparte's plan to renew direct relations between the French government and the Holy See must encounter powerful opposition. Talleyrand and Fouché had placed the First Consul on his guard against Roman presumption, and the members of the council of state were frankly hostile to the

[15] A. Sorel, *L'Europe et la Révolution française*, VI (Paris, 1911), 86.

discussions. More important still, no concordat which reëstablished Catholicism as the favored religion would be ratified by the legislative bodies if it involved the abrogation of religious freedom for minority sects. Irritated by the continued resistance at Rome, and alarmed lest the suspicion aroused by his religious policy overstrain his popularity in France, Bonaparte sent Cacault to the Pope with a final ultimatum in May, 1801. Unless the terms which he offered were accepted as they stood, he declined any longer to guarantee the temporal power. Cacault returned to Paris with a new envoy, Cardinal Consalvi, who disputed the treaty article by article, but finally signed a revised draft on July 15th.

Bonaparte had triumphed in his three major aims. The concordat reconciled the refractory clergy to the Republic, ended the schism in the Gallican church, and reassured the purchasers of church property by validating their title. In return, the Pope was assured possession of his temporal domains in Italy without, however, regaining the Legations ceded in the Treaty of Tolentino of 1797. The French government, having abolished the tithe, assumed responsibility for the payment of clerical salaries, the bishops were to be nominated by the First Consul and consecrated by the Pope, and the lower clergy chosen by the bishops. The concordat recognized Catholicism as the faith of the three consuls and of the great majority of Frenchmen, but the government retained the right to issue police regulations prescribing the manner in which all religious worship was to be safeguarded. This "police clause," left intentionally vague, provided Bonaparte with an excuse to supervise and circumscribe the execution of the concordat in its minutest details, an excuse which he soon found it expedient to invoke.

With the arrival of the formal papal ratification in December, 1801, the legislative councils were invited to approve the new treaty, but Bonaparte took the precaution of weakening the opposition in advance. Yielding to official pressure, the senate retired one-fifth of the tribunes and members of the legislative body, the date having arrived for the annual renewal, and the consuls replaced the retiring deputies by more tractable legislators. The fact that the candidates for dismissal had been designated, not chosen by lot as formerly, afforded the survivors a lesson they could hardly misread.[16] But, as always, Bonaparte combined conciliation with coercion. To render the concordat less objectionable the council of state embodied it in a general law for the regulation of cults, a law which made provision for the Protestant churches in France as well as for the Roman Catholic faith. The government also assumed the authority to edit the catechism, limit the establishment of seminaries, and exclude papal bulls or legates, thus reasserting in defiant terms the ancient liberties of the Gallican church. Framed by the "Organic Articles," the concordat was approved by the assemblies in the first week of April, 1802. The Peace of Amiens, signed on March 25, had raised the First Consul to a new peak of popularity and the legislators appreciated the danger of opposing his will. Ten days after the law on cults had been voted, a *Te Deum* was celebrated in Notre Dame (April 18th) to signalize the reconciliation of France and the Papacy.

VI. THE PATTERN OF THE CENTRALIZED NATION STATE

In a proclamation issued the nineteenth Brumaire, the "organizers" had sworn to provide France with a constitution, to end the civil conflict in the West, to stabilize the finances, codify the laws, and terminate the foreign war with an honorable peace.[17] By the spring of 1802 the consular government had redeemed these five promises, and Bonaparte, largely on his own initiative, had added a further achievement, the settlement of the religious schism. His popularity and prestige, unmarred by a single reverse, gave him an extraordinary hold upon the loyalty of the French people, and he was determined to consolidate his power before the public enthusiasm waned.

The secret of his appeal rested in his example no less than in his achievements. His devotion to practical and constructive work, his insistence upon the virtues of moderation and economy, his respect for decency and order, suited the tastes of that influential body of middle-class citizens who now formed the dominant class in society.[18] The first years of the Consulate confirmed a social and intel-

---

[16] G. Constant, *L'Église de France sous le Consulat et l'Empire, 1800-1814* (Paris, 1928), 180-183.

[17] Buchez and Roux, *Histoire parlementaire*, XXXVIII, 222-229.

[18] G. Hanotaux, "La transformation sociale à l'époque napoléonienne," *Revue des Deux Mondes* (1926, mai-juin), XXXIII, 89-113, 562-597.

lectual transformation in France, the first signs of which had appeared as early as 1795. A mood of revulsion had developed against the insolent *tutoiement* of the *sans-culottes*, the scurrility of the more obscene journals, the vulgarity of political jobholders. The French people were accustomed to look to their leaders to set the style in manners and deportment, and the reserve and dignity which the First Consul displayed in his communications and his public appearances confirmed the trend towards respectability. When the *Moniteur* hinted that General Bonaparte was understood to disapprove of the extreme *décolletage* affected by women of society, the brief note had the force of a fashion mandate. Parisian society was reverting to the proprieties.

Where opposition towards the new government still survived it was poorly organized and for the most part impotent. An unsuccessful attempt to assassinate Bonaparte in December, 1800, though traced ultimately to royalist conspirators, provided an excuse for the deportation of two score ex-Jacobins and terrorists.[19] A vigilant police force provided the best and almost the only protection against such plots, and the task of frustrating them was relegated to Fouché and Réal. More serious, because more legitimate, was the resistance Bonaparte had to meet from the legislature and from the army. As late as the closing months of 1801 the tribunate and the legislative body retained sufficient independence to reject the first sections of the civil code, and their hostility delayed the ratification of the concordat until April, 1802. But as an effective organ of opposition the councils were weakened by their own divisions, upon which the First Consul played with unscrupulous finesse, and by the fear, constantly renewed, that he might appeal over their heads to the nation at large if they persisted in blocking his reforms.

Jealousy and discontent among the officers of the republican armies alarmed Bonaparte more deeply. With the conclusion of peace his brother generals sought the capital, with sour comments on their lips and the prospect of retirement on halfpay in their minds. "What a beautiful fix we are in now," Bonaparte commented to

---

[19] A biographical list of the deportees may be found in J. Destrem, *Les déportations du consulat et de l'empire* (Paris, 1885).

Talleyrand. "Peace has been declared."[20] The army had become, to a greater degree than the nation, republican and atheistical, and the restoration of the Catholic faith and the inclination towards monarchical customs incited the old soldiers to many bitter jibes and not a little private conspiring.[21] The First Consul's reply took the form of an extravagant and unexpected largesse. Reëstablishment of a general peace in March, 1802, was immediately followed by a decree setting aside part of the national domains to provide annuities ranging from 250 to 5,000 francs a year for members of a new order, the Legion of Honor. The decorations, restricted almost exclusively to military men, constituted a reward and a distinction to be distributed at will by Bonaparte as chief of the legion. Though forced through the councils with difficulty and fiercely criticized in republican circles, the new honors served their purpose brilliantly, softening resentments and knitting the fortunes of the soldiers to the leader who alone had it in his power to gratify their expectations. Towards a few irreconcilables suspected of plotting his overthrow or assassination Bonaparte showed a wise clemency, but several dissatisfied generals were thoughtfully scattered to distant military or diplomatic posts. By a dispensation not entirely fortuitous the regiments most ardent in their republicanism had been dispatched the previous December to Haiti, where the yellow fever was already slaking their lust for equality.

Events in France were marching towards a dictatorship: Bonaparte decided to hasten the consummation. The nation, invited to approve a life consulate for him, responded by a majority announced on August 2, 1802, as 3,568,885 to 8,374. Two days later a new constitution was submitted to the senate and passed without discussion. The *Brumairiens* who had helped Bonaparte into power were now the prisoners of his success, and watched supinely as he assumed the right to make treaties, dissolve at need the tribunate and legislative body, and annul judicial decisions. With the approval of the senate, expressed in a *senatus consultum*, he could amend the constitution itself, and his ascendency over the senate was assured through his exclusive right to nominate candidates to it. As a reward for their compliance the senators were invited to vote themselves further in-

[20] *Memoirs of Chancellor Pasquier*, 2 vols., trans. by C. E. Roche (New York, 1893-1894), I, 172.
[21] E. Guillon, *Les conspirations militaires sous le consulat et l'empire* (Paris, 1894).

creases in salary from a special fund drawn from the income supplied by the national domain.

More certainly than the *coup d'état* of Brumaire or the coronation performed in 1804 at Notre Dame, this constitution of the year X (1802) signalized the establishment of Bonaparte's absolutism. An observant commentator who returned to Paris shortly after it was promulgated found that everything except the word *Consul* had become monarchical. "All was regulated by the most punctilious etiquette, and the Second and Third Consuls were as subservient to it as the rest of the crowd; they were present . . . not as colleagues of the First Consul, but as courtiers."[22]

The machinery of a centralized despotism which Bonaparte had perfected differed greatly in its efficiency and vigor from the ponderous and unwieldy government of the old French monarchy. Better than any of the enlightened princes of the eighteenth century, he had been able to reconstruct and energize the state because all the inherited obstacles to the kingly power had been subordinated or swept away in the Revolution. The relics of feudalism, the privileged church and the privileged nobility, the provincial estates, the conflicting codes and tariffs, the guilds, the corporations and the *parlements*, all had been crippled or abolished. Reorganized through the consular reforms, France became the most powerful state in Europe. It was under this form, as Sorel had pointed out,[23] the form of enlightened despotism, that the French Revolution was consolidated, and it was under this form that Europe comprehended and imitated it. The energies of the French people, released, intensified, and coördinated, gave them an immense advantage over their disorganized and backward neighbors. Never before, not even when Louis XIV united France against a divided Europe, had *la grande nation* enjoyed such an opportunity to play the arbiter, as Bonaparte was swift to appreciate. Believing himself condemned to eclipse the achievements of earlier French monarchs in order to justify his usurpation of their throne, he found himself carried forward on a tide of national policy so successful that, insensibly, it blended into an imperial policy from which there was no retreat. Or so at least he chose to believe.

[22] Miot de Melito, *Memoirs,* trans. by C. Hoey and J. Lillie (New York, 1881), 249.
[23] A. Sorel, *L'Europe et la Révolution française,* I (Paris, 1912), 548.

Chapter Three

EUROPE AND THE REVOLUTION: COMPROMISE

I. THE AIMS OF THE SECOND COALITION

WHEN the Girondist firebrands of 1792 clamored in the legislative assembly for a war against *all* tyrants, they startled Europe for the first time with the specter of the Revolution militant. The execution of Louis XVI in January, 1793, made revolutionary France an outcast among the nations, and the "war against kings" became a desperate struggle on the part of the regicide nation to preserve itself from dismemberment. But revolutionary enthusiasm, transmuted into an aggressive patriotism, enabled the French armies to check the invasions of 1792-1793, reclaim the initiative, and pass by 1794 from a war of defense to a war of conquest. Austria, Prussia, Great Britain, Holland, Spain, and the Kingdom of Sardinia, all menaced in greater or less degree by the French expansion, organized a loose coalition to check it, but their efforts, ill-concerted and irresolute, invited failure. By 1795 the governments of Europe were prepared to come to terms. The French Republic had proved its capacity to survive.

To statesmen trained in the traditions of eighteenth-century diplomacy, revolutionary France constituted a danger after 1793, not primarily because the nation had established a republican régime, but because the French victories threatened to destroy the European balance of power. Some moderate annexations the allied governments were prepared to allow. Austria, Prussia, and Russia had all made substantial gains between 1772 and 1795 through the partitioning of Poland, and the principle of reciprocal compensation entitled France to claim some sort of territorial equivalent. In the Committee of Public Safety the level-headed Carnot suggested the Meuse as a reasonable limit of conquest, but the advocates of the "natural frontiers" were more ambitious, and insisted upon claiming the left

36

bank of the Rhine as well as Belgium.[1] In May, 1795, the Prussian government, preoccupied with Polish affairs, conceded the French demands. Holland, conquered and reconstructed as the Batavian Republic, submitted in the same month; Spain made peace a few weeks later. But to bring Austria to acknowledge the French aggrandizement proved a more difficult task. The Vienna court, though tempted, refused the suggestion that Bavaria might be considered a just compensation for the loss of the Austrian Netherlands. This stalemate was broken by Bonaparte's first Italian campaign, which replaced Austrian influence in northern Italy by a French hegemony. At Campoformio, the young general proved his familiarity with the traditions of eighteenth-century diplomacy by offering the Austrians the territories of the Venetian Republic to sweeten their defeat. In return France gained the Emperor's secret permission to retain the left bank of the Rhine. The problems created by a disproportionate expansion of French influence were already manifest in this Campoformio settlement of 1797. To secure the Rhine frontier the French armies had advanced to the Po; to retain control of the Po Valley they were shortly to revolutionize Italy as far as Naples. Pressed in this logical and relentless fashion the French policy carried within itself the seeds of its own destruction, for to secure the ever-extending frontiers was to transcend them, to transcend them was to excite fiercer opposition and to inspire the formation of larger and more determined coalitions.

By the close of 1797 Great Britain alone, the sole survivor of the First Coalition, had refused to recognize the fruits of the French ascendency. Yet it is not improbable that the British government would likewise have conceded France her acquisitions if the hotheads at Paris had refrained from further conquests. But the subjugation of Switzerland (1798), the establishment of French-controlled republics at Rome and Naples (1799), and Bonaparte's expedition to Egypt (1798-1799) disturbed the European equilibrium so seriously that a Second Coalition formed itself spontaneously. Russia could not permit the dismemberment of the Ottoman Empire without protest, and Austria was easily persuaded to reënter the

[1] P. Sagnac, "Les limites de la France et la théorie des frontières naturelles du XVIIe au XXe siècle," *The Franco-American Review*, I (1936), 116-134.

conflict on the chance that a revised settlement would restore her lost influence in Italy. By the autumn of 1798, Great Britain, Austria, and Russia had dedicated themselves, temporarily at least, to a common offensive. The "rampart of republics," erected by the Directory, crumbled under the renewed attack, and in 1799 the French armies were forced back almost to the "natural limits." Once again the government of the Directory had the opportunity to choose between a reasonably just balance of power with a fair promise of peace, or a program of unlimited expansion and the certainty of war. But to forswear all revolutionary activity beyond the Rhine and the Alps meant to abandon the fruits of Bonaparte's Italian victories and to forsake the local patriots who had helped the French to establish revolutionary governments in Holland, Switzerland, and Italy. Even in the hour of defeat such a sacrifice was too humiliating for republican pride. The revival, in the summer of 1799, of a spirit of uncompromising Jacobin fanaticism at Paris, and the decision taken by the government to press the struggle with increased vigor, committed France once again to a war of conquest.[2]

This war was Bonaparte's inescapable heritage from the Directory. The problem, and the solution to it, were prescribed in advance; throughout the Napoleonic period the essential issues did not alter. Pitt's proposals, offered in 1798 as a program for the Second Coalition, prefigured in outline the final settlement of 1814-1815. To restore Holland and Switzerland to independence, unite Belgium to Holland under the rule of the stadtholder, return Savoy and Piedmont to the King of Sardinia, compensate Austria with Italian provinces and Prussia with North German annexations—such were, in effect, the articles of Pitt's memorandum.[3] Add to them a tacit understanding that the tsar might reward himself with Turkish territory, while Great Britain retained any colonies appropriated in the course of the struggle, and the note of November, 1798, may be taken as summarizing the aims of the second and all subsequent coalitions. The program was designed to correct an extraordinary situation, the ascendency of revolutionary France, by restoring a balance of power in Europe with reciprocal compensations for the

[2] R. Guyot, *Le Directoire et la paix de l'Europe* (Paris, 1911), 902.
[3] R. B. Mowat, *The Diplomacy of Napoleon* (London, 1924), 61-62.

victors, but as a program it possessed several defects. The induce-
ments offered Russia were inadequate, for neither the British nor
the Austrians were prepared to concede Constantinople. The territorial gains proposed for Prussia could not include Hanover because
that electorate was subject to George III. Bound by no such restriction in disposing of Hanover, the French diplomats kept Prussia
neutral from 1795 to 1806 by dangling that and other territorial bait
before the eyes of the expansionists at Berlin. Finally, the program
was deficient because it provided no satisfactory formula to assure
the effective coöperation of the allied forces, and no guarantees to
bind the coalition together until its objectives were realized in a
general peace. The only sentiment which could unite four jealous
and selfish powers, Austria, Russia, Prussia, and England, was a fear
of France so compelling that it would subdue all lesser rivalries, and
such an over-mastering fear developed only when Napoleon's spreading influence had made a French domination of Europe seem not
merely possible, but imminent. Each of the allies knew, throughout
the wars of the earlier coalitions, that its partners were susceptible,
and that Napoleon knew they were susceptible, to a sufficiently
tempting French bribe. If, in the end, they learned to keep faith with
one another, it was because they had been convinced through repeated experiences that Napoleon's pledges became valueless the
moment he found himself in a safe position to ignore them, and he
was certain to achieve that position if he could deal with his adversaries separately. There is interesting matter for thought here for
the moralist. And for the cynic.

II. THE WITHDRAWAL OF RUSSIA

Russia in the eighteenth century resembled an oriental satrapy
rather than a European state. The vast personal authority of the
ruler, absolute in theory, was largely nullified in operation by the
passive resistance of a corrupt and apathetic bureaucracy, and by
the opposition of a landed nobility jealous and privileged. Over nine-
tenths of the people remained peasants or serfs, the townsmen were
insignificant in numbers and influence, and the nobles and clergy,
although they represented less than three per cent of the population,
formed the only independent groups in the empire. The core of this

amorphous social organism was the imperial court, where state policies were determined by the caprice of the ruler or the machinations of a dominant cabal. No organic laws, no comprehensive administrative mechanism, no national institutions, had yet been devised except on paper. Despite the arbitrary reforms of Peter the Great and the enlightened projects of Catherine II, the government of Russia remained in effect a personal despotism tempered by inertia.

The lack of constitutional checks and guarantees left the autocrat free to indulge his whims, while the absence of any effective machinery of state foredoomed all far-reaching enterprises to failure. Catherine II, raised to the throne by a palace revolution in 1762, comprehended the situation and accepted it. Though she liked to pose as an enlightened despot, and courted the praise of Voltaire and Diderot, she did not venture to displease the nobles or the bureaucrats by drastic innovations. All the major evils of the imperial régime, the exploitation of the serfs, the lack of an efficient administrative structure, the disorder in juristic and state relationships, the arbitrary fiscal system, she left much as she found them. Paul I, her pathologically unbalanced son, who succeeded her in 1796, was more courageous and less fortunate. Eager to reverse his mother's policies, he suspended the privileges which she had granted the nobles, reduced the compulsory labor of the serfs, and fortified the throne by fixing the imperial succession in the male line. Paul's erratic experiments in executive reform opened a new period in Russian history, which Kluchevsky has called "a supremely bureaucratic period."[4] But this unhappy tsar's mental instability made his reign a nightmare for his courtiers and officials, and his violent death in 1801 constituted, with due allowance for Russian precedents, a more or less normal end to an abnormal situation.

Paul's eldest son, the twenty-three-year-old Alexander, accepted the throne which the conspirators had cleared for him. He had imagined, apparently, that his father could be deposed peacefully, and the strangling of Paul filled him with horror and remorse. It is characteristic of this "crowned Hamlet" that he should have com-

[4] V. O. Kluchevsky, *A History of Russia*, trans. by C. J. Hogarth, V (London, 1931), 122.

menced his reign in this ambiguous guise, protesting reluctance, seductive in his grief, inscrutable at heart. His new subjects, however, welcomed him without reserve, chanting prayers of thanksgiving for their deliverance.[5] "Russia breathes again" the Grand Duke Constantine confided to a friend, and in this universal mood of expectation Alexander recognized a mandate which he could not ignore. His education, supervised by his grandmother, Catherine II, had familiarized him with the works of the *philosophes* and with their reform program. To apply that program to Russia, to organize and invigorate that vast, amorphous, and torpid society by reducing it to the rule of law, by gearing the cumbrous mechanism to run harmoniously under the drive of a single mainspring, was an ideal worth fighting for, and Alexander's desire to bring the Revolution to Russia in this form was the most sincere and ardent impulse of his complex nature. A true son of his century, he saw despotism as the safeguard, not the antithesis, of liberty. The autocrat who extended his authority in accordance with just and invariable principles might not only assure the welfare of his subjects, but make himself their liberator. In the company of congenial spirits—Stroganov, Kochubei, Czartoryski, Novossiltzov—the young tsar discussed a constitutional charter for Russia, a bill of rights, the proclamation of organic laws, and the liberation of the serfs. From the opening of Alexander's reign this unofficial cabinet of his personal friends formed the nucleus of a liberal party at court, but its power for good was limited by the suspicion of conservative groups hostile to foreign ideas, by the apathy of the bureaucrats, and by the unpredictable vagaries of Alexander's moods and loyalties.

As a consequence, it is not surprising that the lofty projects so eagerly debated in the first months of the new reign terminated in nothing more serious than some cautious administrative tinkering. The senate was invited to interest itself in the administration of justice, and was granted the privilege of remonstrating against unpopular laws, but the first attempts to exercise these functions earned it a prompt rebuke. In 1802 eight ministers were appointed to head the government boards, but the significance of the change proved

[5] K. Waliszewski, *La Russie il y a cent ans: le règne d'Alexandre I*, I (Paris, 1923), 30.

almost exclusively titular save in the department of public instruction, where some minor reforms were attempted, and three new universities founded at Dorpat, Kharkov, and Kazan. The fundamental abuses, such as serfdom, were left untouched, and the landlords of Russia, who had observed with alarm the attacks on serfdom and privilege in western Europe, soon convinced themselves that Alexander's liberalism was a pose no more dangerous to their pretensions than that of his grandmother had been.

Napoleon's success in centralizing French institutions under the form of a popular dictatorship stirred Alexander to admiration and envy. Following the Franco-Russian alliance of 1807 he appointed the brutal and dynamic Arakcheiev minister of war, with instructions to unify and modernize the Russian army, and in 1809 he entrusted to Michael Speranski, as secretary of state, the duty of consolidating the civil administration under a formula of democratic despotism. Speranski's proposals, modeled largely on the French constitution of 1799, provided for units of local self-government, an all-Russian diet to sanction the imperial decrees, and a council of state to assist the tsar in forming decisions and drafting legislation. The council was organized in 1810, but the remainder of Speranski's reform program, the most intelligent and comprehensive yet suggested for Russia, was revised, debated and adjourned, until Alexander laid it aside in perplexity and irritation, to plunge himself into the more absorbing game of international politics. When the break came with Napoleon in 1812 Speranski was dismissed from office as pro-French, a victim of Alexander's desire to conciliate the conservatives.

Since the death of Catherine II in 1796, Russian foreign policy had lacked consistency and had vacillated in bewildering fashion. Paul I opened his reign with a declaration of pacifistic intentions, but Bonaparte's occupation of Egypt in 1798 offered a challenge which he found it impossible to disregard. For a century Russian statesmen had anticipated and endeavored to hasten the dismemberment of the Turkish Empire; but Paul assumed the unconventional rôle of protector, offered the Sultan an alliance, and obtained permission to send a Russian fleet through the Dardanelles. In a military and naval campaign remarkable for its rapidity and success, the Ionian

Islands (acquired by the French in 1797)[6] were "liberated" and organized as a republic under the tsar's protection. Russian armies operating in Naples and Piedmont helped to free Italy from French control. The inspired generalship of Suvarov, and the generous sacrifices of the Russian troops, entitled Paul to a voice in the projected reconstruction of the Italian peninsula, but the Austrian court, with customary arrogance, insisted upon the right to dispose of the Piedmontese realm as it saw fit, and subordinated Suvarov to the orders of the war council at Vienna. The Second Coalition, never firmly jointed, speedily fell apart as jealousy of the Russian successes alarmed the ministers at London and the councilors at Schönbrunn. When the Russian corps, reinforced, moved into Switzerland in the summer of 1799, errors in strategy and lack of Austrian support exposed them to costly defeats. Paul's protest to Francis II, canceling the alliance, possessed both dignity and justice. He could not, he wrote, remain the ally of a power which sacrificed the welfare of Europe to its own selfish aims.

Towards Great Britain the tsar's sentiments remained more friendly for another year, although the failure of an Anglo-Russian expedition, dispatched for the liberation of Holland in the autumn of 1799, excited his disappointment. But when the French garrison holding Malta surrendered to the British (September, 1800) Paul's patience snapped, for he had taken the Knights of Malta under his protection and coveted the island for the furtherance of his Mediterranean schemes. Already irritated at the high-handed use the British made of their maritime preponderance, he revived the League of Armed Neutrality which Catherine II had first organized in 1780, and he sought, in collaboration with the Swedish, Danish, and Prussian governments, to protect neutral vessels against the arbitrary right of search exercised by British cruisers. He was meditating an alliance with France, and had ordered an expedition of Cossacks to march on India, when his assassination in March, 1801, cut short his ambitious and fantastic plans.

Bonaparte, who in less than a year had seduced the tsar with flattery and laid the promising basis for a Franco-Russian union against Great Britain, attributed Paul's death to English machina-

[6] E. Rodocanachi, *Bonaparte et les îles ioniennes* (Paris, 1899).

tions and cursed the unpredictable vagaries of Russian policy. French ambitions had, indeed, suffered a sharp check, though Napoleon was never one to confess such reverses, for with Alexander's accession the League of Armed Neutrality collapsed and the expedition against India was abandoned. The British government, prompt to exploit the new shift in Russian sympathies, made discreet overtures which soon reached the point of proposing an attractive treaty of alliance to the new tsar. By April, 1802, the French agent at St. Petersburg, Hédouville, was warning Paris that Russian court circles had grown dangerously cordial towards the English, a development hastened by the judicious distribution of £60,000 among the imperial advisers.[7] Bonaparte was quick to appreciate the import of these pourparlers. His hostilities with the English had been suspended by a preliminary truce in the previous autumn, and negotiations were pending upon which he had relied sufficiently to disptach expeditions to Haiti and Louisiana. But if the cabinet at London drew the tsar into an alliance, its peace demands might rise sharply and his own colonial commitments would make him vulnerable. One month later he accepted the Treaty of Amiens, a treaty which reëstablished a general truce among all the great powers of Europe for the first time in ten years, and, by gratifying the desire of the French people for a victorious peace, raised Bonaparte's popularity and prestige to a new level. It is necessary to turn back a little and pursue the complementary strands of French diplomacy to appreciate how this result had been achieved.

III. THE DEFEAT OF AUSTRIA

The influences which, by 1815, were to make Vienna the headquarters of the reactionary forces of Europe had already manifested their strength by 1800. Throughout the revolutionary era the peoples under Hapsburg rule remained surprisingly unresponsive to the seductive creed of liberty, equality, and fraternity, and the ruling classes asserted their profound hostility towards the revolution from the first. For this uncompromising spirit of resistance there are sev-

---

[7] H. Beeley, "A Project of Alliance with Russia in 1802," *English Historical Review*, XLIX (1934), 497-502. For a penetrating survey of Franco-Russian relations in 1800 and 1801 see H. C. Deutsch, *The Genesis of Napoleonic Imperialism* (Cambridge, Mass., 1938), pp. 14-22.

eral explanations. The empire on the Danube was still, at the close
of the eighteenth century, a semi-feudal domain. No ambitious,
rich, and influential middle class had yet arisen, as in France, to
challenge the privileges of the landed aristocracy or resent the prerogatives of the priesthood. A majority of the peasants lived con-
tentedly, in varying stages of thralldom, on the entailed estates of
the nobles. Political agitation and even political discussion were almost unknown; illiteracy protected the lower orders against revolutionary ideas, while the police maintained a constant guard against
every form of social ferment. A well-endowed but not too officious
Catholic clergy guided the consciences of the faithful, paternal landlords pocketed their feudal dues and distributed justice with casual
and uncontested authority, and the provincial estates, dominated by
the great landowners, adjusted the taxes, deliberated on local affairs,
and resisted the encroachments of the imperial officials with the
bland particularism of their medieval predecessors.

The same languid and procrastinating spirit softened, as a general
rule, the despotism of the imperial régime. No effective central
administration had yet been organized; the ministers reported individually to the emperor, but the latter exercised his authority as
much through his personal influence as through his executive orders.
His contacts with his subjects were restricted very largely to social
encounters with members of the privileged groups, but this did not
weaken the sentimental loyalty of the people, who felt for the Hapsburg dynasty a deep and genuine devotion. Despite the archaic
inefficiency of the administration and the inequality of the social
system the unprivileged classes were not discontented. In education,
in industry, in commerce the Hapsburg realm might lag behind the
rest of Europe, but it included some of the richest agricultural lands
of the continent, the climate was mild and beneficent, food cheap
and adequate, taxation not too oppressive, and life secure and tranquil. With its loosely knit institutions, its cumbrous and disjointed
federal machinery, this great power resembled an oriental empire
rather than a modern European state, and even Metternich was
moved to confess that Asia began on the *Landstrasse*. Yet its dis-
organization and inertia disguised a surprising resiliency, which
enabled Austria to survive remarkably well the defeats, indemnities,

and mutilations inflicted upon it by the French between 1796 and 1810.

Nor should it be forgotten, in any analysis of Austrian conservatism during the revolutionary era, that the population of the Hapsburg dominions had learned before 1789 how objectionable over-hasty reforms could prove. The program of innovations which Joseph II attempted to crowd through between 1780 and 1790 so antagonized the nobles, disconcerted the bureaucrats, offended the clergy and irritated the provincial officials, that Joseph recognized on his deathbed the insurmountable resistance he had stirred up, and thereupon canceled his edicts. His defeated program included many of the social and political measures later introduced by the revolutionary assemblies in France, but the Austrian lands were not yet ripe for them, and the emperor's arrogant and precipitate methods thoroughly inoculated his people against the reform fever.

Of all the continental powers, Austria suffered most heavily from the aggrandizement of revolutionary France. In Bonaparte's crude expression, Austria and France were two bulls competing for the possession of two cows, Italy and Germany. French annexation of the Austrian Netherlands and of Savoy, French domination of the left bank of the Rhine, of Switzerland, and of the greater part of Italy, meant a reverse of fortune for the Hapsburgs which they could never be expected to endure willingly. Nevertheless, it is by no means unthinkable that the court of Vienna might have been persuaded to acquiesce in these changes if suitable compensation had been forthcoming. At Campoformio Bonaparte had recognized this possibility by handing over Venetia.[8] Permission to Austria to add Dalmatia or Bavaria would no doubt have gone far to pacify the imperial resentment. But Bonaparte had no intention of strengthening Austrian influence in central Germany and he planned to utilize the ports of the Adriatic littoral as bases for his eastern projects. So, despite his overture to Vienna in December, 1799 with its assurance that he believed it possible to conciliate the interests of the two countries, he fully expected that the spring of 1800 would see

[8] E. Driault, La Politique extérieure du premier consul, 1800-1803 (Paris, 1910), 32. For the French subjugation of the Venetian Republic and Bonaparte's adroit use of it as a pawn in his dealings with Austria after the first Italian campaign see G. B. Maclellan, Venice and Bonaparte (Princeton, 1931).

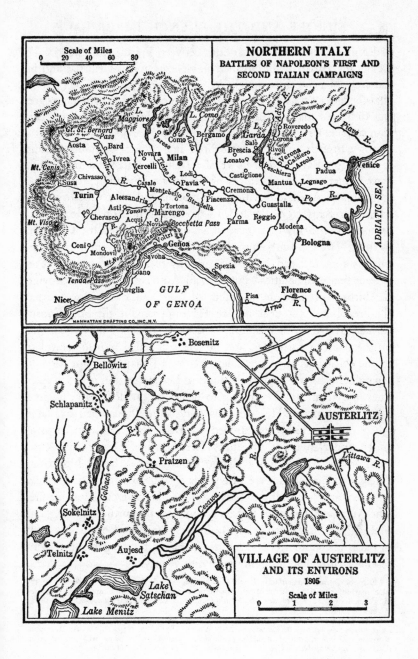

Scale of Miles
0 20 40 60 80

NORTHERN ITALY
BATTLES OF NAPOLEON'S FIRST AND
SECOND ITALIAN CAMPAIGNS

L. Maggiore
Gt. St. Bernard Pass
Aosta
Bard
Dora Baltea R.
Ivrea
Novara
Varese
Como
L. Como
Bergamo
Adda R.
L. Garda
Roveredo
Corona
Salò
Rivoli
Brescia
Lonato
Verona
Caldiero
Peschiera
D'Arcola
Piava R.
Mt. Cenis
Chivasso
Susa
Vercelli
Ticino R.
Milan
Lodi
Pavia
Castiglione
Mantua
Legnago
Padua
Venice
Turin
Casale
Montebello
Cremona
Stradella
Piacenza
Alessandria
Asti
Tanaro
Tortona
Marengo
Guastalla
Po R.
ADRIATIC SEA
Mt. Viso
Cherasco
Acqui
Novi
Bocchetta Pass
Parma
Reggio
Modena
Coni
Mondovi
Ceva
Montenotte
Voltri
Genoa
Po R.
Bologna
Mt. Negro
Savona
Spezia
Tenda Pass
Loano
Oneglia
GULF
OF GENOA
Pisa
Florence
Arno R.
Nice

MANHATTAN DRAFTING CO., INC., N.Y.

Bosenitz
Bellowitz
Schlapanitz
AUSTERLITZ
Littawa R.
R.
Pratzen
Cescawa
Sokelnitz
Golbach
Telnitz
Aujesd
Lake
Satschan
Lake Menitz

VILLAGE OF AUSTERLITZ
AND ITS ENVIRONS
1805

Scale of Miles
0 1 2 3

a decisive resumption of hostilities between France and Austria. To isolate the Austrians in advance he wooed Paul I of Russia, and he flattered the neutral Frederick William III of Prussia by a suggestion that the latter act as mediator, a move which failed to promote peace, but disguised his own imperious plans and helped to disarm Prussian suspicions.

For a French army the most direct line of attack against Vienna lay through Bavaria and down the Danube Valley. Moreau, with 120,000 men, the major forces of the French Republic, opened the campaign in April, and within two months had driven the Imperialists under Kray from Bavaria. In the meantime Bonaparte, having assembled an army of reserve at Dijon, led it across the Great St. Bernard (May 15-20) into the Po Valley. This venture, so frequently romanticized, had been carefully planned and presented no extraordinary difficulties,[9] but a small Austrian garrison occupying the fortress of Bard in the valley of the Dora Baltea disconcerted the French by its stout resistance. Having passed it, the First Consul turned towards Milan, although Masséna, besieged at Genoa, was on the point of surrender, and hunger compelled him to capitulate to the Austrians two weeks later. It was Bonaparte's intention to separate the enemy from their stores in Lombardy and to block their lines of retreat, but in striving to do so he divided his army into three detachments. He had thus only some 18,000 men available when, on June 14th, he stumbled upon the main Austrian corps of 30,000 under Melas at Marengo. The return of Desaix with 5,000 fresh troops, and a lucky charge by Kellerman saved him from defeat, but his losses were heavy, his fortune for the moment had wavered, and in helping to retrieve it the gallant Desaix lost his life. The Austrians, however, had no enthusiasm for further fighting and Melas agreed to an armistice. By July 1st the First Consul was back in Paris, his popularity enormously increased by the general misconception that he had brought peace with victory.[10]

[9] European, and particularly French highways, had been greatly improved in the latter part of the eighteenth century. For communications between France and Italy see M. Blanchard, *Les routes des Alpes occidentales à l'époque napoléonienne, 1796-1815* (Grenoble, 1920).

[10] For the second Italian campaign the reader may consult Capitaine de Cugnac, *La campagne de l'armée de réserve en 1800*, 2 vols. (Paris, 1900-1901), and A. Hermann, *Marengo* (Münster, 1903). A brief professional account with maps will be found in R. G. Burton, *Napoleon's Campaigns in Italy, 1796-97 and 1800* (London, 1912).

In reality the promise of peace was as premature as the victory had been precarious. Six days after the battle of Marengo the Austrian government accepted a new subsidy from Great Britain and pledged itself not to make a separate peace with France. Negotiations which began at Lunéville in September consequently came to nothing, and in November the French armies resumed their offensive. Moreau's cautious advance in Bavaria brought him into collision with the Imperialists on December 3rd at Hohenlinden, where his smashing victory opened the road to Vienna. Bonaparte, ready two months earlier to compromise on Italian questions, immediately stiffened his demands. But worse fortune was in store for the Austrians. Further French successes in Italy, and the increasing friendliness of Tsar Paul towards France, nerved Bonaparte to dictate terms which left the Hapsburgs without consolation. The imperial envoy, Cobenzl, parried and protested; even Joseph Bonaparte and Talleyrand advised more equitable conditions on the ground that they were likely to prove more durable.[11] But the visions opened up by French military and diplomatic triumphs had intoxicated the First Consul. With Moreau moving towards Vienna and the Russians preparing to defy Great Britain he saw no reason why he should not press his advantage against Austria to the utmost.

The Treaty of Lunéville (February 9, 1801) is frequently described as a recapitulation of the Treaty of Campoformio which had closed the first Italian campaign four years earlier. Its terms, however, and its implications, were more severe. The emperor abandoned all Italy beyond the Adige to French domination, recognized the Batavian, Helvetic, Cisalpine and Ligurian Republics, and agreed that German princes dispossessed by French annexation of the left bank of the Rhine should find compensation on the right bank. Thugut, the Austrian foreign minister who had pressed on the war, was supplanted by the more conciliatory Cobenzl, and a peace partly resumed the ascendency at Vienna. With Austria passive, Prussia neutral, and Russia friendly, Bonaparte was free to clear up any disputes with the lesser continental states. This he hastened to do in the early months of 1801.[12]

[11] P. Marmottan, "Joseph Bonaparte diplomate: Lunéville, Amiens, 1801-1802," *Revue d'histoire diplomatique*, XLI (1927), 276.
[12] M. Sepet, "La politique extérieure de Bonaparte. Origine et progrès de l'hégémonie française en Europe," *Revue des questions historiques*, LVIII (1930), 397-412.

Spain, which had ceded Haiti to France in 1795, yielded Louisiana likewise by the Treaty of Aranjuez (March 21, 1801), in return for Napoleon's assurance that the Infante of Parma should succeed to the Grand Duchy of Tuscany. A week later the King of Naples agreed to close his ports to English vessels, to admit French troops into his domains, and to place ships and guns at their disposal (Treaty of Florence, March 28, 1801). Peace with Portugal, which ceded a large portion of Portuguese Guiana to France, was signed on June 6, 1801, the Portuguese government giving at least nominal assurance that English ships would be barred from Lisbon and other ports. The isolation of Great Britain was now complete. Even the United States, which had maintained an attitude of pseudo-hostility towards France since 1798, yielded to the diplomacy of Talleyrand and Joseph Bonaparte in September, 1800, and concluded a treaty of peace and friendship. British statesmen, recognizing at last that if they insisted upon prolonging the war they might have to fight it entirely alone, opened sulky negotiations with France in the spring of 1801.[13]

IV. THE TRUCE WITH GREAT BRITAIN

On February 5, 1801, William Pitt the Younger resigned the post of prime minister which he had held since 1783. His retirement, on the relatively minor issue of Catholic emancipation, to which George III was inflexibly opposed, came at an inauspicious moment, for Austria accepted the Peace of Lunéville the same week and Britain was left without an ally in her duel with France. A reconstructed cabinet, with Addington as prime minister and Hawkesbury at the foreign office, undertook in March to open negotiations for peace, negotiations which culminated exactly one year later in the Treaty of Amiens. Throughout months of haggling the British attitude of resolution weakened steadily, and Addington's reputation for incapacity would be justified even if it rested on these negotiations alone. Opening with the suggestion that Great Britain should retain all her colonial conquests (except possibly Minorca and the Cape of Good Hope), as fitting compensation for the recent French aggrandizement on the continent, he ended by endorsing a treaty

[13] R. B. Mowat, *The Diplomacy of Napoleon* (London, 1924), 89.

which surrendered everything except Ceylon and Trinidad, and ignored, where European affairs were concerned, every essential point at issue.

Hostilities were suspended, as a prelude to diplomatic discussion, by the Preliminaries of London, signed October 1, 1801. Bonaparte's immediate notice of ratification, commencing with the phrase *"En conséquence du rétablissement de la paix . . ."* should have warned Addington and Hawkesbury that he was determined to regard the preliminary agreement as definitive, and that if they permitted this interpretation they would compromise their case in advance. But they contented themselves with ratifying the clauses more cautiously as *"préliminaires qui ont pour objet le rétablissement de la paix,"*[14] and clung to the hope that they would be able to improve their claims in the subsequent discussions. British diplomacy proved singularly ineffectual in this critical hour. To match the recent French successes in Europe, the London cabinet could have pointed to naval triumphs by no means negligible. The Cape of Good Hope, Ceylon and Trinidad were in British hands; the French garrison at Malta had capitulated on September 5, 1800; and the remnant of Bonaparte's Egyptian force had laid down its arms in September, 1801. With the assassination of Paul I on March 24th and Nelson's destruction of the Danish fleet at Copenhagen on April 2nd, the League of Armed Neutrality, which had almost succeeded in excluding British shipping from the Baltic, had broken down.[15] Yet at the close of a year marked by these successive triumphs, a year which so clearly reflected the supremacy of British naval resources, the cabinet consented to a truce which restored all British conquests save Trinidad and Ceylon, tacitly conceded the French supremacy in Europe, and excluded the vital question of commercial relations from the discussions.

For five months, from November, 1801, to March, 1802, the British plenipotentiaries sought to improve by bargaining a position that had already been compromised through ineptitude. Financial

14 G. F. Martens, *Recueil des principaux traités . . . de l'Europe* (Göttingen, 1831), VII, 381-383.
15 The relevant documents on the League of Armed Neutrality have been edited by J. B. Scott, *The Armed Neutralities of 1780 and 1800* (New York, 1918), and by F. Piggott and G. W. T. Ormond, *Documentary History of the Armed Neutralities of 1780 and 1800*, "Law of the Sea" series, Vol. I (London, 1919).

perplexities account in part for the weakness of the Addington cabinet, for the annual budget of the United Kingdom had tripled in eight years of war, the national debt exceeded £500,000,000, and new loans were difficult to negotiate with the treaty still unsigned. Pitt, in 1797-1798, had withstood the French demands when Britain found herself similarly isolated, but Addington was as inferior to Pitt as Bonaparte was superior to the irresolute Directory.[16] At Amiens the conscientious and gouty Cornwallis dined with Joseph Bonaparte, pondered the duplicities of French diplomacy, and acknowledged himself outmatched in the battle of wits. Never, he confessed, as viceroy in Ireland, governor-general in India, or commander of the British forces at Yorktown, had he experienced such painful anxiety of mind.[17] On March 27, 1802, he finally attached his signature to a treaty which embodied concessions more extensive than he was authorized to make. The cabinet ratified them after painful hesitation rather than disown its distinguished and well-meaning envoy.

More important than the items included in the Treaty of Amiens were the items most singularly and ostentatiously omitted. The house of Savoy, the claims of which Great Britain had consistently championed, was not mentioned. For the house of Orange compensation was mentioned but not specifically defined. No assurance was received that French aggression on the continent would cease; Belgium remained in French hands without benefit of British recognition; and, most important of all, no guarantee was secured that French-controlled continental markets would be reopened to British trade. It is puzzling to conceive why the British cabinet consented to exclude such a vital issue from the negotiations, and the failure to provide for a trade pact was the principal factor in the subsequent rupture of 1803, as Bonaparte apparently recognized. At least Talleyrand conceded as much in a note to Fox during the abortive parleys of 1806: "The Emperor [he wrote] does not imagine that any particular article in the Treaty of Amiens produced the war. He is convinced that the true cause was the refusal to make a treaty of commerce, which would necessarily have been prejudicial

[16] For the Anglo-French negotiations of 1797 consult the preceding volume of this series, C. Brinton, *A Decade of Revolution* (New York, 1934), 224-227.
[17] R. B. Mowat, *The Diplomacy of Napoleon* (London, 1924), 100.

to the manufactures and industry of this country (i.e., France)."[18]
The merchants of London, for their part, recognized this flaw in
the settlement from the first, and protested that the omission of a
commerce clause rendered Article I, promising peace, friendship,
and good intelligence between the contracting parties, an empty
and hypocritical phrase.

The terms of the Treaty of Amiens proved, on publication, a
deepening disappointment to the British people. As they scanned
the clauses it appeared to them that Britain had made all the concessions and had gained nothing in return. Egypt, which the French
had already lost, was restored to Turkish sovereignty. Malta, which
the English had captured, was to be handed back to the Knights
of Saint John of Jerusalem. All the stations in the Mediterranean
which the British had taken by force of arms were to be surrendered, and the same applied to almost all the colonial conquests.
For Britain the treaty meant in substance a restoration of the *status
quo ante bellum.* For France it meant tacit recognition of the hegemony which French arms had established in Europe. Bonaparte
had refused stubbornly and successfully to sign away an inch of
territory if it was still held by French forces; his only concessions
were embodied in an agreement to withdraw his garrison from the
Neapolitan Kingdom and the Papal States, and to acknowledge the
Republic of the Ionian Isles, organized in 1799 under Russo-Turkish
protection. He had brought to the French people that general, honorable, and victorious peace which he had promised on his accession to office. Aside from the British, the only victims of the treaty
were the Spaniards, who surrendered Trinidad, and the Dutch,
who failed to regain Ceylon. But these were concessions which the
French found it easy to forgive Napoleon. They could endure the
losses suffered by their allies with commendable fortitude.

It was more difficult for the British to find a cause for self-con-
gratulation, but the desire for peace was so widespread that even
Pitt, who had continued to advise his friend Addington and to
defend his policies, joined in urging ratification of the pact. Hawkesbury, when defending the preliminaries, had touched upon the vital

[18] C. Gill, "The relations between England and France in 1802," *The English Historical
Review,* XXIV (1909), 78.

point which every thoughtful Englishman was pondering in those dangerous days. Nothing essential was lost, nothing essential could be lost, so long as Britain remained mistress of the seas. Her gain from eight years of war had not been a gain in territories, nor in new markets, it had been a gain in the form of security conferred by naval supremacy. The treaty had not jeopardized that; it had left Britain in a favorable position to renew hostilities whenever she chose, should the truce fail to work satisfactorily. At the beginning of the war Great Britain had possessed some 135 ships of the line and 133 frigates, but by its close these numbers had been raised to 202 and 277, respectively. And while the United Kingdom was thus almost doubling its naval forces, the French had seen their 80 ships of the line cut to 39 and their 66 frigates decline to 35.[19] The reassurance of this naval strength made the peace the British so ardently desired seem a safe experiment, and in some quarters there could be found an optimistic faith that Bonaparte would rest content with the conquests which he had already gained. The island nation decided, philosophically, to give the treaty a trial. If it failed, Great Britain would, at the least, have gained an interval in which to seek allies for a new coalition.

V. THE EUROPEAN BALANCE OF POWER

With the establishment of the general peace in 1802 Bonaparte began for the first time to reveal those moments of blind arrogance which, more than any other failing, invalidate his boast that he never neglected to base his calculations upon the "nature of things." In domestic politics his touch remained unerring, and the consolidation of his dictatorship under the constitution of 1802, though somewhat abrupt, was executed with dexterity. But his management of foreign affairs, hitherto characterized by such superb and successful blending of force and suavity, betrayed more frequent flashes of impatient egotism which in a lesser nature would have been called petulance. "At Amiens," he insisted later, ". . . I had

---

[19] A. T. Mahan, *The Influence of Sea Power upon the French Revolution and Empire*, 14th ed., 2 vols. (Boston, 1919), II, 73. It should be noted, however, in connection with these figures, that the French gained an advantage by the Preliminaries of London, as the British released 25,000 French and 10,000 Dutch and Spanish prisoners, many of them trained seamen. See H. C. Deutsch, *The Genesis of Napoleonic Imperialism* (Cambridge, Mass., 1938), 31.

achieved the moral conquest of Europe,"[20] a statement which is at least half true. But in the six months that followed Amiens he permitted himself the first callous repudiation of pledges which forewarned the powers that no treaty with Napoleon could ever be regarded as more than a temporary truce, which he might be planning to violate even while he signed it.

The statesmen of Vienna, St. Petersburg and London, when concluding peace with France between 1800 and 1802, had clung firmly to the hope that the Rhine, the Alps, and the Pyrenees were to set the final limits to French annexations. They could not disguise from themselves the unwelcome truth that the republican governments lately established in Holland, Switzerland, and Italy were subject to undue influence from Paris, but they pretended to regard these satellites as autonomous states, and assumed that Bonaparte would respect and preserve this convenient diplomatic fiction. How unfounded the hope must prove was soon apparent. The Treaty of Lunéville, signed February 9, 1801, expressly stipulated that the Batavian, Helvetic, Cisalpine and Ligurian Republics should remain independent,[21] but Bonaparte prepared to evade this clause before the ink was dry. On April 12th, the day when he learned of the murder of Tsar Paul, he decided upon the annexation of Piedmont, a step which placed the passes of the western Alps in the hands of the French, and extended their dominion into the Po Valley.[22] A week later he issued an order which, in substance, transformed the Ligurian Republic into a French military department.[23] These encroachments were instituted with some pretense at circumspection, but no secrecy surrounded his next move. At the close of 1801 he summoned the leading notables of the Cisalpine Republic to Lyons, where they were persuaded, under the subtle manipulation of Talleyrand, to offer him the presidency. On January 26, 1802, he accepted, and the European courts were invited to recognize the First Consul, already the undisputed master of thirty million French citizens, as head of an (independent) "Italian Republic" also, a republic which included the richest provinces of the Po Valley and

[20] A. Sorel, *L'Europe et la Révolution française*, VI (Paris, 1911), 202.

[21] M. de Clercq, *Recueil des traités de la France*, 2 vols. (Paris, 1864), I, 427.

[22] *Correspondance de Napoléon Ier*, VII, 116-119, 121-122. Nos. 5525, 5526. The incorporation of Piedmont was not formally announced until September 11, 1802.

[23] *Ibid.*, VII, 128-130. No. 5538.

a population of four million souls. The Grand Duchy of Tuscany, reconstructed as the Kingdom of Etruria, extended the French influence into Central Italy, for it supported a French army and Bonaparte treated it as part of his system. "It will be in order," he had notified Talleyrand on June 17, 1801, "for the Batavian, Helvetic, Cisalpine and Ligurian Republics to recognize the King of Etruria."[24] Foreign observers, noting the high degree of coördination which distinguished the policies of France and her "sister republics" could not doubt that it arose from the direction of a single will, and they resented Napoleon's disingenuous protests that the vassal states were to be regarded as autonomous. The pretense was not an easy one to maintain with any consistency, and the developments which occurred in Holland and Switzerland, between 1801 and 1803, exposed its insincerity in a fashion which demonstrated how little regard Napoleon had for it even as a diplomatic convenience.

Following their "liberation" by a French revolutionary army, the Dutch had accepted a treaty of alliance with the French in 1795. Reorganized as the Batavian Republic, Holland submitted to French control to the extent of placing its best ships and its harbors at the disposal of its ally, and permitted the Directory to quarter 25,000 French troops in Dutch territory for a purpose which might be termed either defense or intimidation depending on the point of view. Despite French exactions and English raids on their commerce and colonies, the United Provinces enjoyed a moderate prosperity until 1799, when the mounting taxes and requisitions discredited the pro-French régime and aroused popular feeling against the conditions of the alliance. In 1801 Bonaparte decided to offer the Batavian Republic a new treaty and a revised constitution, proposing at the same time to reduce the French forces in Holland to 10,000 men, in return for a compensation of 5,000,000 florins. To his surprise and annoyance the Batavian legislators voted against the project. Without hesitation, he instructed General Augereau, commanding the French garrison, to dissolve the legislative chambers and submit the constitution to a popular plebiscite. Less than one-sixth of the electors went to the polls and these rejected the new constitution by a vote of three to one. Bonaparte's patience was

<hr/>

[24] *Correspondance de Napoléon I*, VII, 174. No. 5608.

at an end, and his insight assured him that he could afford to ignore the opposition. On October 6, 1801, the constitution was promulgated on the ground that the abstention of the majority from the polls constituted a tacit act of endorsement.[25] To an inquiry from London whether France would continue to respect the Treaty of Lunéville, which guaranteed the independence of the Batavian Republic, Bonaparte replied with superb effrontery that every state had the right to organize its government as it saw fit. The Addington cabinet forebore to press the point, and the Dutch resigned themselves philosophically to accept the new dispensation. Their interest, as Bonaparte had rightly guessed, centered in the commercial opportunities opened up by the restoration of peace, and many of them welcomed the firmer administration decreed for them by the genius who had reconstructed France.

On the settlement of Swiss affairs Talleyrand and Bonaparte expended more earnest thought and achieved a more permanent triumph. Switzerland had fallen a victim to the rapacity of the Directory in 1798, when a popular insurrection provided a scarcely needed excuse for French military intervention. "O impious war!," lamented the honorable Carnot. ". . . The waters of the Rhine, the Rhone and the Adda have carried to all the oceans the tears of desolated widows."[26] But the civic treasure which the invaders confiscated at Berne helped to provide funds for Bonaparte's Egyptian expedition, and General Brune consolidated the French advantage by proclaiming a Helvetic Republic of eighteen cantons, under a constitution which respected neither the geographic peculiarities of the region nor the historical traditions of the inhabitants.[27] Only the presence of the French forces enabled the party favoring the unitary democratic régime to sustain itself against the aristocratically-minded federalists. Bonaparte's decision, after the Peace of Amiens, to withdraw the French army of occupation from Helvetia has been de-

[25] H. T. Colenbrander, *De Bataafsche Republiek* (Amsterdam, 1908), 235-236. All four constitutions promulgated in Holland during the revolutionary era may be found in W. C. J. van Hasselt, *Verzameling van nederlandsche Staatsregelingen en Grondwetten*, 6th ed. (1904).

[26] E. Chapuisat, "L'Influence de la Révolution française sur les suisses," *Cahiers de la Révolution française*, II (Paris, 1936), 26.

[27] For a thoughtful expression of the sentiments which stirred Swiss patriots at this foreign interference and pillaging consult the contemporary account by A. F. von Mutach, *Revolutions-Geschichte der Republik Bern*, re-edited (Berne, 1934), especially pp. 87, 117-118.

nounced as one of the most perfidious masterstrokes of his statecraft, for his sudden pretense of solicitude for Swiss independence
plunged the country into renewed civil strife.[28] Before the close of
the year 1802 he found it necessary to order 30,000 French soldiers
into Switzerland once more.[29] The temporary evacuation had
brought him a threefold advantage: it had freed the French government from its commitments to the unitary party, advertised the
First Consul's concern for Swiss autonomy, and demonstrated the
apparent inability of the cantons to settle their dissensions peacefully without the aid of French military advisers backed up by
French bayonets.

Accepting the familiar rôle of arbiter, Bonaparte next summoned
the Helvetian notables to Paris and outlined the principles which
ought to guide their deliberations in the settlement of Swiss politics.
A new constitution was needed, he suggested, under which the
patrician families would voluntarily renounce their privileges, while
the eighteen cantons retained sovereign rights within the framework of a federal union. Only thus was it possible to preserve the
gains of the Revolution and still respect local peculiarities of religion, language, and custom.[30] "Thus to the advocates of the old
order he sacrificed unity, while to the revolutionary party he sacrificed autocracy, and incontestably in this way he satisfied the majority on both sides."[31] The act of mediation was signed on February
19, 1803, and in the following September the Helvetic Confederation concluded a new treaty of alliance with France, an ironclad
accord which assured Napoleon that the Alpine passes would remain open to French armies and closed to those of his enemies.
He took the precaution, however, of detaching the Valais, which
safeguarded the route through the Simplon Pass, and this district
was later annexed to France. It was not, perhaps, an excessive commission to charge for his labors. No other instrument which he

[28] W. Oechsli, *History of Switzerland, 1499-1914* (Cambridge, 1922), 347.

[29] *Correspondance de Napoléon Ier*, VIII, 64-66. No. 6370. Instructions of October
15, 1802.

[30] F. Guillon, *Napoléon et les suisses, 1803-1815* (Paris, 1910), 77-114. Napoleon's recommendations to the Swiss delegates are in his *Correspondance*, VIII, 124-127, under
date of December 10, 1802. The section of the act of mediation (chap. XX) embodying
the federal accord is reprinted in K. Hilty, ed., *Les constitutions fédérales de la Con-
fédération suisse* (Neuchâtel, 1891), 417-422. The complete *Acte* may be found in
Martens, *Recueil des traités*, VII, 567-656.

[31] Oechsli, *op. cit.*, 348.

outlined for the government of a non-French people has been more highly or more deservedly praised than the act of mediation, and none reflected more clearly his genius for a political compromise founded upon the realities of the situation and free from the warping effect of ideological absolutes.

Throughout Europe these latest proofs that French interference in Italy, Holland, and Switzerland might be expected to continue after the conclusion of a general peace induced a profound sense of insecurity. There was no precedent in modern European history for such rapid expansion by one great power without reasonable compensation to its rivals. Even the "gnawing peace" which had followed the Treaty of Nijmegen had brought Louis XIV no such extension of influence in ten years as Consular France had achieved in ten months. Only the prospect of proportional gains for Austria, Russia, Prussia, and Great Britain could have dispelled the apprehension and jealousy excited by these French encroachments. Bonaparte's refusal to recognize this truth in 1802 and 1803 must be considered the primary threat which doomed the precarious peace. The compromise which had restored tranquillity to Europe in 1802 failed because it was not, in the sense in which statesmen understand the term, a compromise.

No one can read Bonaparte's instructions to his minister of foreign affairs during the critical months before and after Amiens without recognizing the singular conceit of his diplomacy. He was prepared to respect what he chose to consider the special interests of each of his opponents, but he would share with none of them the universal field of action which he claimed for France. With the British cabinet, for instance, he consented to bargain on colonial matters; he furnished on demand no less than three conciliatory notes explaining the scope and purpose of his expedition to Haiti;[32] but he refused insolently to tolerate questions or criticism from London on his European projects. To inquiries from Tsar Alexander regarding Swiss and Italian affairs he responded with cordial reassurances, but the only spheres in which he intimated that he would consider the possibility of Russian coöperation were the eastern Mediterranean and the Germanies. Prussian interests he

[32] *Correspondance de Napoléon Ier*, VII, 295, 307, 319. Nos. 5820, 5845, 5863.

discussed as if they were confined exclusively to North Germany; one of his chief objections to Lucchesini as Prussian ambassador to Paris was the latter's Italian birth and unwarranted preoccupation with, and knowledge of, Italian politics.[33] The Emperor Francis II at Vienna received even less generous consideration when he protested against the French designs to enhance the prestige of Baden, Bavaria, and Württemberg, states which were still, technically at least, part of the Holy Roman Empire of which Francis was the nominal head. "Your Majesty will realize," Napoleon warned him bluntly, "that the present position of France, which has agreements with Russia, Prussia, and Bavaria respecting German affairs, makes it impossible for me to renounce the system which I have adopted."[34] Such a communication, to a ruler whose authority in the disposition of German problems was, traditionally at least, paramount if not exclusive, reveals how completely the First Consul was thinking in terms of power diplomacy, how resolutely he planned to use his military advantage ("the present position of France," as he phrased it with small concession to diplomatic tact) to extend his system and his influence.

For he had set himself to follow in international affairs the method by which he had triumphed in domestic politics, the method of reconciling all factions to his larger aims by playing upon their individual hopes and fears. But in pursuing this course in France he was asserting a tradition centuries old, the tradition that the whole was superior to any of its parts, whereas in applying such a system to Europe he was defying a tradition almost as ancient, a tradition which taught that no first class power can afford to subordinate itself to the imperial designs of its neighbor. None of the leading diplomats of the age, not Talleyrand nor Fouché nor Caulaincort, Pitt, Stadion, Stein, or Metternich, believed in the durability of the international hegemony which the Corsican established. For to believe in it meant to disregard the most pointed lessons taught by international politics since the close of the middle ages.

The habit of disregarding the force of historical precedents was the most common fault of the eighteenth-century ideologists. They

<hr>

[33] *Correspondance*, XII, 159. No. 5589.
[34] Napoleon to Francis II, October 19, 1802. *Correspondance de Napoléon I*ᵉʳ, VIII, 73-74. No. 6382.

dismissed the warnings of the past on the ground that history was a record of mistakes, and they reasoned as if their discovery of the true and universal principles of human society would so change the situation that the ancient precepts and prejudices would no longer apply. In this naïve and optimistic faith they foreshadowed their twentieth-century successors, who, while agreeing that the exploitation of one class by another has been the common theme of history since the beginning of civilization, nevertheless assume that they can find a principle which will terminate the long sequence of revolutionary changes by the creation of a classless society in which the ancient logic will no longer operate. Napoleon frequently proclaimed his scorn for the ideologists, but his precocious mind had ripened in a doctrinaire age and he never wholly freed himself from that early conditioning. His dream of a European empire which would ignore national boundaries defied modern historical trends and in the end he was vanquished by the force of the political traditions which he had slighted.

Chapter Four

IMPERIAL FRANCE: THE REVOLUTION DISCIPLINED

I. "THE GOVERNMENT OF THE REPUBLIC IS CONFIDED TO AN EMPEROR."

THE Treaty of Amiens had promised the reëstablishment of "peace, friendship and good intelligence" between the French and British governments. Bonaparte considered this clause dishonored from the first because the British authorities failed to silence hostile attacks against him in the London press, and declined to expel from England several notorious enemies of his régime. The French populace, conditioned by ten years of war propaganda to regard England as the arch-enemy of the Revolution, willingly credited such charges of bad faith and treaty violation. When, after 1803, the resumption of hostilities between the two nations was followed by the most dangerous and widespread conspiracy yet organized against the life of the First Consul, French opinion was inflamed to an extraordinary degree. Hatred of England, fear of a Bourbon restoration, and alarm for the stability of the consular reforms united the nation behind Bonaparte in a spirit of patriotic defiance.

Proofs that British officials were implicated in the royalist conspiracy of 1803-1804 have been uncovered in the archives of the foreign and home offices.[1] The plot called for the "removal" of the First Consul and a simultaneous uprising in Normandy, but an *agent provocateur* betrayed the plans in advance. "Be in no hurry about the arrests," Bonaparte warned his minister of justice on November 1, 1803, for he wished to complete the evidence before closing the net.[2] In February and March, 1804, the police seized Moreau, the victor of Hohenlinden, Pichegru, who had returned to Paris secretly, and also that resolute Breton, Georges Cadoudal. Yet Bonaparte felt that his stroke had missed, for he had hoped to implicate the Bourbons di-

---

[1] J. H. Rose, *The Life of Napoleon I*, 2 vols. (London, 1913), I, 450.
[2] *Correspondance de Napoléon Ier*, IX, 73. No. 7240.

62

rectly by arresting the Comte d'Artois on French territory. But d'Artois had not appeared, and misinformation turned Napoleon's suspicions instead upon the young Duc d'Enghien, then residing at Ettenheim in Baden. On March 15th French troops violated this neutral state to arrest the prince, and on March 20th he was tried by a military court at Vincennes and shot. In the light of historical study Bonaparte's responsibility for this execution is as clear as d'Enghien's innocence.[3] Two weeks later Pichegru was found strangled in his cell; the evidence pointed to suicide, but the suspicious called it murder. Cadoudal and seven accomplices were guillotined in June, but in Moreau's case the heaviest sentence which official pressure could exact from the judges was two years' imprisonment, which Bonaparte wisely commuted to banishment. He could afford a gesture of clemency, for the frustrated plot had crystallized public opinion and brought an imperial crown within his reach. "We have done better than we intended," declared the defiant Cadoudal. "We came to give France a king and we have given her an emperor." A disillusioned republican who watched the prisoners at their trial was struck by the same ironic thought. "They were accused of having conspired against a Republic, and it was in the name of an absolute emperor that they were threatened with the scaffold."[4]

The regicides could now count Bonaparte one of theirs: he too had shed Bourbon blood. It is worth noting that the tribunate, hitherto the most recalcitrant chamber, was the first to approve the project for a return to "hereditary" rule, and this only one month after d'Enghien's death. The council of state raised objections, and the senate recommended no more than a "modification" of the existing régime, but Bonaparte easily gauged the significance of these pourparlers. The senators aspired to hereditary privileges of their own, the members of the tribunate and legislative body wanted an increase in salary and tenure. "Senators, you have concluded that heredity in the supreme magistracy is an essential," Napoleon prompted them on April 25th,[5] and the senators, who had omitted to mention that

---

[3] A summary of the most important literature on this famous case will be found in the bibliographical notes under "Diplomatic History."

[4] C. Fauriel, *The Last Days of the Consulate*, ed. by L. Lalanne (New York, 1886), 239.

[5] *Correspondance de Napoléon Ier*, IX, 341. No. 7713.

essential in their report, hastened to draft the requisite *consultum*. A national plebiscite confirmed by 3,572,329 to 2,569 the establishment of an hereditary empire.

To bind the notables of France to the imperial régime Bonaparte repeated the tactics of 1802 on a grander scale. The failure of the royalist plot had proclaimed the futility of opposition; the creation of a new hereditary nobility advertised the profits of conformity. A decree of May 14, 1804, listed the first fourteen marshals of the Empire; the first crosses of the Legion of Honor were publicly distributed on July 14th; and the new constitution guaranteed all public officials who attained the rank of grand dignitary a permanent title and pension. Members of the council of state who completed five years of service were promised the distinction of *conseiller d'état à vie*, legislators became eligible for indefinite reëlection, and tribunes won a ten-year term.[6] By 1812 the imperial almanac was to list four princes, thirty dukes, nearly four hundred counts, and over a thousand barons, in addition to the titles bestowed on members of the imperial family. It was, as Napoleon insisted at St. Helena, a fine empire. But it was never, in its upper circles at least, a genuinely loyal or grateful empire. Men are not grateful for bribes; and the devotion of the dignitaries, as Napoleon himself admitted with his unsparing insight, was always proportional to the favors they had not yet received.

For the French nation the Empire signified stability and order under an enlightened despot who had proved himself first in war and first in peace.[7] Royalists who had rallied to the new régime were consoled by the reappearance of monarchical forms and observances. Jacobins found the hereditary empire a guarantee against the return of the Bourbons. The Pope consented to sanctify the new Charlemagne, and Bonaparte carefully planned the pageantry at Nôtre Dame on December 2, 1804, to impress Europe with the fact that he was emperor *par la grâce de Dieu et les constitutions de la République*. The European chancelleries, satisfied to see the revolutionary spirit disciplined, compromised their principles for the promise of

[6] The constitution of the year XII is printed in *Archives parlementaires*, 2° Série, VIII, 343-352.

[7] The political amalgam under the Empire has been brilliantly analyzed by L. Madelin, *Le contre-révolution sous la révolution, 1789-1815* (Paris, 1935), 211-225.

repose, as the French people had already done, and prepared to recognize a new French dynasty. But Napoleon's genius, that *longue impatience* as Pariset has termed it, made repose impossible. The first anniversary of his coronation was to find him at Austerlitz.

II. ADMINISTRATION

Governments born of a revolution are almost always provisory. Bonaparte had spent four years since Brumaire in consolidating his position, and by 1804 he was prepared to give the administration a permanent form. In its broad outlines the imperial régime rested upon the great constructive innovations of 1800-1802, but the screen of popular deceptions which had veiled the return to despotism was largely abandoned, and the principle of enlightened paternalism more frankly avowed. The order in which the constitution of the year XII listed the organs of state is suggestive, for it fixed their place in the bureaucratic hierarchy. After the emperor came the senate, then the council of state, the legislative body, and finally the tribunate. The function of the conservative senate was primarily consultative; its opinions, furnished at the invitation of the emperor, could be issued with the effect of laws. The legislative body and the tribunate had declined in importance, *le pouvoir législatif* was no longer mentioned after 1804 and the tribunate was destined to disappear in 1808. In effect this meant that all power of decision had passed to the executive branch of the government. Even the *consulta* of the senate, expressed, like most French revolutionary legislation, as general formulas rather than specific bills, lent themselves to broad interpretation and implementation. With the transition to the Empire the subservient senate, the impotent legislative body and the expiring tribunate became no more than impressive adornments for the imperial machine. The brain of the organism was the council of state, its arms, the ministers, the generals, and the prefects. The voice of the assemblies sank to a meaningless murmur of assent until they became, in Thibaudeau's caustic phrase, "an echo in a desert of silence."

Though mentioned but briefly in the constitutions of the year VIII and the year X, the council of state had been from the first a cabinet of experts upon whose knowledge Bonaparte drew constantly in formulating his projects. Seven ministers (the number had increased to eleven by 1812) formed the nucleus, twenty-five councilors present constituted a quorum. At the meetings, frequently presided over by the emperor in person, the *redacteurs* of the day's agenda bore the brunt of the discussion, but the *auditeurs,* young men in training for administrative posts, were encouraged to profit by attendance. Bonaparte well knew that no form of bribery is so seductive as that which offers a man brave work in his chosen craft, and the *élite* of the civil service, authorized to attend a session of the council, were as grateful to their chief as a soldier honored on the battlefield. "The council of state," one of them recorded later, moved to lyricism by the recollection of those great days, "the council of state was then the axis of the government, the unique voice of France, the torch of the law, and the soul of the emperor."[8] It was there, among men more nearly his equals than any others he ever knew, that Bonaparte exerted to the utmost that power of analysis and lucidity of expression which constituted the essential quality of his genius. He himself was attracted, as Lefebvre has truly observed, less by the deeds of great men than by the spiritual ardor to which those deeds bear witness,[9] and in council he could be at his best, compelling his colleagues to admiration by the sheer intensity of his intellectual conceptions. In the presence of that prodigious and unwearied schemer able spirits were electrified and lesser minds caught the fire. The council of state was more than the soul of the emperor; it was the reservoir of the living forces of France.[10]

The dearth of able subordinates is a perennial plaint with most despots. Bonaparte's first generation of officials, trained in the pragmatic school of the Revolution, formed a group unique in character and experience. His second generation, the product of deliberate selection and discipline, was by his own confession less capable and less enterprising. It may be that his barrack-room methods drilled the initiative out of them, but this explanation, so gratifying to liberal historians, tells only half the story. The international empire developed too rapidly for French institutions to furnish sufficient officers

[8] J. L. Aucoc, *Le Conseil d'État avant et depuis 1789* (Paris, 1876), 95.
[9] G. Lefebvre, *Napoléon* (Paris, 1935), 64.
[10] F. Masson, *Le Département des affaires étrangères pendant la Révolution, 1787-1804* (Paris, 1903), 453.

for the armies or civilian personnel for the expanding administration. Young men who had barely completed their schooling in civil law and attended the council of state for a year were hurried on to important administrative or diplomatic posts. All the secretaries of legation, for instance, were chosen from this source after 1807, but the demand outran the supply, and the lower ranks had to be filled up with appointees unknown to the emperor and less adequately trained. It has often been charged against Napoleon that the imperial university and the military colleges which he organized were no more than factories designed to transform the youth of France into civil or military functionaries. The charge is justified, but it is important to realize that a century and a half ago, when nine-tenths of the European population was illiterate, the lack of competent officials might cripple a government more seriously than the lack of funds. In attacking this difficulty Bonaparte displayed again his clear perception of essential needs, but no educational reforms which he instituted could have rectified the situation in his time.

This paucity of administrative personnel largely explains the readiness shown, under the Consulate, to ignore a man's precedents, and the lenience sometimes displayed by the emperor towards disloyalty or graft. It was not easy to find or to retain competent subordinates. A decree of Floréal 3, year VIII (1800) promised all civil servants security of tenure and a comfortable retirement annuity. If accused of incompetence or corruption they could submit their case to a committee of their colleagues, and were liable to dismissal only if the charges were clearly sustained. By this enlightened policy, which left each department jurisdiction over its own employees and assured government officials promotion and salary proportional to their merit and length of service, Bonaparte sought to create an *esprit de corps* in the services, free them from the vicissitudes of politics, and attract to them young men ambitious for an honorable career. The responsibility rested on each bureau to set its house in order, and even when the impulse came from above the revisions were carried through in the guise of a voluntary purge. A typical example of such reform is provided by the "purification" of the judiciary instituted in 1808. A committee of legists, nominated at the suggestion of the emperor, recommended the retirement of ninety-four judges on the ground that they had failed to maintain the standard of dignity and impartiality which the public had a right to expect of the magistracy. Napoleon, in accepting the recommendations, congratulated the commission for its zeal in maintaining the ideals of the profession.[11]

The ablest civilians in the imperial service, outside the council of state, were the prefects. It was their task to execute the emperor's will in the *départements* and to guide public opinion. "Napoleon wished his rule to be a dictatorship of persuasion founded upon popularity,"[12] and he struck this note from the first with his challenging proclamation: "Citizens, we have indicated our duties; it will be for you to tell us if we fulfill them." The irony implicit in such a motto, under a régime which thoughtfully relieved the public of all means of telling the government anything at all, occasioned little comment at the time. For the French people realized that the true principles of the new régime had been more frankly defined in the maxim of Siéyès: "Confidence from below, authority from above." But it must be enlightened authority, responsive to the needs, if not to the clamor, of the people. It was at this point that the rôle of the prefects became significant. They were warned never to court a demagogue's popularity by inviting the public to criticize their acts, nor to raise unauthorized hopes by misrepresenting their influence with the national government. They were also warned to keep their constituents tranquil and loyal by practicing all the arts of cajolery, and to avoid all appearance of compulsion save in exceptional and individual cases. In carrying out official instructions they had the assurance that the government would stand back of them, that any reprimand they incurred would be administered privately, and that they would never be sacrificed to popular pressure or political jobbery. But in their case also the principle "confidence from below, authority from above" held true; their instructions from Paris were always curt and sometimes peremptory, their confidential reports were seldom reciprocated in kind, and they were occasionally left in complete ignorance of the imperial plans, even those affecting their own *département*.

[11] G. Vauthier, "L'épuration de la magistrature en 1808," *Revue des études napoléoniennes*, XI (1917), 218-23.
[12] A. Aulard, "La centralization napoléonienne: les préfets," *Études et leçons*, VII (Paris, 1913), 146.

III. THE ARMY

The successes won by the French revolutionary armies after 1793 were attributable chiefly to a new spirit and new tactics. *Élan* came to be prized more highly than discipline, and the process known as the *amalgame* replaced years of formal training. Compelled to turn citizens into soldiers in the shortest possible time, the republican government filled the gaps in the ranks with raw volunteers who picked up the tricks of their trade on the march from comrades who had seen a campaign or two. In action it proved impossible to match the precision and stolidity with which the well-trained automatons of the old régime advanced in rank formation, so the republicans developed a column charge with bayonets ready. As the muskets of the time had an effective range of less than two hundred yards and could be fired only four times in three minutes, the attackers could close with the foe after facing a couple of volleys. Conspicuous bravery in action was the surest pass to promotion and vacancies in the lower grades were filled promptly by recommendation of the colonel commanding. After twelve years of warfare this system reached its maximum effectiveness in 1805. The French armies which shattered the Third Coalition represented an equal amalgam of veterans and recruits and were by Napoleon's admission the finest divisions he ever led. In the later years of the Empire the carnage of Eylau and Aspern, the increasing dilution of the imperial forces by raw or foreign levies, and the profitless campaigns in Spain and Russia sharply reduced the efficiency of that superb fighting machine which Napoleon had inherited and brought to perfection.

In addition to new tactics, the mobile unit and the column charge, the revolutionary wars introduced a new strategy. Professional armies of the eighteenth century had been limited in size, and generals seldom took the field with more than fifty or sixty thousand men, for existing methods of organization and supply made a larger force difficult to maneuver or articulate. When the *levée en masse* and later the conscription law swelled the French armies beyond manageable limits, the war ministry broke them down into divisions of ten to twenty thousand men. Under the Directory a new organism, the army corps, emerged, a discrete unit composed of two or three divisions, with its own reserves of cavalry and artillery. Bonaparte was the first commander to appreciate the full possibilities of this new instrument of war. His favorite strategy was to concert the movement of several army corps behind a range of hills, a forest, or a screen of skirmishers, and then concentrate them suddenly by converging routes in the presence of a startled enemy. Against inferior numbers the fighting qualities of the French infantry and cavalry could be relied upon to achieve a decisive victory, and it was ever the major aim of Napoleon's strategy to compel the foe to fight at a numerical disadvantage. Marengo and Austerlitz are exceptions, and stand out as two decisive battles which he risked and won with odds of six to five against him. It is worth noting that in each case the political situation was more exigent than the military. As a *chef d'œuvre* neither of these conflicts can be held to surpass Hohenlinden, where Moreau won an equally conclusive victory by similar methods against similar odds and followed it up more swiftly. Moreover, Moreau's casualties were only five per cent of his effectives, whereas Napoleon's losses were twenty per cent at Marengo and ten per cent at Austerlitz.[13] If, despite these figures, the legend still persists that Napoleon constantly achieved miracles against superior forces, and possessed a secret formula for victory which no contemporary general could apply, the answer must be sought in his genius for self-advertisement. He seldom gave his subordinates public credit for performances which might dim the glory of his own; neither Kellerman at Marengo, Moreau at Hohenlinden, nor Davout at Auerstädt received full credit for the initiative and courage which brought them victory.

The myth that Napoleon conducted war according to esoteric principles which his genius had divined provides one more illustration of "the leaning of sophists towards apocrypha." As a child of the Enlightenment he was not immune to such a pretense himself, and insisted upon occasion that "every well-conducted war is a war of method" and "the military art is an art subject to rules which it is never permissible to violate." But in franker moods he repudiated such doctrinaire claims. "There are no precise or determined rules; everything depends on the character which nature has bestowed upon

[13] Otto Berndt, *Die Zahl im Kriege* (Vienna, 1897), tables 18-21.

the commander; on his talents and his defects, on the temper of the troops, the disposition of forces, the season of the year, and a thousand contingencies which make no two actions alike." The lessons of history and of his own experience confirmed his belief that nothing succeeds like success and that a bold front is half the battle. "My whole plan of campaign," he confessed in a moment of unusual candor, "is a battle, my whole policy a victory."[14] When victories could no longer be improvised the game was over.

The legend that Napoleon's genius for organization made the grand army a marvel of efficiency is another tradition which has been dimmed by recent scrutiny. Studies on draft evasion and desertion prove that these evils remained perpetual problems for which no remedy could be found. Pay, especially after 1806, was almost always in arrears, and the resultant mutinies were usually condoned or repressed with leniency. The commissariat and transportation services, entrusted under contract to civilian profiteers, were wretchedly inadequate, and the troops were handicapped by a recurrent insufficiency of muskets, shoes, and bread. When they campaigned in populous and fertile regions, like the Po and Rhine valleys, their privations could be eased by confiscation, and few armies have practiced more successfully the art of living off the country. But in northern Germany, and especially in Poland, Spain, and Russia this hazardous method failed with gruesome consequences. On all Napoleon's campaigns, soldiers of the French armies, weakened by an alternation of gorging and fasting, fell ready victims to disease, and the deaths from this cause exceeded the battle casualties. The medical corps remained to the end of the Empire the most inadequate, under-staffed, and generally incompetent branch of the service, and the handling of the sick and wounded was only surpassed in its brutality by the treatment accorded the horses.[15]

The deterioration of the grand army after 1806 was due in no small measure to the deficiencies of French industry. To supply weapons and equipment for an army of half a million men would tax the productive machinery of a modern state. In Napoleonic

[14] E. Kessel, "Die Wandlung der Kriegskunst im Zeitalter der französischen Revolution," *Historische Zeitschrift*, CXLVIII (1933), 248-276.

[15] J. Bourdon, "L'Administration militaire sous Napoléon Ier," *Revue des études napoléoniennes*, XI (1917), 17-47.

France handworkers failed to provide the muskets and bayonets needed, the number of forges was insufficient and the standards low, and the artisans, poorly paid and resentful of their disabilities, had little incentive to speed their output. When, as in the case of the artillery, the output was successfully augmented, the quality declined. Further study is needed to determine whether it was not lack of *matériel* rather than lack of men which brought the Empire to defeat; for modern investigations tend to show that Napoleon's battle losses have been greatly overestimated, and that French man power was far from exhausted in 1814. Taine's approximation of 1,700,000 French war dead under the Consulate and Empire, a figure which has been quoted and requoted for half a century, represents an historical error of possibly five hundred per cent. More recent calculations place the number of Frenchmen *recruited* within the ancient boundaries of France from 1800 to 1815 at about 2,000,000, or seven per cent of the population, and the number killed or died of wounds at approximately 400,000.[16] During the World War, twenty-one per cent of the French population was called to the colors, a conscription three times as exacting, and spread over four years instead of fifteen, while the decimation of the conscript levies proceeded from 1914 to 1918 at a rate proportionately eight times as murderous. To estimate the total number of men who were killed or died of wounds in all the European armies during the Napoleonic struggles is a more difficult task, but 1,000,000 has been offered as a rational approximation.[17] These estimates must no doubt be doubled if they are to include the soldiers who fell victims to disease, but such as they are they refute the supposition that the Napoleonic holocausts permanently weakened the stamina of the French nation. The loss of three per cent of the population (six per cent of the male population) over a period of fifteen years, though shocking to humanitarian sentiments, probably

[16] A. Meynier, "Levées et pertes des hommes sous la Consulat et l'Empire," *Revue des études napoléoniennes,* XXX (1930), 46. P. A. Sorokin, *Social and Cultural Dynamics,* 4 vols. (New York, 1937—), III, 551-553, presents independent computations which support the same conclusions. French casualties are estimated at approximately twenty-eight per cent of effectives in the campaigns of 1801-1815, against forty-seven per cent for the years 1914-1918. Total French casualties for the Napoleonic period (excluding foreign levies) are fixed at some 1,270,000, but as casualties in the military sense include losses from death, wounds, capture, or desertion, the same man can figure in the lists several times, and the battle fatalities may well have been no more than one-third the total. In the World War the French dead represented approximately one-fifth of the total casualties.

[17] G. Bodart, *Losses of Life in Modern Wars* (Oxford, 1916), 133.

affected the French birth rate less in these years than a few bad harvests or a sharp rise in the cost of living.

IV. FINANCE AND TAXATION

The fiscal system of the Empire has been singled out for more uncritical praise than any other feature of the Napoleonic régime, but authorities are far from agreement regarding the ultimate wisdom of Napoleon's economic measures. Two factors make a final judgment peculiarly difficult: the constant repercussion of political and military events upon French national credit, and the part played by that irregular fund, the *domaine extraordinaire*, which was built up from the indemnities and confiscations inflicted upon vanquished foes. These contributions have been estimated at a thousand million francs for the years 1806-1810 alone.[18] Napoleon drew on the fund for a variety of disbursements, for the maintenance of the army while in the field, the expenses of the imperial household, occasional subsidies for public works or special services. As Defermon, who administered the *domaine extraordinaire*, was responsible to the emperor alone and made public no details of its operations, the official government budget annually submitted to the nation offered an incomplete and untrustworthy picture of the true condition of receipts and expenditures.

Deprived of these receipts from abroad, it is highly improbable that the imperial government could have undertaken its program of public works without floating long-term loans, an expedient which Napoleon refused to countenance on the ground that it laid a curse upon succeeding generations. He had been fortified in this resolution by the exorbitant rates—three per cent per month—which bankers demanded when the Consular government sought financial assistance in its first months.[19] After the establishment of the Bank of France, the treasury utilized this new institution almost exclusively for temporary accommodations, the bank advancing a total of 722,000,000 francs to the government between 1800 and 1805, chiefly by discounting the obligations of the collectors-

[18] P. Darmstädter, "Studien zur Napoleonischen Wirtschaftspolitik," *Vierteljahrschrift für Sozial und Wirtschaftsgeschichte* II (1904), 563.
[19] A. Liesse, *Evolution of Credit and Banks in France*, Government Printing Office (Washington, 1909), 16.

general at six per cent *per annum*. In 1807, at the emperor's insistence, the rate was cut to four per cent and by 1813 the treasury was indebted to the bank for some 340,000,000 francs.[20] The impression that Napoleon avoided every form of borrowing is therefore incorrect; his veto was limited to bond issues and annuities which would have permanently increased the national debt.

The close association existing between the bank and the treasury exposed the bank to grave risks. In 1801 the ministry of finance was split into two departments, with Gaudin in charge of receipts and Barbé-Marbois to supervise expenditures. The campaign of 1805 threw such a heavy burden upon the treasury that Barbé-Marbois could not pay the purveyors to the army, especially a company known as the *Négociants Reunis*, which had also speculated on Spanish colonial shipments now halted by the British blockade. To save the *United Merchants* from ruin Marbois urged the bank to advance them credits which rose ultimately to 141,000,000 francs. In order to oblige, the bank raised its note issue to the unwarranted sum of 80,000,000 francs; a panic followed, and in September, 1805, it was driven to a partial suspension of payments, its specie having fallen to 782,000 francs with notes for 63,000,000 still unredeemed.[21] The victory of Austerlitz in December saved the situation, and Napoleon's first act on returning to Paris in January, 1806, was to replace Marbois by Mollien, who restored the bank to solvency. The main force of Napoleon's wrath fell upon the *United Merchants* whose leader, Ouvrard, was later imprisoned for bankruptcy.

Public confidence in the financial stability of the Empire, weakened at all times by the suspicion that the budgets told only part of the story, vacillated nervously in response to the wars and rumors of war that filled the period. French consolidated government bonds, interest upon which remained a first charge against the revenue, fluctuated between 70 and 80, touching 93 briefly in 1807 after the Peace of Tilsit. Market quotations on these five-per-cents cannot be taken as an infallible barometer, for the treasury had orders to peg them on the Bourse by secret buying when they threatened to decline. Nevertheless, the fact that they were still quoted at 45

[20] Liesse, *op. cit.*, 40.
[21] Liesse, *op. cit.*, 29-30.

in the week of Napoleon's abdication in 1814 suggests that France had reëstablished some degree of national credit during the later Empire. Louis XVIII, before his return, hastened to reassure the bondholders that the debt would be honored by the Restoration government, and the Bank of France resumed its normal course of operations as soon as the political crisis was over.

With the department of receipts, administered by the industrious Gaudin, Napoleon had little fault to find. The collection of internal revenue was reduced to order under the Consulate[22] and underwent no important modifications under the Empire. A gradual increase in the excise on liquors, salt, and tobacco rendered these *droits reunis* unpopular and protests against them had grown vehement by 1813. Land and personal taxes were lightened, but this reduction was nullified by shifting a larger share of the expenditure for religion, charity, and local administration to the municipalities, which had no option but to raise local taxes. Despite the disappearance of the most vexatious tolls and imposts of the old régime, and the energetic prosecution of the public works program, Frenchmen suspected that the government of Napoleon, while more efficient, was also more expensive to support than that of Louis XVI had been, and they were probably correct. For even with the contributions from abroad swelling the war chest, military needs devoured over half the national revenues in years of peace. To undertake foreign ventures which would transfer the cost of supporting the army divisions onto alien shoulders and at the same time augment the war indemnities remained a perpetual temptation. For the Empire peace was an extravagance, and it is not without significance that the two most serious business depressions which struck France in this era—that of 1804-1805 and 1810-1811—followed on the two intervals when the nation had been at peace for over a year.

V. AGRICULTURE, INDUSTRY, AND COMMERCE

Four chapters of Napoleonic history, the political, military, diplomatic, and religious, were sketched in the nineteenth century; a fifth, on the economic background, was largely neglected until the

[22] See above, pp. 21-25.

twentieth.[23] Today, thanks to the research of recent decades, the blueprints of Napoleon's imperial design stand forth in sharper outline as the conflict of economic forces is more definitely traced. Political economy, the last major field of administration which he sought to master, proved the most recalcitrant to his methods. Translated into economic formulas, his plans for the aggrandizement of France reveal the arbitrary and doctrinaire qualities of his mind at their worst. It is not necessary to cite the "continental blockade," that "monstrosity" as Levasseur termed it,[24] to emphasize this thesis. From the outset he adopted a course which, if successful, would have imposed upon Europe an economic disequilibrium more contrary to historic trends and more onerous to the subject peoples than his political hegemony. Later, in an empire which he pretended to consider international, he pursued the same policy of intensified mercantilism, exercising his authority to bend the economic forces of Europe exclusively towards the enrichment of France.

Years spent under the pressure of dispatching administrative decisions induces the mental habit, so baneful if indulged to excess, of classifying issues categorically in order to expedite judgment. In economic as in other matters Napoleon found it convenient to evaluate French national activities in a fixed order of importance. Agriculture he accepted as the primary economic interest of the state, industry he placed second, and commerce third. In similar fashion, when regulating tariffs he considered the prosperity of France the paramount issue, that of Italy came next, Belgium, Holland, the Hanse Towns and Illyria third, and the rest of the European states fourth.[25] It is significant that these gradations reflect approximately the degree of devotion which the populations concerned in these several groups and regions developed towards him as emperor. The French peasants were in general the best contented class in France; the industrialists welcomed the high protection and occasional subsidies provided by the imperial government, though the workers had less reason for gratitude; while the merchants and traders, es-

[23] W. E. Lingelbach, "Historical investigation and the commercial history of the Napoleonic Era," *American Historical Review*, XIX (1914), 256-279.

[24] E. Levasseur, *Histoire du commerce de la France*, II (Paris, 1912), 93.

[25] E. Tarlé, "Napoléon Ier et les interêts économiques de la France," *Revue des études napoléoniennes*, XXVI (1926), 117-137.

pecially those who had formerly handled colonial wares, preserved a chronic grievance. Outside the boundaries of ancient France the Italian people were the most completely reconciled to the French preponderance; in Holland and the Hanse Towns French commercial regulations proved difficult to enforce and discontent mounted steadily; while Spain, Austria, and finally Russia defied the continental blockade. This centrifugal disintegration of Napoleon's influence has commonly been explained on the ground that his power varied in direct proportion to the distance which his armies must march to exact a reckoning, a formula which ignores entirely the economic motives for resistance. What part these motives played in the growth of opposition towards France is an intricate question which must depend for its final solution on regional studies not yet completed.

French agriculture, left largely to itself, suffered least from Napoleon's passion for regulation. Crops were still produced in large measure for local consumption, and when there was a wheat surplus permission was accorded to export it, even to England. The main exception to this liberal policy was the legislation covering the food supply of Paris, where the butchers and bakers operated under strict control. Dread of discontent arising from excessive commodity prices moved Napoleon to fix a maximum for grains in 1812, but in general the economic policies of the Empire gratified and enriched the peasants. The exclusion of colonial imports, and the encouragement of new crops, like woad for an indigo substitute and beets for sugar (250,000 acres were set aside for the latter after 1810) increased the profits of agriculture. Had the government offer of a million francs for a machine which would spin flax thread borne prompt fruit a further profit might have accrued to the landowner. Official encouragement of the silk industry led to an impressive increase in the mulberry crop in France and Italy before the close of the Empire.

For French industry the years between 1789 and 1814 were a critical quarter of a century, but manufacturers benefited more from the effects of the revolutionary wars than has been commonly supposed. When the French Republic revoked the moderate preferential duties which had been established between France and Britain in 1786, and sought instead to exclude British products from Europe, French industrialists were protected from their most aggressive competitors. This was no small advantage at a time when many manufacturers were undertaking the costly and hazardous transition to machine and power production. With the advent of Bonaparte this change was deliberately accelerated. He sought to assure plentiful credit at four per cent for industrial expansion, opened neighboring countries to French manufactures by tariff agreements, and exhorted chemists and agriculturalists to find substitutes for the raw materials cut off by the British blockade. These policies produced some notable results, especially after 1806. Leblanc's process for making sodium carbonate from sodium chloride freed France from dependence upon imported soda, the cost of which had averaged over 5,000,000 francs a year. The Jacquard loom, rights to which were acquired by the state in 1806, executed intricate patterns in silk. Most remarkable of all was the progress in cotton-spinning; the output of French mills, estimated at some 4,500,000 pounds in 1806, had quadrupled by 1810, and the exports for that year alone were valued at 11,668,800 francs. These are official figures and may be suspected of some exaggeration, but they suggest remarkable progress and indicate that French industry responded to the impulse of mechanization contemporaneously with that of Great Britain, though less extensively. The activity of the French cotton industry particularly alarmed the British, and orders in council specifically listed raw cotton as contraband, a step which barred the American supply from the French mills but could not hinder imports from the Levant. By the close of the Empire the introduction of machinery in French industry was so far advanced that one of the most conscientious investigators in this field has ventured to style it *un fait accompli*.[26]

This favorable estimate of French industrial progress does not hold for the metallurgical trades. The transition from wood to coke smelting was delayed in France, and the lack of vigorous competition enabled many small and primitive hand foundries to continue in operation, and permitted, under the lax standards prevailing, the

[26] Ch. Ballot, *L'introduction du machinisme dans l'industrie française* (Lille, 1923), 2-3. Ballot was killed at Verdun in 1917 before he could complete his researches, but his general thesis is brilliantly substantiated.

output of much low-grade work. As a consequence the French iron industry made comfortable profits, but failed to meet the national needs, and in 1815 it was still almost half a century behind that of Great Britain in method, quality, and production. Lack of greater enterprise in a field so vital to the welfare of the state in peace and especially in war suggests the limitations of the imperial policy. In the world of business Napoleon could flatter and encourage, he could restrict and destroy, but he could not create or command. There liberty of action remained the rule, though it was a rule corrupted by a multitude of detailed and often irritating ordinances. Manufacturers, while recognizing the emperor's zeal for their welfare, constantly deplored the arbitrary and impetuous decrees which issued from his cabinet, and never ceased to petition, with increasing petulance, for less supervision of manufacturing methods and less versatility in tariff legislation.[27]

Similar protests were raised by the *négociants* and with more reason for commerce was the Cinderella of the imperial household. Before the Revolution one-third of the French imports, and one-fifth of the export trade, had depended upon the colonies.[28] With the closing of the ocean routes to French vessels the sea ports became death towns, a fact which helps to explain the persistence of royalist sentiment from Rouen to Marseilles. So long as the war continued against the mistress of the seas the only remedy for the situation was to seek substitutes at home for materials previously drawn from the colonies, and to divert to European markets the products formerly sold abroad. To carry out this readjustment without undue dislocation of trade became Napoleon's major economic aim; the markets of Europe, he insisted, were richer and nearer to hand than markets overseas, and he could open them to French wares by securing preferential tariffs. When the merchants argued for free trade, and deplored his attempts to canalize the flow of commerce as unwise and unworkable, he scolded them for lack of devotion to the national welfare, and warned them to take example from the industrialists who were growing rich by seconding his projects.

[27] Tarlé, *op cit.*, 134-135.
[28] P. Darmstädter, "Studien zur Napoleonischen Wirtschaftspolitik" *Vierteljahrschrift für Sozial und Wirtschaftsgeschichte*, II (1904), 565-570.

Not all commercial centers suffered equally; the misfortune of the western ports was the good fortune of several inland cities. The plan to abandon sea routes for land routes shifted the head-quarters for commercial activity from the west to the east of France, and Lyons and Strasbourg, which became clearing houses for the Italian and German trade, prospered from the new dispensation. But despite the official and often officious encouragement, despite the extension of French influence throughout Europe, the foreign trade of France never achieved under the Empire the total it had maintained during the closing years of the old régime. Existing routes of communication were too inadequate, the obstacles hindering the transfer of heavy cargoes like lumber were too severe for the internal lines of transport to compete successfully with the ocean lanes, especially in an age before railroads. One of the few permanent advantages which the new system brought to France was the network of new roads and canals which it necessitated. Improved means of transportation were vital to the success of the emperor's commercial policies, and his famous imperial roads were designed to serve the legions of Mercury no less than the hosts of Mars.

VI. TRANSPORT AND COMMUNICATION

"I would have changed the route of commerce and the face of industry," Napoleon boasted at St. Helena, listing with pride the details of the communication system which his engineers had drawn up.[29] Plans for the construction of stone-surfaced roads linking Paris to the frontiers had been discussed under the old régime; the Directory had endeavored to put them into execution (law of the 24 Fructidor, year V), but the taxes assessed for the purpose were diverted to more pressing needs and the highways sank by 1799 into a deplorable condition. Here once again the new Cæsar was able to crown the projects of his predecessors and reap the glory. Between 1804 and 1812 over 300,000,000 francs were spent on roads and bridges. Two hundred and twenty-nine imperial routes, leading from Paris to all parts of Europe, formed the radii of a network which, when complete, was to include main arteries from Paris to

---

[29] W. E. Lingelbach, "Historical investigation and the commercial history of the Napoleonic Era," *American Historical Review*, XIX (1914), 258.

Hamburg, Paris to Amsterdam, and Paris to Madrid. At the close of the Empire 30,000 kilometers of the 33,162 proposed were at least open to travel, and an additional 18,600 kilometers of departmental highways were in use. All the routes were reclassified under Napoleon and it is not easy to decide how this total—51,762 kilometers of imperial and departmental roads—compares with the mileage available under the Monarchy. If the imperial and departmental routes are regarded as corresponding roughly to what were termed first- and second-class roads before 1789, then the revolutionary era witnessed an increase from 32,000 to nearly 52,000 kilometers. Neither figure includes the 20,000 to 40,000 kilometers of dirt roads connecting one town with another, for these local highways degenerated at times into cow paths that foiled the statisticians.

The completion of a new and speedier highway was to the emperor a victory won against his great enemy Time, and the Roman element in his nature exulted at leaving such monuments to posterity. Yet here again he obeyed a tradition established under the Bourbons. France, the leader in modern road construction, had already possessed the finest highway system in Europe before the Revolution. Arthur Young was by no means the only foreigner to comment on the splendid French roads, so smooth and pleasant under their poplar shade, and so little traveled. Stone roadbeds with a convex surface had been introduced by Tresaguet as early as 1780, and were speedily supplanted by the improved construction devised by Macadam in England. By the close of the eighteenth century England had overtaken and was rapidly outstripping France in such road construction, but the rest of Europe lagged half a century behind and as late as 1815 few stone-faced roads existed beyond the French frontiers.

As engineering feats the mountain roads constructed by French enterprise made the strongest impression upon contemporaries. The Simplon Pass was opened to carriages in 1805, the Mont Cenis Pass in 1806. To further facilitate intercourse with Italy Bonaparte sought additional routes, and the famous Corniche Road, renowned since Roman times, which he had followed in 1796 on his first invasion of Italy, was reconstructed from Nice to Genoa, with extensions planned to Spezzia and Florence. But for commerce in bulk the cost of land transportation remained prohibitively high on the best roads, and rivers or canals offered the only available alternative. France boasted 1,000 kilometers of canals in 1800; by 1814 the figure had doubled, and vital connections from the Rhine to the Rhone, the Scheldt to the Somme, the Rance to the Vilaine and the Ourcq had been completed. Though stimulated, no doubt, by the strain which the British blockade threw upon all internal lines of communication, this development of roads and canals in France under the Consulate and Empire must be regarded primarily as the normal acceleration of a process already manifest in the eighteenth century. The British, whose sea-borne trade suffered no interruption between 1800 and 1815 and increased fifty per cent in volume, nevertheless found it expedient to better their internal communications system, and the new roads and canals which they constructed in these years exceeded in mileage those built in France.

A similar speeding up of passenger and mail transportation distinguished this period, and here likewise the English services excelled. Coaches from London to Edinburgh cut their time to forty-two hours by 1800, when it still required six days for a journey of approximately the same distance from Paris to Bordeaux.[30] In the last years of the eighteenth century a schedule of regular departures was established for the principal stage lines in both countries and the comfort and security of the passengers were greatly enhanced. Fares averaged about eight cents a mile for an inside seat and half as much for outside accommodation. Postal charges still varied with the distance to be covered, a letter from London to Edinburgh costing fourteenpence, and proportional rates prevailed in France. The visual telegraph, perfected during the Revolution by the brothers Chiappe, made it possible for Napoleon to transmit brief messages across France in a few hours, weather permitting, but this new system of communication remained a government monopoly and was still too expensive to prove of commercial value.

[30] B. Nogaro and W. Oualid, L'Evolution du commerce, du crédit et des transports (Paris, 1914), 49.

Chapter Five

THE ECONOMIC CONFLICT: FRANCE AND GREAT BRITAIN

I. FRENCH COLONIAL ASPIRATIONS

THE wars of the eighteenth century stripped France of all but a trivial fraction of what had been an extensive colonial empire. By the Peace of Utrecht (1713-1714) Newfoundland, Acadia, and Hudson Bay Territory passed to Great Britain; by the Peace of Paris (1763) Canada was likewise lost, while the French claims to the Mississippi River and the lands west of it were transferred to Spain. The same treaty permanently blighted the French dreams of imperial expansion in India. To millions of Frenchmen, living inland, these losses appeared negligible, for the half-explored lands beyond the Atlantic had never seemed worth fighting for, and their potential value was considered almost as problematical as that attached today to segments of Antarctica. But in the maritime centers of France colonial interest was keen and the reverses of the eighteenth century did not extinguish it. In the outburst of national pride and energy released by the Revolution an active element in commercial and shipping circles pressed for the resumption of an aggressive colonial policy.

All the auguries, in the first decade of the Revolution, seemed unfavorable to such a course. The outbreak of war with England in 1793 made sea voyages hazardous; and of the colonies still remaining Martinique was captured, while Guadaloupe and Haiti were devastated by civil war resulting from the ill-managed attempts to abolish slavery. It is not surprising that French hopes turned to projects nearer home, and that writers lauded the Egyptian expedition of 1798 as laying the cornerstone for a new colonial empire. "No colony has ever offered greater advantages," Bonaparte wrote from Cairo in September; but the audacious venture was wrecked in the storms of the Second Coalition and the new conquest had to be abandoned.[1] Undeterred by the failure, the First Consul seized the chance which came with the restoration of order in France and peace with Great Britain to dispatch Colonel Sebastiani on a tour of the eastern Mediterranean in 1802. Sebastiani had orders to observe the state of the defenses, the attitude of the populace, and the opportunities for French intervention in Egypt, Syria, and the Ionian Islands. His report, published in January, 1803, helped to arouse the apprehensions of the British.[2] Two months later General Decaen started for India, ostensibly for the purpose of administering the French posts returned by the Peace of Amiens, though his title of captain-general and the small flotilla which accompanied him hinted at a more ambitious program. But the renewal of war with England in the spring of 1803 nullified these preparations.

The most ambitious and the most costly colonial effort which France put forth in this period was the attempt to reconquer Haiti. The western part of the island had been a French possession since 1677, and Spain had ceded to France the title to the eastern half by the Treaty of Basel in 1795. It was Bonaparte's intention to make Haiti a stepping-stone to Louisiana, which he induced the Spanish government to retrocede by the secret treaty of San Ildefonso, negotiated in 1800. His leaping imagination pictured a French empire in America, the Antilles its gateway, New Orleans commanding the mouth of the Mississippi, French Guiana, enlarged by a section of Brazilian coast gained from Portugal in 1801, commanding the northern outlet of the Amazon.[3] But this insubstantial pageant faded with the destruction of Leclerc's expedition to Haiti, where the obduracy of the blacks and the malignance of the yellow fever dimmed the French hopes of reconquest by the close of 1802. Even a major part of the troops intended for New Orleans had to be deflected to the island and sacrificed to the hostility of man and nature.[4]

The disaster at Haiti helped to settle the fate of Louisiana. This

---

[1] C. L. Lokke, "French Dreams of Colonial Empire under Directory and Consulate," *Journal of Modern History*, II (1930), 246.
[2] The report appeared in the official *Moniteur*, January 30, 1803.
[3] The Franco-Portuguese treaty extending French Guiana is in De Clercq, *Recueil des traités de la France*, I, 455-457.
[4] E. W. Lyon, *Bonaparte's proposed Louisiana Expedition* (Chicago, 1934), 10-14.

vast territory had been ceded by France to Spain in 1763 at the close of the Seven Years' War, but the cost of administration and the westward expansion of the young United States convinced Spanish statesmen by 1795 that the colony was a liability. The Spanish minister of foreign affairs, Manuel de Godoy, when arranging the Treaty of Basel with the French Republic in that year, offered to sacrifice Louisiana for the sake of peace, but in the end the Spanish half of Haiti[5] was ceded to France instead. Five years later, after Bonaparte's victory at Marengo, negotiations for the transfer were renewed, and on October 1, 1800, Spain retroceded Louisiana to France in return for the First Consul's promise that a scion of the Spanish Bourbons should reign at Florence as King of Etruria. This Treaty of San Ildefonso was kept secret lest it arouse premature opposition in England and the United States, and Spain retained possession of the colony two years longer. Far from being bullied into a craven surrender, the Spaniards could persuade themselves that they had exchanged a colonial liability for an Italian kingdom.[6]

In the United States fear that the monopoly of the Mississippi might pass from the feeble authority of Spain to the masterful control of France moved Jefferson to dispatch James Monroe to Paris to effect a compromise. Monroe arrived on April 12, 1803, and found Napoleon already resolved to sell not merely a portion but all of the Louisiana territory. The motives for this change of attitude have been much debated. No doubt the gloomy news from Haiti at the close of 1802 had prepared the way, and Sebastiani's optimistic report on the eastern Mediterranean lands, coming at the same time, may have confirmed Napoleon's preference for colonial ventures in regions more glamorous and more accessible. Furthermore, the imminence of renewed war with England exposed Louisiana to conquest from the sea. But Barbé-Marbois, Napoleon's minister of the treasury, urged a more cogent argu-

[5] The island, variously known as Hispaniola, Santo Domingo, and Hayti, is styled Haiti here throughout, in conformity with the recent decision of the United States Geographic Board.

[6] A. P. Whitaker, in "The Retrocession of Louisiana in Spanish Diplomacy," *American Historical Review*, XXXIX (1934), 454-476, and "Louisiana in the Treaty of Basel," *Journal of Modern History*, VIII (1936), 1-26, has shed new light on the Spanish motives. For the French position, see E. W. Lyon, *Louisiana in French Diplomacy* (Norman, Okla., 1923).

ment upon his imperial master. "That conquest would be even more simple for the Americans. They are arriving on the Mississippi by several navigable rivers and to be masters of the country they have only to enter it."[7] Marbois may not have ventured at this time his later surprising prophecy that the United States would have a population of 100,000,000 by 1900,[8] but if he called attention to the second American census, the figures for which had lately come to hand,[9] Napoleon must have appreciated their import, for the tide of settlers in Kentucky had swollen from 73,677 to 220,955 in ten years. On April 30, 1803, Barbé-Marbois for France, Livingston (who deserves chief credit for pressing the American claims) and Monroe for the United States, signed the convention whereby Louisiana was to become American territory in exchange for a payment of 60,000,000 francs ($11,250,000). The following November the Spanish governor of the province yielded formal possession to a French official who in turn transferred it to the United States commissioners. The American flag was raised at New Orleans on December 20, 1803.

II. BRITISH MARITIME STRENGTH

The defeat of French colonial projects during the revolutionary wars tells but half the story; more costly and even more complete was the destruction of the French merchant marine. Before 1789 over 2,000 French ships had been engaged in European and colonial trade; ten years later there was not a merchant ship on the high seas flying the French flag. Some 800 had been captured by the British, the remainder lay rotting in the harbors, or, if of light enough tonnage, flitted hastily from port to port in coastal waters. The heaviest losses had befallen ships of 200 tons and over. By 1800 France retained only 200 such vessels, less than one-fifth the number employed before the Revolution.

[7] Barbé-Marbois, *Histoire de la Louisiane* (Paris, 1829), 288.

[8] E. W. Lyon, "Barbé-Marbois and his *Histoire de la Louisiane*," Franco-American *Review*, I (1937), 359.

[9] The *Moniteur* for 10 Vendémiaire, an X (October 2, 1801) published the increases in the population of Kentucky and Georgia, giving the item the place of honor on page one, column one. Marbois may himself have provided the copy, for he was in the habit of furnishing the editor with cogent information on colonial matters (*Vide Correspondance de Napoléon Ier*, VIII, 199-200. No. 6566).

In striking contrast, the British merchant marine had continued to expand despite the hazards of war. The eighteenth century brought a five-hundred-per-cent increase in British merchant tonnage, and by 1800 it stood at nearly 1,500,000 tons.[10] Even in the seven years of war from 1793 to 1800, years which all but swept French trade from the ocean, the number of ships under British ownership rose from 15,000 to nearly 18,000. Nothing better indicates the energy and the recuperative power of the British merchant marine. With ample supplies of English oak and Scandinavian or American pine to draw upon, with a monopoly of the world's colonial products available, not to mention a superior metallurgical industry to arm the men-of-war, Great Britain enjoyed an advantage in naval construction which France could not seriously challenge. The unequal competition helped to destroy the fiscal balance which Napoleon had achieved, and the three years which followed the renewal of war in 1803 saw the French naval expenditures leap from a projected total of 240,000,000 francs for the triennium to more than 440,000,000, an extravagant indulgence of hopes that were doomed to founder at Trafalgar.[11] Raids upon British commerce and the interception of convoys in the narrow seas the French might indeed attempt, and the tonnage captured in this manner was by no means negligible. Mahan has calculated that on the average some 524 British merchant ships a year fell into the hands of the French and their allies between 1795 and 1810.[12] But this constituted, even in the worst years, no more than three per cent of the total British tonnage, and the percentage of captures declined to two and one-half per cent toward the close of the period. Marine insurance rates, the readiest index of the risk involved, touched twenty-five per cent in the 1790's, but by 1806 the average had fallen to twelve per cent and by 1810 to six per cent.[13] The fact that the rate declined as the struggle advanced, and never approached the fifty-per-cent charge quoted by London insurance

---

[10] B. Nogaro and W. Oualid, L'Évolution du commerce, du credit et des transports (Paris, 1914), 40.
[11] Simon de la Rupelle, "Les finances de la guerre de 1796 à 1815," Revue des sciences politiques, VII (1892), 62.
[12] A. T. Mahan, The Influence of Sea Power on the French Revolution and Empire, 14th ed. (Boston, 1919), II, 226.
[13] G. Lefebvre, Napoléon (Paris, 1935), 314.

brokers during the American War of Independence, provides the best comment on the British achievement.

As in the anti-submarine campaign of the World War, the British found the convoy method the surest defense against enemy depredations. This system involved a risky dispersal of naval reserves and often delayed or prolonged merchant voyages, for it required time to assemble the five hundred or more merchant ships, which sometimes put to sea in company, and the speed of such a flotilla was the speed of its slowest members. But the protection thus afforded was welcomed by all save a few captains, who relied upon superior mobility in eluding the French cruisers. Neither the risks of war nor Napoleon's attempt to close the continent to British goods could arrest the growth of British foreign trade, the value of which rose fifty per cent between 1800 and 1815. French foreign trade, in tragic contrast, languished incurably and did not recover until 1830 the billion francs a year average which it had attained at the close of the old régime.[14]

The *naval* superiority which Britain maintained over France throughout this period, as distinguished from the *mercantile* superiority, appears, superficially at least, much less definitive and overwhelming. Neither side was adequately prepared for a contest on the seas in 1793. The morale of the French naval personnel had suffered greatly in the opening years of the Revolution from civilian interference, the demotion of royalist officers, and the growing insubordination of the crews. But a similar spirit of unrest also infected the British sailors, many of them victims of the notorious press-gang system. Numerous outbreaks, culminating in the mutinies at Spithead and the Nore in 1797, threatened to paralyze the operations of the home fleet. In ships Great Britain possessed a clear though not an incontestable advantage. When the revolutionary war opened the French had eighty-six ships of the line and seventy-eight frigates, but less than one-third of them were in condition to put to sea. The British navy was in a somewhat more efficient state; of 141 ships of the line 115 were ready for action, as well as the greater part of the 157 frigates. When both sides had serviced the

[14] Nogaro and Oualid, *op. cit.,* 137.

dismantled vessels the British were still left with an advantage of something like two to one for ships of the first and second class, which enabled them to spread their forces from the Baltic to the Mediterranean. Yet their naval operations in the war of 1793-1801 were, on the whole, carried on in a mediocre and inconclusive fashion. The outstanding exception was Nelson's victory at the Nile in 1798, which cost the French ten of their best ships and doomed Napoleon's Egyptian expedition.

The renewal of hostilities in 1803 found the adversaries with their relative strength little changed. The British government could send forth two armed ships to Napoleon's one, and could equip two more for each one he might build and commission in French or Dutch harbors. It takes longer, moreover, to train officers than to build ships, and here the British superiority was incontestable. Blockading cruisers now hung off the French ports from Boulogne to Bayonne in all weathers, and the few French squadrons which put to sea were, almost without exception, hunted down and badly mangled before they could return. It seems clear, too, that the French commanders failed to safeguard the health of their crews, either because of faulty sanitation or a deficient diet, and their ships frequently returned from a prolonged voyage with half the men unfit for duty. The British tar was more intelligently provided for, especially in the matter of fresh fruits, a fact which his sobriquet of limey (from lime-juicer) still serves to recall.

In the face of the tenacious vigil which the English captains maintained, Napoleon's warlike preparations at Boulogne for the invasion of England had small chance of success, and many contemporaries, including Metternich and the Archduke Charles, believed the whole project a disguise for a contemplated struggle with Austria. But it is difficult to hold this view after reading Napoleon's correspondence for 1803 and 1804.[15] To divert some of the British flotillas to the eastern Mediterranean or to the West Indies by a series of excentric maneuvers, and then to concentrate a

[15] French historians are still in sharp disagreement regarding the real aims of Napoleon's naval policy. See in this connection E. Desbrière and H. Dufestre, "La manœuvre de Boulogne," *Revue des études napoléoniennes*, XX (1923), 170-176. A judicious appraisement of the value and purpose of the Boulogne flotilla may be found in H. C. Deutsch, "Napoleonic policy and the project of a descent upon England," *The Journal of Modern History*, II (1930), 541-568.

superior French fleet in the Channel before the British ships could reassemble, remained the chief aim of Napoleon's naval strategy for over two years. The details of the plan varied with each passing month, and French squadrons, in their efforts to execute it, duly feinted at Egypt and twice sailed to the West Indies and back. The results, from the French point of view, proved wearisome and inconclusive. When Napoleon hastened to Boulogne in the first week of August, 1805, his naval forces still remained divided, with twenty-nine ships of the line at Corunna and twenty-one at Brest. Hovering between these ports with thirty-five well-armed ships, Cornwallis dominated the Bay of Biscay, confident that the same wind would never bring both the enemy detachments against him at one time and that he could deal with either separately. Yet when he learned that Villeneuve had left Corunna on August 13th, the British admiral divided his command, a blunder likely to give the French heavy odds in any engagement they might have to fight before gaining Brest. Villeneuve, however, lacked information and audacity, and two days out of port his resolution failed. Instead of risking all in a dash for Brest, which might have given him fifty ships with which to dominate the Channel, he turned south and fled to Cadiz. His action gave the final blow to Napoleon's grand design.

For at Cadiz Villeneuve found himself promptly blockaded by a hastily assembled British force. Before the end of August, Napoleon's Boulogne divisions were on the march, but they were headed for Vienna instead of London, and the war of the Third Coalition had begun. As part of his new campaign the emperor decided to order the Cadiz squadron to the Mediterranean to attack Naples. Villeneuve, knowing he was about to be recalled in disgrace, put to sea precipitately on October 19th in a final effort to redeem his failures. But fortune proved even harsher than the court martial he feared to face, for the British blockading force had risen to twenty-seven ships and Nelson himself had arrived to command it. On October 21, 1805, while Napoleon was receiving the surrender of 30,000 Austrians at Ulm, Villeneuve found the enemy waiting for him before the Straits of Gibraltar. He accepted battle with his thirty-three Franco-Spanish ships disposed in a single line five miles in length. Without hesitation the twenty-seven British men-of-war drove at his center from the left in a double column. The wisdom of thus advancing a numerically inferior force in parallel column against the middle of the opposing line has been severely criticised by some authorities, but it was this prompt utilization of a sluggish breeze and this audacious example of the "Nelson touch" that decided the battle.

The story of Trafalgar remains an epitome of those tactics and advantages which had given the British command of the sea. Superior equipment, superior seamanship, superior gunnery, and the initiative of individual British captains extended the scope of the victory and made it a classical example of the *Vernichtungs-schlacht*. Only one-third of the Franco-Spanish ships regained their harbor. Deprived of twenty-two of their heaviest vessels, the French were forced to abandon all hope of equaling their opponents on the sea during the remainder of the war, for the British lost not a single ship at Trafalgar. In a material sense, no naval victory of similar importance was ever more cheaply gained, but Nelson had been mortally wounded in the first hour of the engagement and England had only one Nelson.

A grateful nation buried its most brilliant naval strategist in St. Paul's Cathedral and transmuted his fame into a schoolboy legend of impetuous daring. The breadth and vigor of his strategical conceptions, which constituted the real proof of his genius, formed only a small part of the legend, his flashes of un-British emotionalism and theatricality were carefully edited, and the ill-savor of his *affaire* with Lady Hamilton was passed over in embarrassed silence. Fame, which was to raise his effigy to the top of the Nelson Monument in 1849, dealt cruelly with his adversary. Villeneuve, whose chief failing had been his sound recognition that the French, with their poorly-fitted vessels and their sickly and ill-trained crews, could not beat the British even when they had a numerical advantage, survived the battle of Trafalgar but could not survive his disgrace. He committed suicide in 1806, and a reputation for timidity and incompetence, only partly deserved, still clings to his name.

III. THE BATTLE FOR MARKETS

No simple theory can explain why Britain so definitely out-stripped France in the economic race of the eighteenth century.[16] The material advantages appeared to lie with France, which had excellent harbors on the Atlantic and the Mediterranean, navigable rivers, fertile soil, and a favored geographical position. In area and population France exceeded the United Kingdom at the opening of the eighteenth century by nearly three to one, yet by the close of it Britain had emerged as the world's leading maritime and manufacturing power and France had lost an extensive colonial empire. Contemporaries, faced with the problem of accounting for this outcome, attributed it in part to the superiority of the British political system, and extolled the benefits of a limited as opposed to an absolute monarchy. It would have seemed more relevant to seek the answer in the economic structure of the two states, for in England a more flexible banking system, the accumulation of disposable capital, and the freedom allowed to individual initiative favored the new economy. In France, where the eighteenth century opened with Louis XIV's fiscal extravagances and John Law's speculative experiments, and closed with the repudiation of the *assignats*, capital remained more timid, and industry, further handicapped until the Revolution by the shackles of an obsolete guild system, was slower in responding to the golden opportunities created by the improvements in mechanical production and the expanding markets.

But if French economic enterprise, when compared with that of Great Britain, appeared to lag, compared with that of the remaining European states it marched rapidly. French foreign trade quadrupled in the eighteenth century, and maritime reverses, when they came, were partly offset by the invasion of continental markets, particularly those of Germany, Italy, and the Levant. But here, too, British competition was growing keener, and the negotiation of the Eden Treaty in 1786 made France itself a profitable market for the active islanders. British exports to France, which had aver-

[16] For a more detailed study of the question consult Volume XI of this series, Edwin F. Gay, *The Economic Revolution*.

aged £87,000 a year for the six years ending in 1774, leaped to
£717,000 a year for the six years ending in 1792.[17] The mutual reduction of tariffs provided by the pact spurred French trade also,
particularly in wines and luxury products, but open competition
with the more advanced English factory system proved ruinous to
French industrials. As a consequence they denounced the Eden
Treaty vigorously and the national convention cited abuse of its
provisions as one of the reasons for going to war with England
in 1793. For twenty years thereafter French industry enjoyed the
maximum protection provided by an almost unbroken period of
armed strife, but this immunity did not equip it to meet British
competition on equal terms when peace was restored in 1814. A
trade agreement negotiated by the Restoration government, which
admitted British goods once more on favorable terms, spread ruin
and consternation among French manufacturers whose markets on
the continent Napoleon had so long guaranteed and extended.

Contrasted with Napoleon's articulate and grandiose projects for
the advancement of French trade, the course pursued by the British government in the war years seems almost inconsistent and half
absent-minded. Parliament was still more of a debating society than
a bureaucracy, and British fear of categorical measures lent to most
legislative acts an air of experiment, of irresolution. It is difficult to
find the clue to England's greatness during this epoch in the policies of the government, because it is difficult to find the policies.
The regulations passed for the control of trade, for the protection
of agriculture or the prevention of workingmen's combinations, may
seem easy to explain *post hoc*, but the motives which inspired them,
when analyzed, are likely to confound the investigator. Thus the
workingmen's combination acts of 1799 and 1800, which forbade
collective bargaining for higher wages, were apparently due less to
the self-interest of employers (who were not yet strongly represented) than to a rooted antipathy towards anything savoring of
restraint or engrossment of the economic man. Yet this principle
did not operate against the corn law of 1804, which raised the duty
on imported wheat to 24s 3d a quarter except when domestic wheat
passed 63s, and provided a bounty of 5s a quarter on exported

---

[17] W. Smart, *Economic Annals of the Nineteenth Century,* I (London, 1910), 3.

wheat if the home price fell below 48s. This generosity to the farmers, who made excessive profits throughout the war years, was defended as a measure to protect the consumer, and the industrial interests, which were to attack the corn laws so viciously a generation later, made little effort to combat the act.

There is a more modern note about the traitorous correspondence bill introduced by the government in 1793 to prohibit, among other things, the sale of arms to the enemy. The bill finally passed the house by a majority of one vote, and legislators today would blush to repeat some of the arguments which Fox used in opposing it. ". . . Considering all wars of late years in Europe as contests of revenue rather than of arms, he questioned whether it would not be of advantage to the country to trade with its enemies, and perhaps to sell to them even articles of arms whilst we had prompt payment, at our own prices, for them."[18] Twenty years later the British merchant was still pursuing his profits with the same fine objectivity, if the editor of *Nile's Weekly Register* can be trusted. "If Bonaparte were to grant a *licence* for the purpose," wrote the irate Baltimorean, "I cannot doubt but that certain London merchants could obtain leave to supply him with *arms* and *ammunition*, so zealous are they for a *trade with the enemy*."[19]

The remarkable profit which the British manufacturer and trader could accumulate if assured a fair field and no favors was clear to the business man and to a few economists, but the reasons for it had not yet penetrated the consciousness of the nation. Englishmen contemplated the prosperity of their country in these years with a sort of delighted awe, and attributed the advantages they drew from war conditions and a *laissez faire* economy to their natural and innate superiority rather than to the benefits of a specific system or the lack of it. Less given to logic than the French, less fond of theorizing than the Germans, they felt little incentive to speculate about economic doctrines. But on the continent it was less easy to remain indifferent. The Prussian who was denied his coffee, the merchant confined to a Westphalian enclave, the Weimar artisan forbidden to sell his wares in Erfurt, had reason to ponder

[18] *Parliamentary History*, XXX (London, 1817), 585.
[19] Quoted in F. E. Melvin, *Napoleon's Navigation System* (New York, 1919), 314.

and deplore the evil of irrational restrictions. Fichte had already given voice to the exasperation excited by this system of petty checks: "To be brief, this haphazard method of half-excluding foreign products without any attempt to measure the total to be admitted against the needs of the nation does not achieve the result desired and leads to worse evils."[20] Blind, useless, and destructive interference with commerce and manufacture had come to be recognized under the old régime as one of the distinctive features of a tyrannical order. It was a matter of profound importance that so much of the tariff legislation which Napoleon was driven to impose wore this same appearance. In his efforts to force French goods upon Europe and to bar English goods from the continent he resorted to arbitrary tariffs, and condemned confiscated articles of British or colonial origin to public destruction. In the eyes of the consuming public this was the act of a tyrant. Throughout the Anglo-French battle for markets it was the unpremeditated good fortune of the British that they were able to goad their great enemy into opposing them by measures which could not fail to weaken his authority and undermine his popularity and his pretensions.

IV. THE CONTINENTAL SYSTEM

The "continental system," whereby Napoleon sought after 1807 to close Europe to English commerce, has been denounced by some critics as a monstrosity and hailed by others as the grandest conception of his brain. Both interpretations overrate the importance of his share in the project, for neither the idea nor its application was new. Since the time of Colbert French statesmen had striven persistently to render France independent of foreign imports while developing French export trade as extensively as possible. Every war in which France engaged in the later seventeenth and the eighteenth centuries was in part a tariff war, induced by this rigid application of protectionist principles. Even the lowering of barriers provided by the Anglo-French commercial pact of 1786 did not mark an abandonment of mercantilist practices, but rather a

[20] J. G. Fichte, *Der geschlossene Handelstaat* (Tübingen, 1800), 198.

compromise, for Calonne hoped to raise a larger revenue for the exhausted treasury from a lowered duty on a greatly expanded trade.

The war with England after 1793 called forth numerous plans for promoting French industry and deflating the commercial greatness of "the modern Carthage." British ships were driven from French ports; then all goods of British origin were excluded. As Holland and northern Italy came under French control the vassal governments were induced to extend the system. The treaties which Napoleon wrung from Portugal and the Neapolitan Kingdom in 1801 required the exclusion of English ships from Lisbon and Naples. In a letter to Tsar Paul, then in the act of reviving the Armed Neutrality of the North in an effort to preserve the freedom of the seas, Napoleon proposed that all continental harbors should be closed to English ships, "so that the English would have no communication whatever with Europe."[21] Paul's assassination a few weeks later, and the Anglo-French truce signed before the close of the year, postponed any further extension of the proposal at the time, but the letter is evidence that the germ of the continental system was in Napoleon's mind as early as 1801.

Following the conclusion of the Peace of Amiens in 1802 the British cabinet proposed a return to the low tariffs of 1786. French merchants were not unfavorable, but the manufacturers, especially in the cotton trades, protested that such a step would ruin them and would probably induce a passive trade balance that must ultimately drain France of specie. For some months Bonaparte hesitated; then the mercantilist tradition prevailed and British goods were excluded by prohibitive tariffs and the threat of confiscation. Renewal of the war in 1803 made the destruction of enemy commerce once again a paramount issue. When ceding Hanover to Prussia by the treaty of February 15, 1806, Napoleon insisted that in return Prussia close all ports to the British; the articles of the Rhine Confederation, enacted in July, 1806, required the exclusion of British products from all the member states; and the occupation of Naples in the same year sealed, at least nominally, the southern half of Italy. The blockade had thus become almost continental in concept when the defeat of Prussia at Jena brought all northern Germany under

[21] *Correspondance de Napoléon Ier*, February 27, 1801, VII, 49-50. No. 5417.

French control and enabled Napoleon to formulate a constitution for the system in his Berlin decree of November, 1806.

"We have been compelled," the emperor informed the French senate, "for the good of our people and of our allies, to oppose to the enemy the same arms which they have invoked against us." The British Isles were declared in a state of blockade, all commerce or correspondence with them, or trade in British merchandise, was forbidden, and subjects of England found in any country occupied by the French troops or allied with France were made prisoners of war. The emperor confessed that he had signed the decrees with repugnance, and regretted that the interests of individuals should thus become dependent upon the quarrels of princes. But he failed to make clear what he meant by opposing to the enemy the same arms that they had used, nor did he explain that the seizure of British subjects and the prohibition of British merchandise, justified as "retaliation," had been decreed in France as early as 1803. Nor, it need hardly be said, did he stress the profit which France, as the most highly industrialized state after England, might draw from the markets of the continent if the blockade proved effective.

The first British reply, contained in the orders in council of January 7, 1807, declared that all ships trading between European ports from which English ships were excluded would be liable to capture and condemnation as lawful prizes. The measure was designed to penalize those states subservient to France. Holland and Spain had already learned how costly such subservience could be, for the British cruisers had chased their merchant flags from the ocean and British merchants were diverting their colonial trade. Rather than see their colonial products go to London, the Dutch and Spanish (and the French) governments were prepared to authorize neutrals to enter the exclusive fields which the mother countries sought to monopolize in peace time. American ships in particular made a quick profit conveying the products of French, Dutch, and Spanish colonies in the New World to Europe. Thereupon the British sought to interpose the "rule of 1756" which declared in effect that "a neutral has no right to deliver a belligerent from the pressure of his enemy's hostilities by trading with his

colonies in time of war in a way prohibited in time of peace."[22]
For a year the American skippers evaded this provision by inter-
rupting their voyage at a port in the United States, unloading, re-
loading, and sailing with new clearance papers. But in 1805 a British court decided that the interrupted voyage was in substance a
continuous voyage and confiscated the *Essex* as a test case, whereupon congress retaliated with the non-importation act of April 18,
1806, excluding many articles of British origin from this country.

Indignation against England, which ran high in the United States
after the *Essex* case, was speedily diluted by further grievances
against France. On December 17, 1807, Napoleon ordained that
any ship which had touched at a British port, paid a tax to the
British government, or even submitted to search by a British cruiser,
was thereby *denationalized* and rendered liable to confiscation. The
aim of this Milan decree was to exclude from European waters the
ships under neutral registry which the British had pressed into
service to carry their wares into ports from which their own ships
were barred. Jefferson's embargo act of 1807 and the non-intercourse
act of 1809 reflect the despair and confusion to which neutrals were
reduced by the policies of the two great belligerents, each determined to regulate commerce to its own profit, each ruthless in
penalizing states which submitted to its adversary's regulations. On
learning that the United States had closed its harbors to French
(as well as British) vessels by the non-intercourse act of March 1,
1809, Napoleon retaliated by a decision, dated March 23, 1810, to
seize all American ships entering the ports of the Empire. Five
weeks later congress passed Macon's Bill No. 2, offering to revoke
the non-intercourse act in favor of whichever belligerent first abandoned its edicts against American commerce. Making astute use
of this olive branch, Napoleon succeeded in persuading Madison
that the Berlin and Milan decrees would be withdrawn,[23] and so
turned the force of American indignation upon Great Britain, which
maintained its orders in council in full vigor.

The British practice of searching neutral ships on the high seas

---

[22] E. F. Heckscher, *The Continental System: an Economic Interpretation* (Oxford,
1922), 36.
[23] Napoleon to the Duc de Cadore, August 2, 1810. *Correspondance de Napoléon Ier*.
XXI, 1-2. No. 16743.

and of sometimes impressing American sailors for service on the ground that they were fugitives from the royal navy, added an inexcusable crime against persons to the already flagrant crimes against property, and it was this "crying enormity" which Madison skillfully invoked when he recommended that congress take action (message of June 1, 1812). The British cabinet appears to have accepted the sincerity of this protest without question, ignoring, as American historians tended to do for three-quarters of a century, the part played by the "expansionists," with their dreams of conquering Florida and Canada, in promoting the conflict.[24] On June 23rd, the cabinet revoked the orders in council of 1807 as they applied to American commerce, but the concession came too late, for congress had voted for war five days earlier. The inconclusive course of that Anglo-American conflict and the even more inconclusive Treaty of Ghent which terminated it,[25] passed all but unnoted in Europe, where the attention of contemporaries was focused upon the Moscow expedition and the War of Liberation.

Aside from his effort to conciliate the United States, Napoleon pursued his project for the self-blockade of Europe with increasing ruthlessness. The invasion of Portugal in 1807, the violation of Spain in 1808, the annexation of Holland and the German coastline to the Elbe in 1810 were logical but increasingly hazardous moves in his campaign. For a successful blockade of Europe from the land side was impracticable without the coöperation of the civilian population, and this Napoleon never won. His calculation that British credit must collapse if British commerce could be excluded from Europe was probably sound; but British commerce was never excluded. It continued to flow, under neutral flags, under licenses, through the bribery or negligence of customs officers and the audacity of smugglers. With European prices on many lines of manufactured and colonial products one hundred per cent above normal, the profits remained greater than the risk. The British

[24] The "commerce and empressment" explanation of the war has received classical expression in A. T. Mahan's *Sea Power in its relation to the War of 1812,* 2 vols. (Boston, 1905). For a more recent and contrasting interpretation see J. W. Pratt, *Expansionists of 1812* (New York, 1925).
[25] G. F. Martens, *Nouveau recueil de traités,* II, 76-84. The treaty settled some disputes concerning the border line between Canadian and American territory and the activities of the Indians, but left out of consideration the naval issues, the ostensible motive for hostility.

government not only avoided the predicted insolvency; it increased
its revenues, and the greater part of its expanding budget was met
by duties on an expanding trade.

V. BRITISH FINANCIAL STABILITY

To French economists, predisposed like the physiocrats to regard land as the basic and durable form of wealth and agriculture
as the primary interest of the state, the commercial prosperity of
Great Britain in the early nineteenth century seemed spurious and
artificial. Napoleon did not stand alone in his dislike and distrust
of *négociants*, whom he ranked with speculators and profiteers. Like
their patron Mercury in the fable they stole away the fatness and
increase of the land, growing rich by secret and invisible ways. Yet
a structure of commercial greatness, such as England boasted, rested
upon a shifty and precarious foundation; it was dependent upon
the steady flow of trade and might be expected to collapse in a
wave of financial panic and business failure if that trade were even
briefly interrupted. Government revenues, drawn largely from customs and income taxes, would shrink immediately, national credit
would fall, and the carrying charges of the public debt, growing
like St. Christopher's burden, would break the back of the exhausted government. To hasten this result, it would be sufficient
to reduce the British export trade. As imports poured in and unsold
manufactures and colonial products glutted the London warehouses,
England's trade balance would turn adverse. Unable to purchase
supplies, especially wheat, with surplus exports, the nation would
have no choice but to pay in specie, thus exhausting its gold reserve.
When the Bank of England confessed itself unable to redeem its
notes, the fragile structure of British credit would collapse and the
national greatness founder in a sea of inflation.[26]

Year after year throughout the revolutionary wars the exponents
of this thesis scanned the British budgets for corroboration of their
hopes, and year after year they found increasing evidence to support their prophecies of doom. The total of the national debt, which

---

[26] *"Je désirerais avoir le plus de détails possibles sur la situation des finances."* Bonaparte to Andréossy, French ambassador at London, March 7, 1803. A week later came his
defiant attempt to intimidate the British ambassador, Whitworth: "So you are determined
to go to war!" Cf. *Correspondance de Napoléon*, VIII, 228, 230, 246. Nos. 6611, 6616,
6630.

had alarmed Adam Smith in 1775, stood by 1793 at £230,000,000.
Nine years later, when the Peace of Amiens was signed, it had
more than doubled, reaching the total, staggering for that epoch,
of £507,000,000. A threatened run on the Bank of England in 1797
had forced the cabinet to authorize suspension of gold payments.
With the annual budget rising from £27,000,000 for 1792 to nearly
£100,000,000 in 1802 and £174,000,000 in 1813, the collapse of this
gigantic credit structure seemed inevitable. Continental observers
failed for the most part to comprehend the prestidigitation by which
His Britannic Majesty's government not only persuaded the public
to accept irredeemable bank notes, but continued to borrow at will
to meet the cost of the war. In England itself the performance excited some lively criticism. When the bank ceased to pay in specie
and issued notes of one pound denomination, Pitt's enemies contrasted him with Augustus, who had found Rome of brick and left
it of marble, whereas

> Of Pitt and of England
> Men may say without vapor
> That he found it of gold
> And left it of paper.[27]

But their scorn was confounded by the confidence of the business
world, and foreigners with capital to hoard continued to ship it to
London for investment. Nor was the confidence misplaced. A comparison of British fiscal policy during the Napoleonic epoch with
that of World War days yields some interesting conclusions.

From 1793 to 1816, despite the unprecedented increase in expenditures, the government revenue accounted for about forty-
seven per cent, or almost half, the annual disbursements. The average *differential* war expenditure was about £65,000,000 *per annum*,
against £1,720,000,000 *per annum* for the four years of the World
War. Even for the period 1811-1815, when the differential rose to
£120,000,000, the effort compares very favorably with the annual
World War differential, which was fourteen times as great. A
comparison of the loans or subsidies which Britain advanced to her
allies in the two wars is more difficult to make. For the revolution-

[27] P. W. Wilson, *William Pitt the Younger* (New York, 1934), 263.

ary period the total has been calculated at £59,300,000 for subsidies, a sum which compares modestly with the £99,500,000 expended in the same years for the maintenance of British armed
forces in Europe. Wellington's Peninsular campaign proved especially costly, for he could not confiscate supplies in a friendly country and had to discharge obligations chiefly in silver. The favorable
trade balance which Britain maintained throughout the war enabled the government to provide specie for this purpose and also
for the wheat imports, which rose as high as £6,000,000 in years of
lean domestic harvests. Napoleon has been criticized for permitting
the sale of French wheat to the English for cash in 1810, when
further privation added to the financial strain and discouragement
might have induced serious disturbances among the English workers. But it seems highly improbable that Napoleon had it in his
power to bring England near to starvation,[28] and he was consistent
according to his principles in selling perishable wheat for irreplaceable specie. His reasoning was sound and logical; the miscal-
culation which ruined the system lay in the premises. Napoleon
assumed that he could close the continent to English merchandise,
force England to an adverse trade balance, and condemn the government to the disastrous expedient of an uncontrollable inflation.
All these assumptions proved false. Though the British government was early forced to suspend gold payments, to increase the
circulation of paper, and to float loans for unprecedented amounts,
British national credit remained sound. In the opinion of a recent
investigator this fiscal achievement, coming at a time when the
fiasco of the *assignats* in France had shaken public confidence in
paper currency, was a remarkable triumph. "It is difficult, in the
light of these facts, to charge the men who were responsible for
Great Britain's security in the Napoleonic days with having neglected reasonable precautions against inflation."[29]

[28] W. F. Galpin, *The Grain Supply of England during the Napoleonic period* (Philadelphia, 1925), 193-201. Galpin concludes that England was then far less vulnerable in
the matter of a grain supply than has been commonly supposed, and could have survived
any restrictions Napoleon could have imposed, had it occurred to him to attempt such a
maneuver.

[29] N. J. Silberling, "Financial and Monetary Policy of Great Britain during the Napoleonic Wars," *Quarterly Journal of Economics*, XXXVIII (1923-1924), 220. The statistics quoted in this paragraph are drawn in great measure from the tables presented in
this valuable analysis.

That the British trade balance remained favorable throughout this era is reasonably certain, but there is, unfortunately, no satisfactory means of estimating the total exports and imports. For the customs house still imposed fixed official valuations based in general on prices which had prevailed a century earlier, and the annual figures have in consequence little more than relative value. As such, they testify to the steady rise in exports and imports, and reflect the diversion towards England of the world's colonial produce. British reëxports of foreign (which meant substantially colonial) goods increased from twenty-one per cent to over thirty-six per cent of the annual total between 1792 and 1800.[30] The new docks and warehouses rushed to completion on the Thames in these years are a further testimony to the middleman's profit accruing to English wholesale merchants from this trade. The order in council of November 11, 1807, declaring all European states in alliance with France or under French control, together with their colonies and dependencies, in a state of blockade, opened the colonial trade of the world to British control and exploitation. The European states caught in the struggles of the successive coalitions could give scant attention to distant colonies, but Europe's extremity was England's opportunity, and the consequence was a matter of profound historical importance, not only for Great Britain, but for America, for Africa, and even for Asia and Australia.

VI. THE RESULTS OF THE REVOLUTIONARY WARS FOR THE WORLD OUTSIDE EUROPE

For a quarter of a century the European powers, absorbed in the struggle with France, were forced to relinquish colonial enterprise to Great Britain. The other continents passed out of the spotlight of history, momentarily, until the Napoleonic armies had ceased to march, and the diplomats who reconstructed the map of Europe gave only passing attention to colonial questions. It is possible to argue, however, from the point of view of world history, that the changes which took place during this era in each of the other continents had more permanent significance than the Declaration

[30] E. F. Heckscher, *The Continental System: an Economic Interpretation* (Oxford, 1922), 39.

of the Rights of Man or the Battle of the Nations. Certainly in the territorial sense the minor readjustments effected in the political map of Europe have little meaning when contrasted with the areas overtaken by more radical changes in other parts of the world.

In North America the extremity of France set the stage for the sale of Louisiana in 1803, an event of supreme importance for the future of the United States. The crippling of Spain, resulting from her unhappy alliance with France and war with England, and her even more costly war with France and alliance with England, provided the Spanish-American colonies with an opportunity to slip the leash, and prepared the way for the cession of Florida to the United States in 1819. Less critical, perhaps, for the future of America, and less easily related to the course of events in Europe, were the conflicting Spanish, English, and Russian efforts to establish a claim to the west coast from California to Alaska. After bringing Spain and England close to war in 1790, at the time of the Nootka Convention, these competing claims were pursued but languidly for several decades while the three governments were preoccupied with more imperious problems in Europe. With the retrocession of Louisiana to France (1800) and the proclamation of Mexican independence a generation later, Spanish title to the Pacific region lost significance. The Russian claims might easily have proved a more serious challenge to American westward expansion if the Russians had pressed their colonization projects more energetically. A Russian-American Company, active as early as 1790, had founded several posts in Alaska by 1803. The reëstablishment of peace in Europe in 1802 encouraged eastward adventures, and two Russian cruisers were dispatched to the Pacific in that year. Plans had been drawn up for Russian settlements in California and a fort was constructed near the site of San Francisco, but the distance and the lack of firm official encouragement doomed the project. In the same years British traders invaded the Oregon territory, and the British claims to the coast, based upon the explorations of Drake in 1579, Cook in 1778, and Vancouver from 1788 to 1792, were so strong that the United States in 1818 conceded the right of joint occupation as far south as the California boundary. Here again a few decades of priority in colonization might have confided the ultimate destiny of the territory into the hands of the British, but Jefferson's promptness in dispatching the Lewis and Clarke expedition (1804) to explore the Louisiana purchase and to find a way to the Pacific overland established a strong American counterclaim to the Columbia River valley and opened the route for American settlers.[31]

South as well as north of the Rio Grande the revolutionary era brought changes of permanent significance. Through the eighteenth century discontent had steadily deepened among the Spanish colonists of the two Americas. Spain still ruled her viceroyalties in the New World for her own profit, insisted upon monopolizing their trade, and excluded native-born whites, the Creole class, from the administration.[32] By preserving a neutral stand in the continual strife between the Creoles and the Indians, Spanish officials thought it possible to keep both in check, but this policy of *divide et impera* broke down after 1800. For the revolt of the thirteen English colonies to the north provided an example, and the turmoil in Spain after 1808 provided an opportunity for rebellion. Local juntas in the colonies refused to recognize Joseph Bonaparte as king, and in 1809 Simon Bolívar returned to his native Venezuela to lead a movement for the liberation and unification of all the Spanish colonies of the New World. The struggle shifted back and forth for a generation, and as late as 1823 the possibility that Spain might find means to repress the rebels helped to motivate the proclamation of the Monroe Doctrine. But the political ties, broken during the Napoleonic era, could not be reknit, for the ultimate power of decision lay with the British government. Rather than see the Spanish trade monopoly reëstablished, Great Britain lent the rebels unofficial aid, and later recognized the independence of the new republics. Yielding to the dictation of similar influences, the Portuguese colony of Brazil opened its ports to foreign commerce in 1808 and was declared an independent state in 1822. For the Iberian nations, which had so proudly headed the van of overseas conquest and colonization three centuries earlier, the Napoleonic era was the sunset of empire.

[31] J. Schafer, "The Western Ocean as a determinant in Oregon history," *The Pacific Ocean in History* (New York, 1917), 287-297.

[32] B. C. Moses, "The social revolution of the eighteenth century in South America," *Annual Report of the American Historical Association for 1915* (Washington, 1917), 163-170.

During the fifteen years that Napoleon required to conquer and lose an empire in Europe, the British conquered and kept a larger empire in India. Lord Richard Wellesley, elder brother of the more famous Duke of Wellington, accepted the post of governor-general in 1798, at a moment when Bonaparte's Egyptian expedition had aroused British apprehensions in the east. "Without intending it, French adventurers played the part of *agents provocateurs*," inciting Wellesley to a vigorous policy of expansion which was maintained energetically until his retirement in 1805 and was later resumed by Hastings in 1814.[33] All India from the Bay of Bengal to the Indus became a sphere of British influence, while the attention of the European cabinets was focused upon the problem of combating the French hegemony. For India, and perhaps for England, the opportunity for easy Indian conquests provided by the temporary preoccupation or paralysis of the other colonizing powers was more significant than all the wars of the coalitions.

The future of Australia and New Zealand likewise took its shape from the events of the revolutionary epoch. An expedition under Captain James Cook, who circumnavigated the New Zealand group and touched the Australian coast at Botany Bay in 1770, wakened new interest in this unclaimed continent. The first shipload of British convicts settled at Sidney in 1788, and the southern and eastern shores of Australia were mapped out by Flinders before 1805. Here again the curtailment of competition favored the British, for had peace prevailed the French and the Dutch would certainly have pressed counterclaims. Two weeks after Sidney was founded the ill-fated La Perouse visited the harbor; and in 1802 at "Encounter Bay," near the modern city of Adelaide, Flinders came upon a French expedition which had just named the territory *Terre Napoléon*. But the renewal of the war in 1803 put an end to French explorations. Had the Dutch likewise not been driven from the seas for a generation because of their forced alliance with France, they would hardly have relinquished their claims to western Australia (New Holland) without sharp resistance, nor would Cape Colony, the *point d'appui* for the conquest of South Africa, have passed into British hands in 1806. The Dutch at Capetown, the French at Cairo, saw the founda-

[33] *The Cambridge History of India*, ed. by H. H. Dodwell (New York, 1929), 323.

tion of a promising colony swept away in this decade by the pressure of a naval hegemony against which they were powerless to compete.

For the peoples of the Far East the fact that the European nations dedicated themselves to internecine strife from 1792 until 1815 meant a quarter of a century's reprieve from the inevitable impact of European civilization. Though British frigates chased Dutch ships to cover from Saigon to Nagasaki, British landing-parties met with small success, and the opening of China and Japan to westerners and to western trade was postponed until the middle decades of the nineteenth century. The ultimate effects, if any, resulting from this delay in assaulting the Orient are difficult to weigh; it is possible that earlier, sharper, and more disorganizing intrusions might have shattered Japanese civilization beyond the power of self-conservation; but in general the effects must be counted simply as negative. For other regions of the earth, however, for India, South Africa, Australia, New Zealand, the western United States, Central and South America, the years when Napoleon dominated Europe were years of destiny. The present political coloring of these regions was very largely decided in this period, more definitely than in any similar period of their history. And this meant, as a glance at the map will reveal, the political coloring that now holds for one-fourth the land area of the globe. Napoleon's achievements thus tend to appear predominantly negative when measured by the tenets of any but the Europocentric school of historiography, for it was his least intention to assure and extend Great Britain's position as the leading colonial power. Had the energies of the French, which carried them to Madrid and Moscow, been diverted towards the creation of an overseas empire, there might be several *Terres Napoléoniennes*, many times the area of France, on the world map. In the nineteenth century the French were to demonstrate their capacity for colonial administration by developing a new overseas empire second only to that of Great Britain in extent; but Napoleon's genius was more responsive to traditional than prophetic appeals, and he preferred to concentrate his resources upon that narrow European policy which had brought France to the verge of ruin a century earlier and Louis XIV to a death-bed repentance. A policy of moderation on the continent, which freed him from the hostility of Austria, Prussia, and

Russia, might have left him in a position to press colonial conquests, and to meet the British in armed conflict, if conflict could not be avoided, with a reasonable chance of success. But against England in alliance with the successive European coalitions France ended in 1814 as she had ended in 1714, with colonies confiscated and European conquests reft away. To this better-known and more dramatic aspect of the French bid for supremacy in the years 1799-1814 it is now necessary to return.

Chapter Six

THE FAILURE TO CHECK THE EXPANSION OF
FRENCH INFLUENCE IN EUROPE

I. THE RECONSTRUCTION OF ITALY

ENURED throughout a thousand years to the rapacity of conquerors who descended from the Alps and retired again, the Italians resigned themselves to Napoleon's arbitrament with pliant unconcern. Italy had survived the incursions of the medieval emperors and the forays of Charles VIII and Francis I, had seen the cuirasses of the Spanish infantry yield to the white coats of Austria, and the Austrians retire before the insolent republicans with their tricolor cockades. The sight of a foreign uniform had as yet little power to wring the Italian heart, and the ferment which stirred the peninsula during the revolutionary epoch cannot, save in retrospect, be identified as patriotism or nationalism. Rather it was a spontaneous effervescence, ebullient and destructive, which required discipline and direction unless it was to waste itself in a few generous gestures, a few vicious reprisals. The high-minded Neapolitan liberal, Vicenzo Cuoco, admitted in 1800 that to most Italians the revolutionary urge meant no more than an aping of French manners, an invitation, always welcome, to insult the authorities, an opportunity for the ambitious to seek advancement and for the calculating to seek profit.[1]

All classes responded to the intellectual and emotional stimulus provided by the conflict of fashions and ideas, but no clear call to national union can be detected above the discords of this overture to the Risorgimento. Bonaparte, after a year in Italy, assured the directors confidentially that the Italians were a nation of superstitious, flabby, chicken-hearted buffoons, who hated the French in private

[1] V. Cuoco, *Saggio storico sulla rivoluzione napoletana del 1799*, ed. by F. Landogna (Leghorn, 1927), 87.

but lacked the capacity for self-government or the courage for resistance.[2] As province after province fell under his control he substituted a systematic tribute for the irregular pillage practiced in the
first campaign. The decade of energetic improvisations after 1800
shook Italian society from its torpor, but the French rule was never
popular. In 1809, when for a brief interval an Austrian army threatened to invade Lombardy, the Italians prepared to reverse their
allegiance as casually as they had done on the appearance of Suvarov
ten years earlier. "The existence of the French in Italy" an imperial
functionary wrote from Leghorn in April, "hangs on a bulletin."[3]
Napoleon's entry into Vienna a month later provided the bulletin,
but in 1814 he was to prove less fortunate.

None of the French political creations in Italy lost this aspect of
impermanence, of improvisation. The Cisalpine Republic, over-
thrown in 1799, reconstructed in 1800, renamed the Italian Republic
in 1802 and the Italian Kingdom in 1805, was the first in order of
time and importance, but its frontiers continually shifted, its institutions never crystallized. Situated in the Po Valley, it possessed some
claim to geographic unity, and the addition of Venetia, the Marches,
and the Italian Tyrol raised its area by 1810 to 4,586,000 square
kilometers and its population to 6,703,000 souls.[4] The viceroy, Eugène
Beauharnais, strove to win the loyalty of his subjects while intro-
ducing reforms. Church lands were secularized, monastic orders dissolved, the French civil and commercial codes introduced, seventy
million francs assigned for roads and canals, the coinage stabilized to
match the French franc, and brigandage sternly oppressed. But the
constitution remained a dead letter and Napoleon's exactions multiplied steadily. After 1806, thirty million francs a year, one-fifth of the
state income, was requisitioned for the imperial treasury, with additional assessments for extraordinary military expenses. The budget
of 1812, the last completed, assigned forty-six million francs to defense, twenty-two million for charges on the funded debt, and thirty
million for Napoleon's *domaine extraordinaire*, leaving only thirty-
two per cent of the total for administration, internal improvements

[2] *Correspondance de Napoléon I*, III, 369, 376. Nos. 2292, 2296.

[3] A Pingaud, "Le premier royaume d'Italie: La guerre de 1809," *Revue d'histoire diplomatique*, XLII (1928), 41.

[4] Pingaud, *op. cit.*, 69.

and education.[5] Taxes, which were twice as heavy as under the Austrian hegemony, increased twenty per cent between 1805 and 1812,[6] and approximately half the revenue raised was transmitted to Napoleon or expended for the upkeep of Italian troops fighting in his service. The hatred engendered by this fiscal exploitation broke loose at the news of Napoleon's fall, and on April 20, 1814, a Milanese mob beat the finance minister, Giuseppe Prina, to death, without a hand being raised in his defense.

From the first the French used their preponderance to transform their Italian conquests into economic colonies. Not British goods alone, but all rival manufactures, were to be excluded from the markets, and Italian industry itself was sacrificed to that of France. Commerce with England was forbidden, commerce with Austria discouraged. By 1812 fifty-six per cent of the exports from the Italian Kingdom went to France and forty-eight per cent of its imports came from that country.[7] Tariff regulations were forcing the Italians to exchange their raw silk and grains for French manufactures, and their foreign trade was being driven steadily into a single channel, the control over which rested in Paris. When Austria surrendered Istria and Trieste in 1809, these provinces were joined to Dalmatia to form the Government of Illyria, and suffered the same stagnation of industry and navigation as the Italian Kingdom.[8] The benefits to business which should have resulted from the more competent and energetic French administration, from the simplified laws and improved transportation, were offset by the vexatious tariffs, the perpetual sense of impermanency, and the military conscription.

The precise tribute which Italy paid in men during this period is difficult to reckon. Napoleon complained that he could learn less about the internal affairs of his Italian Kingdom than about those of Great Britain, and students who have attempted to probe the records can sympathize with his exasperation. On paper, the armed forces raised in Italy apparently increased from 30,000 in 1807 to

[5] E. Tarlé, *Le blocus continental et le royaume d'Italie*, Nouvelle ed. (Paris, 1931), 16-24.

[6] A. Pingaud, "Le premier royaume d'Italie: L'œuvre financière," *Revue d'histoire diplomatique*, XLIV (1930), 446-447.

[7] Tarlé, *op. cit.*, 234.

[8] M. Pivec-Stele, *La vie économique des provinces illyriennes, 1809-1813* (Paris, 1930), 335.

90,000 in 1812, but desertions sometimes cut the detachments in half. Of 450 conscripts demanded from the Roman departments in 1810, for example, the prefect, with prodigious efforts, assembled 235, and desertions *en route* reduced this number to 120 before the detachment reached France.[9] It has been estimated that between 1805 and 1814 120,000 Italians were called to the colors and 60,000 perished.[10] These figures, approximate at best, suggest that conscription in Italy took less than one per cent of the population, which is exceptionally light judged by modern standards. On the other hand they imply losses of fifty per cent, which is exceptionally heavy, and with full allowance for desertions they bear out the charge that Napoleon sacrificed his Italian conscripts more recklessly than his French veterans.

All Italy, under the modern Cæsar, was divided into three parts. The segment west of the Apennines from Piedmont to Rome (Lucca excepted) had been organized by 1810 as part of the hundred and twenty-eight *départements* of the empire. The Piedmontese, accustomed to bureaucratic efficiency and military manners, found the French administration supportable. The softer Tuscans submitted sullenly, remembering with regret the gentler rule of the Archduke Leopold, whose enlightened policies had made Tuscany the happiest of the Italian states before 1790. The Romans resented their subordination and scorned Napoleon's favors with all the strength of their ancient and implacable pride. To refuse the oath of allegiance required of all public servants under the imperial régime became in Rome a fashionable gesture, dangerous but intoxicating. Pius VII denounced all who dared to lay profane hands upon the property of St. Peter and was hurried to Savona under arrest. Zingarelli threw down his baton rather than conduct a *Te Deum* to commemorate the birthday of the King of Rome and was thrown into jail. Even Canova, though he protested his loyalty and friendship for Napoleon, resisted the oath. For two years after the decree of annexation in 1809 Napoleon viewed the folly of his Roman subjects with indulgence, confident that the material benefits which he planned for the second city of the empire would dissolve their hostility. Instead the hostility mounted, intensified by economic ills. The cultivation of

[9] L. Madelin, *La Rome de Napoléon* (Paris, 1906), 308.
[10] A. Pingaud, "Le premier royaume d'Italie: L'œuvre militaire," *Revue d'histoire diplomatique*, XLII (1928), 44.

glasswort, from which the Romans extracted as much as three and a half million kilograms of soda in 1810, was ruined by Berthollet's process for manufacturing soda from sea salt. The new cotton culture, from which great profits were expected, expired in the rainy autumn of 1811.[11] Sudden exasperation at the ingratitude of the Romans replaced the emperor's genial paternalism. The prefect, summoned to France, passed a horrible quarter of an hour attempting vain extenuations. Thereafter, to judge by his correspondence, Napoleon did his best to banish Rome and its incorrigible populace from his thoughts. He hated failure.

The Kingdom of Naples retained its nominal independence until 1806. Its court was the most vicious in Europe, for Ferdinand IV, brother of Charles IV of Spain, was a treacherous vulgarian, and Marie Caroline, daughter of Maria Theresa of Austria, matched his vices and surpassed his villainy. Two months after Austerlitz Napoleon announced that the Bourbons had ceased to reign at Naples and offered the throne to his brother Joseph. The ubiquitous British frigates rescued the dethroned pair, who did not overlook the contents of the treasury in their flight, and by May 11, 1806, Joseph had installed himself in their palace. But the auguries were inauspicious; that same night Sir Sidney Smith seized the island of Capri as a visible reminder that French power ended at the water's edge.[12] Joseph's presentation of a diamond collar to St. Januarius in an effort to disarm the superstitious Neapolitans drew from Napoleon the tart reminder that it would be more to the point to disarm the brigands of Calabria. Guerilla warfare that was a foretaste of the Spanish nightmare darkened Joseph's none too hopeful spirit and thwarted all attempts to acquire Sicily, a failure which drew further criticism from Napoleon. Harassed by his brother, depressed by the horror of burned villages and perpetual firing-squads, Joseph sought peace in the multitudinous tasks of administrative reform.

In Naples itself the citizens accepted him with graceful nonchalance, for their leading trait was an invincible indolence. "There, and there alone in Italy, something of the Greek spirit had sur-

---

[11] Madelin, op. cit., 499-501.
[12] E. Driault, Napoléon en Italie (Paris, 1906), 402.

vived—nothing of the Greek virtues, much of the Greek failings."[13]
Had Joseph been free to follow his own inspiration he might have
won their fickle allegiance. His two years' ministry was a world of
paper projects, projects for the clarification of the laws, for the regulation and simplification of the taxes, the liquidation of the state
debt, the reduction of clerical privilege. But the inescapable military
demands devoured two-thirds of the revenue, the British blockade
jeopardized commerce, and the low tariff on French imports discouraged local industries. In 1808 Joseph resigned the throne of
Naples for that of Spain. "When it was realized that he would not
return, he passed all at once for a grand prince, a prince of the *élite*
of the eighteenth century, 'philosophy on the throne.' . . ."[14] But the
attention of the Neapolitans was soon diverted by his successor,
Joachim Murat. This flamboyant captain of cavalry, who had married Caroline Bonaparte, opened his reign with a daring attack on
Capri, which succeeded against all odds and all reason. Murat's *élan*,
his good looks, surpassed by those of Caroline, captured the hearts of
the Neapolitans, who respected wisdom but worshiped beauty.[15]
Had he possessed more political acumen he might perhaps have preserved his throne in the storm which wrecked the Empire, but his
double dealing, less adroit than Bernadotte's, brought him before a
firing-squad in 1815.

II. THE REVOLUTION ON THE RHINE

To promote disunion in the Germanies and paralyze the Holy
Roman Empire by encouraging particularist sentiments among the
German princes had been a cardinal principle of French foreign
policy since the time of Richelieu and Louis XIV. For a century after
the Peace of Westphalia the Bourbon-Hapsburg rivalry divided
Europe, and the lesser states looked for direction to Paris or Vienna.
When, in the middle of the eighteenth century, France and Austria
forgot their traditional rivalry and entered the Seven Years' War as
allies, the event was rightly hailed as a "diplomatic revolution." But
the Austro-French entente of 1756, symbolized by the betrothal of

---

[13] R. M. Johnston, *The Napoleonic Empire in Southern Italy and the Rise of the Secret Societies* (London, 1904), I, 16.
[14] A. Sorel, *L'Europe et la Révolution française*, VII (Paris, 1911), 282.
[15] A. Murat-Rasponi, "A la cour du roi Murat." *Revue de Paris*, V (1928), 481-511.

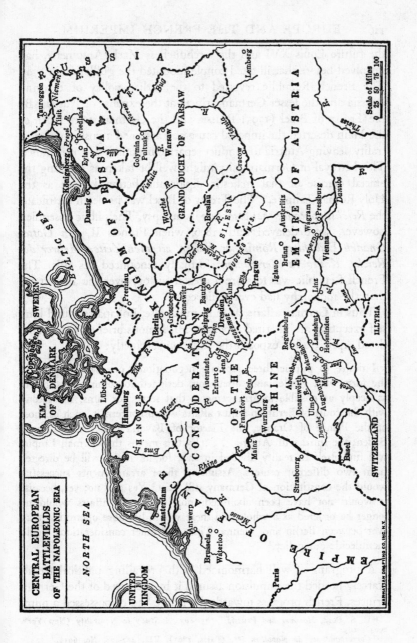

CENTRAL EUROPEAN
BATTLEFIELDS
OF THE NAPOLEONIC ERA

the future Louis XVI and the Archduchess Marie Antoinette, had dissolved before that ill-fated couple mounted the guillotine in 1793. The French Republic reverted to the earlier policy of favoring Prussia and the lesser German princes at the expense of Austria. By the Treaty of Basel (1795) Prussia and the German states north of the Main deserted the imperial cause and assumed a position of neutrality, leaving Austria to conduct separate negotiations with France. This betrayal of German unity might well be taken as marking the official demise of that majestic diplomatic fiction known as the Holy Roman Empire.[16] The Treaty of Basel was its death certificate, the *Reichsdeputationshauptschluss* its autopsy. The public obsequies, however, were delayed until 1806, when Francis II, *von Gottes Gnaden Erwählter Römischer Kaiser, zu allen Zeiten Mehrer des Reichs, König in Germanien,* formally renounced his title. The French Republic was to score a greater victory over the ancient foe than the monarchy had ever achieved.

Thus in German affairs, as in so much else, Bonaparte found himself executing an inherited program. His famous brief to Talleyrand, dated April 3, 1802, exposed the situation succinctly:

I desire to pursue three separate negotiations: one with Russia, in the form of a gentlemanly discussion, designed to commit that power as deeply as possible to arrangements that serve our aims; the second with the court of Berlin to adjust affairs which concern it, such as those of the Prince of Orange, the Elector of Bavaria and the Elector of Baden; the third with Austria. . . . By this means the German Empire will find itself in reality divided in two, for its affairs will be directed from two different centers. Assuming these arrangements successful, would the constitution of Germany still exist? Yes and no; yes, because it would not have been abolished; no, because its affairs would no longer be ordered as a whole and there would be more opposition than ever between Berlin and Vienna. Time and other considerations would then decide our policy.[17]

A program so well harmonized with prevailing political trends scarcely needed the impulsion assured it by the greed of the German princes. French progress towards the Rhine had dispossessed a num-

---

[16] G. S. Ford, *Hanover and Prussia, 1795-1803. A Study in Neutrality* (New York, 1903), 103.
[17] *Correspondance de Napoléon I*er*, (Paris, 1861), VII, 427-428. No. 6019.

ber of hereditary German nobles and compensation had been found for them by secularizing ecclesiastical territories on the right bank. But such a process, once started, proved difficult to arrest. In 1802 the Holy Roman Empire included some ninety secular rulers, seventy ecclesiastical states, fifty-one free cities, and over a thousand imperial knights. A year later the number had been halved, and the chief beneficiaries of the new synthesis were the powerful secular states, Prussia, Bavaria, Württemberg and Baden. A deputation at Regensburg confirmed the settlement by an imperial recess; Russia acquiesced, and the Emperor Francis II submitted under pressure.[18] To Bonaparte, as patron of the new dispensation, the German princes bound themselves by military conventions, realizing that his overthrow would remove their protector and undo their gains. The tsar's approval had been sought at each stage of the proceeding, and Prussia had assimilated two bishoprics, five abbeys, three imperial cities and other estates as compensation for territories ceded to France on the left bank of the Rhine. The only continental power which had lost by the transaction was Austria, but the emperor's protests drew from Paris nothing more satisfactory than a cool note of regret and a suggestion that Austria might find compensation in the Balkans.

Napoleon's assumption of the imperial title "Emperor of the French" in 1804 involved a further humiliation for Francis II. Before the prestige of this new Cæsar, his own orb of office became more than ever a tarnished anachronism, burdensome and vain. Despite assurances from Great Britain, Russia, and Prussia that the dignity of the Holy Roman Emperor should suffer no loss through the Corsican's presumption, the Austrian ministers advised Francis to fortify his position by shifting the emphasis to his hereditary rather than his electoral claims.[19] Without renouncing the title of Holy Roman Emperor (that final salute to Cæsar was to follow Austerlitz), he became *Seine Österreichisch-Kaiserliche und Königlich-Apostolische Majestät*, Francis I of Austria.

[18] The recess, or *Reichsdeputationshauptschluss*, is in Martens, *Recueil des traités*, VII, 435-551. The form of consent extorted from the Emperor of Austria is in De Clercq, I, 596-603.
[19] H. von Srbik, *Das Oesterreichische Kaisertum und das Ende des Heiligen Römischen Reiches, 1804-1806* (Berlin, 1927), 33-38.

Napoleon's confidence, fed by his easy triumphs in Italy and the Germanies, blinded him to the mounting defiance which his course excited. "With Europe in its present state, England cannot reasonably make war on us unaided," he assured Joseph Bonaparte in the spring of 1802;[20] yet a year later, when the French position was even stronger, England did make war. Unforeseen opposition always angered Napoleon unduly; to strike back in the easiest way open to him he arrested all English tourists in France, even diplomatic agents, and moved 12,000 troops into the Electorate of Hanover. The seizure of the Duc d'Enghien in neutral Baden on March 14, 1804, and of the British *chargé d'affaires*, Sir George Rumbold,[21] in neutral Hamburg the following October further advertised his disregard of public law. At St. Petersburg the court donned mourning at the news of d'Enghien's execution, while Frederick William III, despite his love of peace, insisted stubbornly upon Rumbold's release. Pitt's reiterated prophecy (he had returned to power in May, 1804), that all European powers must fight France collectively or prepare to go under one by one, was beginning to wear the guise of an unpleasant truth.

The older dynasties, however, felt the lack of a humane and lofty principle with which to gild their selfish diplomacy and oppose the universality of the revolutionary creed. It was in part a recognition of this lack that moved Alexander to adopt Czartoryski's suggestion and announce himself the protector of the weak and oppressed, the guardian of justice among the nations.[22] Such a policy, born of an exaggerated faith in the possibility of establishing peace and justice, might be above the level of events as another of the tsar's intimates, Kochubei, later admitted,[23] but *Justice* was the only war cry that could be worthily opposed to the revolutionary *Liberty*. Early in 1804 Alexander proposed that the French evacuate all territories beyond the Alps and the Rhine; on Napoleon's refusal, he withdrew

---

[20] *Correspondance de Napoléon Ier*, VII, 410-411. No. 5991.

[21] Rumbold was British *chargé d'affaires* to the Hanse Towns from 1801 to 1804. He was released, after a few weeks' detention in France, on the demand of the King of Prussia, but his papers were retained. *British Diplomatic Representatives, 1789-1852*, Royal Historical Society, Camden third series, vol. L (London, 1934), 66.

[22] *Memoirs of Prince Adam Czartoryski*, ed. by A. Gielgud, 2 vols. (London, 1888), II, 9.

[23] N. Brian-Chaninov, "Alexandre Ier et la paix," *Revue d'histoire diplomatique*, XLVII (1933), 302.

the Russian ambassador from Paris. To London he dispatched his friend and confidant Novossiltsov, with a suggestion that Russia and Britain coöperate to free all conquered provinces from the yoke of France, free France itself from the yoke of Napoleon, and promote a league of European states which would guarantee the right of self-government to all peoples. To what extent this proposal of 1804 may be considered an anticipation of the Holy Alliance of 1815 is still a matter of dispute.[24] The British cabinet distrusted Alexander's metaphysics, but synthesized his ostensibly disinterested aims with their own more practical plans for humbling France, and a Russo-British alliance was concluded at St. Petersburg in April, 1805. Prussia resisted all overtures, but Austria, already bound by secret accord to Russia since November 6, 1804, was persuaded to endorse the St. Petersburg pact, and the Third Coalition against revolutionary France became a reality.[25]

Worsted in the diplomatic duel, Napoleon retrieved himself on the battlefield. The army of Boulogne, four magnificent divisions assembled since 1803 for the invasion of England, was rushed across Europe by forced marches in three weeks. The Austrian general Mack, who had already advanced into Bavaria and Württemberg, found himself surrounded and capitulated with 30,000 men at Ulm (October 17-21, 1805). By November 13th Napoleon was in Vienna. Yet his position remained full of peril, for his corps were scattered in a gigantic semicircle from Brünn to Pressburg, and two Russian armies of unknown strength were hastening to the aid of the Austrians. Winter was at hand, the news of Trafalgar had cheered the allies, and Haugwitz was on his way from Berlin with an offer of "mediation" which was blackmail thinly disguised. Even the dispatches from Paris proved disquieting, for the draft had aroused widespread discontent, and the Bank of France was in grave difficulties.

The chief military danger lay to the north, and before the close of

[24] The best recent discussion on this point is H. Schaeder, *Die dritte Koalition und die Heilige Allianz* (Berlin, 1934), 12-25.

[25] J. H. Rose, ed. *Select Despatches relating to the formation of the Third Coalition against France, 1804-1805.* Royal Historical Society (London, 1904), 265-282. The treaties are reproduced in Martens, *Recueil des traités*, VIII, 330-358. A lucid discussion of the diplomatic framework of the Third Coalition, reconstructed from the archival evidence, may be found in H. C. Deutsch, *The Genesis of Napoleonic Imperialism* (Cambridge, Mass., 1938), pp. 257-316.

November Napoleon had taken up his quarters at Brünn with some 40,000 men. He knew that at Olmütz, fifty miles to the northeast, the Russian and Austrian emperors were debating their next move, while Russian reinforcements, pouring through the narrow gate between the Carpathians and the Sudetes, swelled their forces to double his own. With a show of apprehension not wholly simulated he drew back his outposts, luring the enemy southwards, and inflated Alexander's confidence by requesting a conference. By December 1st the two armies faced each other along a seven-mile front running north and south of the village of Austerlitz. The temptation to sweep around the right wing of the French and sever their connections with Vienna appealed to the allied commanders, and Napoleon encouraged the plan by abandoning the Pratzenberg, a move which convinced them that he still sought to escape, and that their center, based upon this defensible plateau, could be weakened with impunity. The deception succeeded brilliantly, for the Austrians and Russians were confident that for once they had Napoleon thoroughly outnumbered, and they ignored the lesson, so consistently demonstrated for ten years, that French troops could march two miles to their one. In the sixty hours before the battle Napoleon brought up a division from Pressburg, seventy miles to the south, and a corps from Iglau, fifty miles to the east, and this rapid concentration gave him nearly 70,000 men against the allies' 80,000. Satisfied that he had solved the enemy's strategy, he even ventured, on the night of December 1st, to take the army into his confidence, and the delighted soldiers built straw fires in his honor, remembering that the morrow would be the first anniversary of his coronation.

Before the "sun of Austerlitz" had dispersed the morning mists, 30,000 Austro-Russian troops hurled themselves against the French right, driving it from the village of Telnitz and across the Goldbach. Five miles to the north the French left was also falling back, until the allies, stretched over a long arc, began to find their possession of the outside lines a handicap. This was the moment Napoleon chose to push home his drive in the center. Storming the heights of the Pratzenberg, Soult's corps held on grimly, and all attempts of the Russian foot and horse to retake this key position failed. With its center shattered, the allied army fell apart. The right wing, unable to extricate itself in time, was swept into the frozen marshes where hundreds fell through the ice. The total Austro-Russian losses exceeded 25,000 men, against 9,000 casualties for the French. *"Soldats,"* announced Napoleon, *"je suis content de vous!"*

Austerlitz shattered Alexander's self-confidence and forced Francis II to abandon the coalition. By the Treaty of Pressburg Austria recognized Napoleon as King of Italy and yielded Venetia, Istria, and Dalmatia. To the Electors of Bavaria and Württemberg, now raised to the rank of kings, the treaty allotted the Tyrol and Vorarlberg, and some small towns on the Danube, while the Elector of Baden received part of the Breisgau and the city of Constance. All Austrian protests failed to modify Napoleon's greed for territory, but as a concession he reduced the indemnity demanded from one hundred to forty million francs.

It had been a shrewd and successful gamble in which fortune had favored the bold. But Napoleon had few illusions regarding the risk he had run. When Haugwitz congratulated him on the success of his arms, he disconcerted the Prussian ambassador by inquiring what the message would have been had Austerlitz proved a defeat. Prussia still held the scales of the European balance, a fact Napoleon conceded by surrendering Hanover to Frederick William. The bribe prolonged Prussian neutrality but it failed to appease Prussian resentment.

For to the war party at Berlin it was clear that a unique opportunity had slipped away. But Frederick William III still clung stubbornly to his neutrality. "I detest war, as all the world knows," he had written his uncle shortly after his accession in 1797. "I know of nothing on earth more precious than peace and tranquillity."[26] But even for this mild spirit Napoleon's contemptuous disregard of Prussian aspirations during the spring and summer of 1806 proved too much to bear. Bavaria, Württemberg, Baden, and Hesse-Darmstadt, which had aided France in the campaign of 1805, received generous rewards, and a Confederation of the Rhine rapidly took shape under French protection. Austria and Prussia seemed destined to lose all real influence in German affairs outside their own borders.

[26] F. M. Kircheisen, "Pourquoi la guerre éclata en 1806 entre la France et la Prusse," *Revue d'histoire diplomatique*, XLIII (1929), 240.

Most disturbing to Prussian pride was the news, which reached Berlin in July, that Napoleon had secretly offered to restore Hanover to Great Britain as a step towards peace with that power.[27] The execution of the Nürnberg bookseller Palm a few weeks later, for distributing the pamphlet *Deutschland in seiner tiefen Erniedrigung*, was probably a superfluous blunder, for by August Frederick William had consented to the mobilization of the Prussian army.

Napoleon refused to take the agitation in Berlin seriously. "The idea that Prussia could take the field against me by herself seems to me so ridiculous that it does not merit discussion," he wrote Talleyrand on September 10th.[28] But the Prussians were not planning to fight alone. The previous March, at the moment when he was ratifying the Treaty of Alliance with France which had brought him Hanover, Frederick William had also reached a secret accord with Alexander directed *against* France. "My first duties are to you, Sire," he assured the tsar repeatedly as the zero hour approached; and Queen Louise, who appreciated Alexander's aid (and his charm) even more profoundly than her husband, flattered the tsar on September 17th with the tribute, "I believe in you as I believe in God."[29]

For Napoleon, who had persuaded himself that Prussia was his obedient ally, and that Russia was on the point of accepting peace, the dénouement provided a rude shock. On September 3rd he learned that the treaty, signed at Paris the previous July by the tsar's envoy, Oubril, had been repudiated at St. Petersburg. Negotiations with London languished at the same moment, and the Prussians marched an army into Saxony. It seemed to Napoleon that, with the graves at Austerlitz still fresh, his enemies had dared to crown the Third Coalition with a Fourth. "I can have no real alliance with any of the great powers of Europe," he complained to Talleyrand bitterly, and that urbane minister, who had been urging moderation since Ulm and Austerlitz, held his peace.[30] To Talleyrand, the emperor's insistent disregard of the rights and dignities of sovereign states was prophetic of disaster; and indeed Napoleon's repeated protests in the summer of 1806, that he really desired peace, were

---

[27] Sorel, *L'Europe et la Révolution française*, VII (Paris, 1911), 82.
[28] Kircheisen, *op. cit.*, 242.
[29] Kircheisen, *op. cit.*, 246.
[30] Sorel, *op. cit.*, VII, 94.

worse than disingenuous; they were in the existing circumstances no less than insensate. Even John Holland Rose finds such blindness at this point difficult to excuse. "It is perfectly true," he concludes, "that he did not want to make war on Prussia in 1806 any more than on England in 1803. He only made peace impossible."[31]

The folly of the Prussian venture was demonstrated to an astonished Europe in less than a month. By the first week of October the armies were in contact on Saxon territory; by the 14th the Prussian divisions were driven in upon Jena and Auerstädt, with French forces which outnumbered them two to one closing in on the north, west, and south. At Jena, on that date, Napoleon advanced 85,000 men against what he conceived to be the main Prussian army, and swept the opposing lines into a rout after heavy fighting. In reality he had encountered only half the enemy forces, for the King of Prussia and the Duke of Brunswick were twenty miles to the north, retreating towards the Elbe. At Auerstädt they found their escape blocked by Davout's corps, 27,000 strong, and after pounding in vain against his rock-like defense, their lines broke when he counter-attacked. Fugitives from the two battles mingled in a panic-stricken stream. Davout's victory, won against odds of almost two to one, was much more brilliant and decisive than Napoleon's, for it assured the dissolution of the Prussian army. The survivors, carrying panic with them, infected the garrisons of the fortified towns, and Spandau, Stettin, Küstrin, Magdeburg, and Hameln capitulated almost on demand. Two weeks after Jena the French were in Berlin, sharpening their swords on the statue of Frederick the Great.[32]

III. THE FRANCO-RUSSIAN ALLIANCE OF 1807

With three-fourths of his kingdom in French hands, Frederick William fled to East Prussia to seek the protection of a Russian army which had crossed the Vistula too late to aid him. Thither Napoleon followed him, after pausing a few weeks in Berlin to inaugurate the continental blockade against England. But now the

---

[31] J. H. Rose, *Life of Napoleon I* (London, 1913), II, 89.

[32] Even Prussian historians have found it difficult to extenuate the foolhardiness and incompetence of the general staff which invited the disasters of 1806. A sincere but not very successful attempt to modify the general judgment is presented by H. Saring, "Prinz Louis Ferdinand als Führer der Avantgarde im Oktober 1806," *Forschungen zur brandenburgischen und preussischen Geschichte*, XLV (1933), 233-261.

Emperor of the French, to whom prompt decisions had become a habit, advanced with a divided mind. The lust for action urged him to seek a decisive battle with the Russians and the remnants of the Prussian forces, but the misery of his men and the harsh aspect of the countryside warned him what a winter campaign would cost in those muddy reaches between the marshes of Poland and the Baltic dunes. In the end the gambler's impulse triumphed, and on February 8th he found his battle at Eylau. Out of that day's blind slaughter, during which the sky grew black and falling snow re-duced the visibility to a few yards, not even Napoleon's fanciest phrases could improvise a victory. The French lost 15,000 men, over one-fifth of their effectives; the Russians, who had fought like mad-men, suffered still more heavily. Nothing had been settled, and as the grand army fell back in search of winter quarters discourage-ment spread through the ranks. War had lost all glamour, supplies were failing, the wounded had to travel fifty leagues in open sleds to find shelter. "Sire," Murat wrote desperately, "it is time Your Majesty did something. We are absolutely without resources."[33] The finest of the French divisions were wasting away in the Polish mud, seven hundred miles from home, while to the south the garrisons of Austria held their stations, watchful and enigmatic, on the flank of that tenuous line of communications. "Ah, if only I were the Arch-duke Charles!" sighed General Jomini, for the author of the *Précis de l'art de guerre* viewed his trade with an artist's eye. But the Arch-duke Charles had not yet instilled into the Austrian forces the lessons learned at Austerlitz the previous year, and wisely, perhaps, he chose to wait.

With the spring Napoleon's confidence revived. Happy that his proposal for an armistice after Eylau had been rejected, he reverted hopefully to the arbitrament of battle. New levies had raised his forces, including the garrisons left in Prussia, to 300,000, while the Prussians and Russians had not mustered half that number. More-over, the war spirit was waning at Russian headquarters, to be replaced by indignation towards England, which had refused sub-sidies, and towards Prussia, which had proved so feeble an ally. At Friedland on June 14, 1807, the main Russian army was mangled so

[33] H. Butterfield, *Peace Tactics of Napoleon* (Cambridge, 1929), 66.

severely that Bennigsen feared to risk a second engagement. He urged Alexander to request an armistice from Napoleon, and the latter was eager to grant it now that he could pose as victor.

The meeting of the two emperors, June 25th, on a raft moored in the Niemen, has always exercised the imagination of historians. Even in that age of kaleidoscopic shifts, a reversion from open warfare to friendly alliance, consummated within two weeks, squinted at the theatrical. Throughout that duel of personalities each protagonist exhausted his facility in the effort to flatter and deceive the other, and if there was a victor in that double game it was not Napoleon. Vandal, with poetic exaggeration, has pictured two races as well as two individuals face to face. "Napoleon personified the Latin genius in its most forceful expression, its radiant clarity, its alert vigor, its talent for conceptions at once harmonious and precise. With him the gift of imagination, however exuberantly it might burn, was always subordinated to rules and logic. Alexander inherited from the races of the north a bent for lofty aspirations, incalculable and cloudy, which had been intensified in his case by an education wholly speculative."[34] But statesmen in conference seldom remember to act as symbols. In deciding for peace with France Alexander was obeying the dictation of domestic politics, for in 1807 the reform, or pro-French, party in Russia was once more in the ascendent. Russian foreign policy throughout this period veered towards France or towards England, according as reformers or conservatives dominated the imperial council, but European historians have usually preferred to seek the clue to it in the over-emphasized contradictions of Alexander's character.[35]

Napoleon's motives at Tilsit, despite Vandal's tribute to the radiant clarity of his thought, are less easy to penetrate, though it is not difficult to reconstruct the general frame of his design. Throughout his administration he had worked on the assumption that France must retain at least one first-class European power as an ally. The fortunes of war, which had exposed Austria to repeated loss of prestige and territory, appeared to eliminate the Hapsburg Empire

---

[34] A. Vandal, *Napoléon et Alexandre Ier*, I (Paris, 1896), Introd. v.
[35] B. Mirkin-Gecevič, "L'influence de la Révolution française sur le developpement du droit international dans l'Europe orientale," *Recueil des cours de l'Académie de Droit International*, XXII (1928), 374.

from the list of eligibles, and to Prussia had fallen the profitless honor of alliance with republican France from 1795 to 1805. Talleyrand, who viewed every friend as a potential foe and every foe as a potential friend, doubted the value of the Prussian alliance and definitely preferred Austria, for he believed that France could use Austria to better advantage in blocking the Russian pressure in eastern Europe. Such a plan was consistent with traditional French policy. For over a century French diplomats had cultivated the friendship of Sweden, Poland, and Turkey, and this cordon of outposts, though its units were all steadily weakening, had delayed the Russian advance.[36] But with the dismemberment of Poland in the later eighteenth century the system of checks lost cohesion, and Talleyrand believed it could be reëstablished by swinging Austria into the line. For this reason he deplored the outbreak of war with Austria in 1805, and after Austerlitz he besought Napoleon to spare the fallen foe. "Your Majesty is now in a position to shatter the Austrian monarchy or to revive it. Once shattered, it would not be possible even for Your Majesty to recombine the fragments."[37] But Napoleon, confident that Prussia would remain a more satisfactory ally, weakened Austria yet further. When the Prussians attacked him the following autumn his error was apparent, and in his vindictiveness, as he himself called it, he swore to abolish that faithless kingdom. At the same time, he recognized that he must seek a new ally. The superior fighting quality of the Russian troops, and the fact that Russia could help to close the Baltic to English ships, persuaded him to woo the tsar, and he found Alexander in a responsive mood.

All lovers of consistency who seek a unifying aim or motive behind Napoleon's aggressive opportunism find Tilsit a turning-point in his career. To Albert Sorel and his school, who see Napoleon as a man condemned to defend the Rhine frontier for fourteen years against the eternal Anglo-European coalitions,[38] Tilsit was one more, and perhaps the greatest, of the labors of Sisyphus. To Émile Bourgeois, for whom the secret of the emperor's foreign policy lay in his Levantine schemes, Tilsit, which forced him to

[36] E. Driault, *Napoléon et l'Europe: Tilsit* (Paris, 1917), 1-14.
[37] P. H. Olden, *Napoleon und Talleyrand: Die französische Politik während des Feldzuges in Deutschland, 1805* (Tübingen, 1927), 54.
[38] A. Sorel, *L'Europe et la Révolution française*, VII (Paris, 1911), 167-187.

compromise with the tsar on the Turkish question, marked a check to that policy.[39] Frédéric Masson, having consecrated thirteen volumes to the Bonaparte family, came to see Napoleon as primarily concerned with finding thrones for his relatives. Tilsit was, therefore, for him, a confirmation of the dynastic changes wrought between 1803 and 1807.[40] Edouard Driault subordinated the *politique familiale* of Masson and the *secret oriental* of Bourgeois to a vaster concept, a progressive imperial organization of Europe, and this *hypothèse impériale* has the merit of conforming most closely to the Napoleonic gospel according to St. Helena.[41] But none of these theories, when pressed down upon the facts, is wholly satisfactory. "We are guilty of a kind of Hegelian fallacy, we are imputing to Napoleon too much the mind of a philosopher intent upon unifying his thought, we are forgetting how much he made his decisions with the mind of a strategist, if we assume that his policy had one central running purpose to which all his actions can ultimately find reference."[42]

To turn from the divination of Napoleon's ultimate purposes to the terms of the Tilsit treaties is not unlike passing from a medieval exegesis to the curt biblical text upon which it is based. Three major issues commanded the attention of Napoleon and Alexander during those midsummer days of 1807 when they rode together on the banks of the Niemen: the question of Prussia, the question of Turkey, and the question of England. On Prussia they compromised, for Napoleon "out of regard for the Emperor of the Russias" allowed Frederick William to retain his throne and two-thirds of his hereditary dominions. On Turkey they compromised also, and Napoleon, who had spurred the Porte to make war on Russia in 1806, deserted his ally without shame, and secretly consented to leave Moldavia and Wallachia under Russian control. In return, the French were to reoccupy the Ionian Islands, and if the Ottoman government resisted the fate prepared for it, France and Russia might jointly divide all the European territories remaining to the Turks, with the exception of Constantinople. The English question, more than ever in the

[39] E. Bourgeois, *Manuel historique de politique étrangère*, II (Paris, 1898), 277-279.
[40] F. Masson, *Napoléon et sa famille*, 13 vols. (Paris, 1897-1919).
[41] Ed. Driault, "Une conception nouvelle de la politique extérieure de Napoléon," *Revue des études napoléoniennes*, VII (1915), 8-10, 35.
[42] H. Butterfield, *Peace Tactics of Napoleon* (Cambridge, England, 1929), 274.

forefront of Napoleon's thought since Trafalgar, was likewise to be settled by joint action. Unless the British government consented, within one month, to restore all conquests made since 1805, and to respect the flags of all nations upon the seas, Russia was to make common cause with France. As there was little probability that the British government would accept the tsar's mediation on these terms, a secret Franco-Russian treaty of alliance, signed July 7th, provided that the lesser maritime states, Portugal, Sweden and Denmark, should be invited to coöperate against the mistress of the seas, and the Danes in particular should be persuaded to close the Baltic by blocking the Sound.[43] The provisions of this agreement were jealously guarded, but Canning, at the head of the British foreign office since March, guessed their purport. He offered the Danes £100,000 a year for the use of their navy. When the offer was refused, a British force bombarded Copenhagen. Within two months of the Tilsit negotiations what remained of the Danish fleet was in British hands. Napoleon's adversaries were learning to match his methods in speed and exceed them in ruthlessness.

Neither Alexander nor Napoleon honored the pledges which they exchanged at Tilsit. Though Frederick William III was permitted to return to Berlin, French garrisons remained in Prussia until driven out in 1813. Though Russia nominally joined France in the war against Great Britain from 1807 until 1812, it was a war fought with folded arms. The Turks were invited to make peace with Russia on the lines laid down at Tilsit, but Napoleon failed to coerce them and was secretly gratified at their continued resistance. Opposition to the French alliance remained strong in Russia and Alexander before long began to lament his bargain. Napoleon, on his side, soon complained of the languor Alexander showed in fulfilling his obligations as an ally. But there was one clause in the treaty from which Napoleon could draw unmixed satisfaction. The British cabinet might refuse to recognize General Bonaparte as Emperor of the French or to acknowledge the titles and territorial awards which he had bestowed upon his vassals, but with the Tilsit truce all the remaining European powers had yielded to the realities of the situation

[43] The text of the Tilsit treaties, the secret clauses, and the Franco-Russian Alliance are in De Clercq, II, 205-223.

and favored his political system with the benefit of their diplomatic sanction.

IV. THE INTERNATIONAL EMPIRE

The months which followed Tilsit found Napoleon's fortunes at full tide. Only Great Britain remained at war and he was confident that the continental blockade would undermine British prosperity and promote the economic recovery of France. All attempts to overthrow the hegemony of *La Grande Nation* had broken down and Europe appeared ready, as in 1801-1802, to acquiesce in the French domination if acquiescence would assure the blessings of peace and stability.

The territory which Napoleon now controlled, directly or indirectly, had doubled since the general peace of 1802. The Italian Kingdom, under the Viceroy Eugène, had been completely subdued to French policy, and the Kingdom of Naples, assigned to Joseph Bonaparte in 1806, supported a division of French troops. The remainder of the Italian peninsula had been annexed, or was shortly to be annexed, to France, organized in *départements*, and ruled by prefects appointed from Paris. A similar loss of liberty was shortly to overtake Holland. In 1806, under threat of annexation, the Dutch accepted Louis Bonaparte as their king. But Louis' easy-going disposition, which led him to court the goodwill of his Dutch subjects and wink at their evasion of the trade restrictions imposed by Napoleon, led to sharp altercations between the two brothers. In 1810 French troops were ordered into the kingdom, Louis abdicated and fled to Bohemia, and Holland also was split into *départements* and annexed to the French Empire.

In the Germanies a revolution had taken place since 1801. With the dissolution of the Holy Roman Empire Napoleon decided to substitute a new organization, the Confederation of the Rhine, designed to include all German states except Austria and Prussia. A precedent existed for such a scheme, for Mazarin had organized a Rhine League as a temporary device when fighting the Hapsburgs in 1658. Before the war of the Third Coalition opened in 1805 Napoleon therefore took the precaution of concluding treaties with the rulers of Bavaria, Baden, and Württemberg, treaties whereby the princes promised to furnish military aid in return for an assurance of territorial aggrandizement.[44] The aggrandizement came before the close of the year, for the Treaty of Pressburg with Austria (December 26, 1805) enlarged the domains of the three electors and raised Bavaria and Württemberg to the dignity of kingdoms. As the German princes were to enjoy henceforth "the plenitude of sovereignty and all rights which derive from it" they were free to accept Napoleon the following July as protector of the Confederated States of the Rhine.[45] The Duke of Berg, the Landgrave of Hesse-Darmstadt, and half a dozen lesser dignitaries joined at the same time. Napoleon had organized the Duchy of Berg as a reward for Murat, who was married to Caroline Bonaparte, but the move offended the Prussian court, for Berg lay within the line of demarcation whereby North Germany had been neutralized under Prussian protection. After the ill-starred attempt to assert Prussian rights, which led to the catastrophe of Jena, Napoleon was at liberty to reorganize North Germany also. Saxony, which had been an unwilling ally of Prussia, he let off lightly, and the elector joined the Confederation of the Rhine with the title of king. An additional kingdom was constructed between the Ems and the Elbe from Hanoverian, Hessian, and other lesser territories, and confided to Jerome Bonaparte as King of Westphalia. All the Germanies, save the truncated Austrian Empire and the crippled Kingdom of Prussia, now formed part of the French system.

One further creation, or rather resurrection, Napoleon undertook at this time, which undermined from the first the Franco-Russian accord reached at Tilsit. The Polish territory acquired by Prussia from the partitioning of Poland in the eighteenth century was detached in 1807 to form the Grand Duchy of Warsaw, under French protection. Though Alexander acknowledged the independence of this small state, wedged in between the Niemen and Silesia, he knew that Polish aspirations for liberty were strong and might easily embarrass the Russian and Austrian governments, both of which held

[44] De Clercq, *Recueil des traités de la France* (Paris, 1864), 120-124, 126-128.
[45] *Ibid.*, II, 171-179.

sections of the dismembered state and had no desire to yield them up. After the defeat of Austria in the war of 1809, Napoleon added a small section of Austrian Galicia, including Cracow, to the Grand Duchy of Warsaw. Alexander had made clear beforehand that he would view any further step towards the reëstablishment of an independent Poland as directly contrary to the primary interests of Russia, and Napoleon's suggestion that he too annex a slice of Galicia did not reconcile the tsar nor relieve his suspicions.[46] He would never, he assured the French ambassador at St. Petersburg, permit the creation of a French province on the Russian frontier.

Europe was learning after 1807, as it had learned after 1802, that Napoleon could be more arbitrary in peace than in war. When the Portuguese refused to close their ports to English ships a secret treaty for the dismemberment of Portugal was concluded between France and Spain (October 27, 1807). General Junot had already been ordered to march to Lisbon, and he occupied the city by November 30th. The terms of the Franco-Spanish convention authorized the passage of a French army through Spain, a concession won by promising Charles IV a large share of Portugal, the restoration of Gibraltar and Trinidad, and the title "Emperor of the Two Americas." But as Napoleon declined to make the terms public and the French forces in Spain continued to grow, the Spanish court became alarmed. Popular indignation against Charles, and against the favorite, Godoy, enabled the heir to the throne, Ferdinand, to force his father's abdication in March, 1808, and to assume the crown. Such a dénouement, however, formed no part of Napoleon's plan. He enticed both Charles and Ferdinand to France, where he coerced them into resigning all claim to the Spanish throne by the Treaty of Bayonne, May 5, 1808. A French army under Murat had already entered Madrid, and in June Napoleon proclaimed his brother Joseph King of Spain. Morose as ever, Joseph accepted his new assignment. "The King of Naples is recognized as King of Spain," Napoleon informed Talleyrand on June 9th. "There have been disturbances in several Spanish provinces. . . ."[47] In one of

[46] S. Tatistcheff, *Alexandre Ier et Napoléon* (Paris, 1891), 474.
[47] *Correspondance de Napoléon Ier*, XVII, 284. No. 14073.

these disturbances the Madrilenos in a mad outburst of hatred had massacred several hundred French soldiers, and insurgents were already facing the firing-squads with shouts of *Cristo y España*. But Napoleon was never one to believe in anthropomancy.

By 1808 the international empire surpassed in area the European realms of Charlemagne or the Roman emperors. Four kings held their titles by the grace of Napoleon: Joachim of Naples, Joseph of Spain, Jerome of Westphalia, and Louis of Holland; and three others had acquired royal rank by his aid: Maximilian of Bavaria, Frederick of Württemberg, and Frederick Augustus of Saxony. To lesser dignitaries the emperor distributed titles suggesting the continental scope of his system, creating Masséna Duke of Rivoli, Bernadotte Prince of Ponte Corvo, and Talleyrand Prince of Benevento. "It was a fine empire," he insisted, looking back on these great days from the nullity of St. Helena; but even in 1808 there were contemporaries who recognized its artificiality. For Napoleon's successes had been won while he fought governments and they were certain to cease when he began to fight nations. In Italy, in the smaller German states, and in Poland the French interference was not at first unwelcome to populations mortified by division and misrule. But when he sought to refashion sovereign states like Prussia or Spain he was dealing with less plastic political material, and his brutality wakened a fiercer resentment. To meet the increasing opposition which his policy excited he could offer no more cogent argument than force, and all his efforts to secure recognition for his creations, to contract royal marriages for his relatives, to consecrate his conquests with the traditional formulas, brought them no more than a spurious legality. There is more than a touch of irony in his debate with Alexander I at Tilsit, wherein he argued for an hour to persuade that "crowned Jacobin," the Tsar of All the Russias, that hereditary rule was indispensable to the repose and stability of a state.[48] "One thing he always regretted extremely," Metternich observed in his shrewd character sketch of Napoleon, "was that he could not take the principle of Légitimacy as the basis of his power. Few men have been so profoundly conscious as he was that authority

[48] N. Brian-Chaninov, "Alexandre Ier et la paix," *Revue d'histoire diplomatique*, XLVII (1933), 294.

deprived of this foundation is precarious and fragile and open to attack."[49] On more than one count, and on more than one occasion, Napoleon had reason to regret that he could not be his own grandson. Time, as he complained with justice, and time alone, was all that was needed to consecrate a dynasty, and time was the one element he could not control.

[49] *Memoirs of Prince Metternich*, ed. by Prince Richard Metternich, 2 vols. (New York, 1880), I, 275.

Chapter Seven

EUROPEAN SOCIETY UNDER THE INTERNATIONAL EMPIRE

THE only permanent triumphs which the Revolution won beyond the frontiers of France were triumphs of principle, and the way had been made clear for these before 1789. In the van of the French armies, when they first invaded Italy and the Germanies, moved the banner of civil equality and religious toleration, emblem of the new age, a sign by which to conquer. So clear in the minds of enlightened men everywhere was the image of a fairer world, in which all citizens would enjoy equal justice under law and promotion according to merit, that Frenchmen, who had first dared to proclaim these imprescriptible rights of man, seemed children of light and heralds of the future. Among the European middle class this all but universal Gallomania persisted into the Napoleonic era. It was believed that in France courageous men had attempted, in the face of treachery and bloodshed, to found the heavenly city of the philosophers upon earth; what the best of the enlightened despots had prefigured, the Republic had carried out. In Germany the aging Wieland paid tribute to the universality of the revolutionary dream when he compared the decrees of the constituent assembly to the frustrated projects of Joseph II: "He, too, was inspired by that glorious design which the French national assembly is now realizing in its entirety, and he held it long before anyone suspected the possibility that the Revolution would be so rapidly accomplished in France."[1] Despite the reign of terror and the decline of revolutionary idealism under the Directory, France remained to the unprivileged classes of Europe the Great Nation which had first vindicated the principles of liberty

[1] J. Jaurès, *Histoire socialiste de la Révolution française*, ed. by A. Mathiez, 8 vols. (Paris, 1922-1924), V, 47.

and equality, and Napoleon, whose victories spread these principles abroad, was the Man of Destiny. To members of the nobility, the clergy, the religious orders, to functionaries and associates of the exclusive guilds and corporations the march of the Revolution might seem the march of anarchy, but to a majority of the continental bourgeoisie, to artisans and peasants, the *Declaration of the Rights of Man* was the charter of a brave new world, the constitution of a universal society.

"When a people, having become free, establishes wise laws, its revolution is complete," the ardent Saint-Just had proclaimed in 1791.[2] Such faith in the efficacious grace of beneficent legislation was characteristic of the age. Frederick the Great, Maria Theresa and Catherine of Russia had all acknowledged it to be the foremost duty of the sovereign to simplify and codify the laws. Here again France set the example with the *Code Napoléon*, a Koran for the new and conquering creed. Contrasted with the *Declaration of the Rights of Man* the *Code* was a reactionary document, no doubt; the right of resistance against oppression, the right of all citizens to participate directly or indirectly in the making of the laws, the guarantees respecting freedom of speech and freedom of the press had been deleted or curtailed by 1804. But the articles which a despot could endorse without impairing his authority had been retained—article I which asserted that men are born and remain equal in rights, and article X which declared that no citizen should be persecuted for his opinions, even his religious opinions, provided the expression of them did not disturb the public order. Joined with the decrees abolishing feudal privileges, and the inheritance provisions assuring all the children of a family a share in the paternal estate, the Napoleonic legislation represented to Europe a codification of the essential elements of the revolutionary program. The adoption of the *Code* outside France is perhaps the most accurate index available of the spread of the French influence, and the most enduring monument to Napoleon's energy. As the executor, in this respect, of the revolutionary legacy, he came nearest to justifying Goethe's flattering tribute: "Napoleon was the expression of all that was reasonable, legitimate, and European in the revolutionary movement."

[2] L. A. de Saint-Just, *Œuvres complètes,* ed. by C. Vellay, 2 vols. (Paris, 1908), I, 264.

The confidence which Napoleon himself reposed in the transforming virtue of the new legislation is evident from his correspondence. "The *Civil Code* is the code of the age," he reminded the legislative body in 1808. "It not only ordains tolerance but systematizes it, and tolerance is the greatest blessing of mankind."[3] And to his brother Jerome, King of Westphalia, he wrote: "What the people of Germany most ardently desire is that individuals who are not nobly born but possess ability should have an equal right to your consideration and preferment, and that every form of servitude, every intermediate bond that comes between the sovereign and the lowest class of his subjects should be entirely abolished."[4] So, in the interests of tolerance and equality, it was urgent "not to defer in the least the establishment of the *Code Napoléon*." With equal assurance he demanded its adoption in the Hanse Towns, and conveyed tactful suggestions to the rulers of Baden, Bavaria, and Hesse-Darmstadt that they should follow the general example. When Murat at Naples complained that the divorce provisions would offend his subjects the emperor replied firmly, "I cannot, as protector of the constitution, consent to any modification of the Napoleonic code." Protests from Louis of Holland that he felt impelled to drop several provisions to placate Dutch prejudices drew a still sharper rebuke:

If you revise the *Code Napoléon* it will no longer be the *Code Napoléon*. . . . The Romans gave their laws to their allies; why should not France have hers adopted in Holland? It is equally essential that you adopt the French monetary system, a step already taken (*sic*) in Spain, Germany, and the whole of Italy. Why do you not do it? The bonds which hold nations together are knitted more strongly when they have the same civil laws and the same coinage. When I say the same coinage I mean that your coins should carry the arms of Holland and the effigy of the king, but the type, the system, should be the same.[5]

A desire for uniformity in the imperial system frequently led Napoleon to act and write as if that uniformity had actually been achieved. On paper the empire revealed a symmetry which belied

[3] *Correspondance de Napoléon Ier*, XVIII, 9. No. 14394.
[4] *Ibid.*, XVI, 166. No. 13361.
[5] *Ibid.*, XVI, 161. No. 13357.

the facts. By 1811 France had expanded to 128 *départements*, with a population estimated at 43,000,000. In the Italian peninsula the territories of Savoy, Piedmont, Genoa, Tuscany, and Rome had been annexed. In the north and east the Belgian provinces, the Kingdom of Holland, and one-third of Germany, including the left bank of the Rhine, Hanover, Oldenburg, and the Hanseatic towns (Lübeck, Bremen and Hamburg) had shared the same fate. Certain other territories, like the Illyrian Provinces and the departments of Catalonia, Aragon, Navarre, and Viscaya in Spain, were administered by prefects from Paris, though retaining an anomalous character, since they were not formally considered part of France. A second general type of territories comprised the vassal states, like the Italian Kingdom, of which Napoleon himself assumed the crown in 1805; the Kingdom of Naples, ruled by Murat after 1808; Spain, confided to Joseph Bonaparte the same year; Westphalia, a collection of North German provinces organized into a kingdom for Jerome Bonaparte in 1807; and the Duchy of Warsaw, bestowed on Napoleon's ally Frederick Augustus of Saxony. A third category of states accepted Napoleon as protector and were bound to France by military alliances. Among these was the Swiss Confederation, tranquil and fairly prosperous after the mediation of 1803, enjoying nominal independence but guided by France in all matters of foreign policy and pledged to furnish 20,000 men for the imperial armies. The thirty-seven states of the Rhine Confederation, technically allied to France on terms of equality, submitted in varying degree to French control. Their collective quota in case of war amounted to 88,400 men, while France was pledged to furnish 200,000,[6] and their highways remained open for the movement of French forces. The population in the two confederations, the Rhine and the Swiss, had probably less to complain of than any other alien peoples within the sphere of French influence.

Thus summarized, the International Empire gives an impression of cohesion which it never really possessed, an impression fortified for the student of history by colored maps of Europe in 1810 showing the whole continent, with the exception of Russia, a diminished Austria and Prussia, and perhaps Portugal, subordinate to French

[6] R. B. Mowat, *The Diplomacy of Napoleon* (London, 1924), 161.

control. Yet despite the improved communications, the higher economic development and the more effective extortion of tribute, Napoleon's empire was almost as unwieldy as that of Charlemagne, and was even further divorced from the unifying spirit of the Roman tradition. The attempt to hold up the shattered mirror of the Roman example before the Europe of 1810 was a piece of hollow and fantastic plagiarism. The European nations never lost the power to throw off the French hegemony whenever the burden it imposed was found to outweigh the advantages. To believe that Germany, Italy, and Spain, to say nothing of Austria, Prussia, and Russia, would have acquiesced permanently in the French preponderance is as difficult as to suppose that they would have voluntarily shipped their historical archives and records to Paris in the interest of efficiency and centralization. Reason was on the side of political, legal, and linguistic uniformity for Europe, but there are limits to the concessions which men will make in the name of reason. Europe, like France, had been obsessed in 1789 by an intense aspiration for order, but the impulse which in France substituted the eighty-three *départements* of the unitary Republic for the forty discrepant provinces of the old régime could not impose on the political mosaic of Europe the benefits of a continental federation. The arguments in favor, the advantages to be derived from a more perfect union, might be as compelling in the second case as in the first. But national sentiments are stronger obstacles than provincial loyalties, and Europeans as a people had no sense of a common political bond. In France it was the allied invasion of 1792 which, more than any other factor, forged the "Republic One and Indivisible." Christendom, however, had faced no common foe since the decline of the Ottoman power, and Napoleon's efforts to unite the European states against England as the vampire of the north ended by uniting four-fifths of the continent in a coalition against France. The coalition perpetuated itself for a few years after the conclusion of peace, as such coalitions often do, in the form of the quadruple alliance. But of the spirit which inspired the unitary ideal the only authentic vestige was the Holy Alliance of 1815, and that was a pale ghost of the *Imperium Gallicum* sitting on the grave thereof.

"The solitude in which Bonaparte left the world," as Chateaubriand poetically described it, might better have been compared to the dissonance of Babel, for the intensification of national sentiments which resulted from the Wars of Liberation made the political unification of Europe more than ever a chimera. Yet that "empire of reason" with Paris as its capital, dreamed by the philosophers, projected by the revolutionaries, had more than conceptual validity and it has become in moderate degree an intellectual reality in the century since Napoleon's death. Outside France, only the Belgian provinces and the Rhineland had fully accepted the civil code in 1815, but in Holland, Italy, and Portugal the national codes later adopted were modeled upon it, and the legal systems of Spain, the South American republics, Louisiana and French Canada, owe much to its inspiration. "The *Code* stands out as one of the few books which have influenced the whole world."[7] Similarly, the system of decimal coinage, decreed for France early in the Revolution, has since conquered every enlightened country of the globe except Great Britain. The metrical system of weights and measures, proposed at an international conference held in Paris in 1798, is now the official system in twenty-five states and is sanctioned in as many more. These are triumphs of "right reason" that would have delighted the *philosophes*, who liked to hail Euclid as the world's truest despot and Newton as history's greatest legislator. They are triumphs, moreover, which owe more to the labors of a Condorcet or a Cambacérès than to Napoleon, and their benefits will outlast the Corsican's fame.

II. THE EMERGENCE OF THE BOURGEOISIE

For the twentieth-century reader, modern European history has tended in recent decades to become more and more emphatically the drama of the emerging bourgeoisie. The march of the middle classes, particularly of those classes which drew their livelihood from trade, manufacture, or finance, has taken on the appearance of a fated phenomenon, at once the central theme and the motivating force in the evolution of European society. Unhappily, however, for those who would willingly apply the formula of the middle-class revolution as a yardstick of social progress, its dynamics are not yet clearly

---

[7] J. H. Wigmore, *A Panorama of the World's Legal Systems*, Library ed. (Washington, 1936), 1027.

understood, its momentum and intensity appear often to have varied unpredictably, and its conquests were sometimes surprisingly impermanent. To ponder those spasms of business aggressiveness which, in the past six hundred years, have seized upon and transformed European cities and states is still to be impressed chiefly by their unaccountability. Too frequently they appear, at least in the light of present knowledge, to belong among the arbitrary phenomena, the *novae* of the historical firmament.

Thus the Italian cities, where the stimulus of reviving trade produced such marked effects in the thirteenth and fourteenth centuries, failed to retain their leadership, and the shift of commerce to the Atlantic seaways is an inadequate explanation of their decline. As in the analogous decadence which overtook the Iberian countries a century later, the complex factors at work defy any very satisfactory analysis. The business spirit yielded to a pursuit of hollow feudal pageantry, manufacture languished, shopkeeping fell into contempt. By the eighteenth century Italy retained little save the memory of that artistic, intellectual, and commercial primacy which had been hers in the *quattrocento*. No powerful and discontented middle class existed in 1800 to which Napoleon could appeal in his efforts to reconstruct Italian society. A few imaginative business men envied without imitating the audacity of French bankers and capitalists like Ouvrard and Lafitte, and the Italian professional classes, lawyers, doctors, journalists, officers of the civil and military services, supported the new order enthusiastically and formed a small *neoborghesia napoleonica*.[8] But as a class they lacked an adequate economic or political basis for their pretensions, and they were opposed by an ecclesiastical hierarchy and by the ubiquitous influence of a theocratic tradition stronger in Italy than anywhere else in Europe.

For in Italy the most powerful privileged class was not the landed nobility, but the priesthood. To revolutionize Italian institutions meant not merely to liberalize but to *laicize* them. It was not sufficient to decree civil equality, annul the feudal prerogatives of the nobility, cancel immunities and equalize the burden of taxation. So long as the ecclesiastics retained their lands and revenues, supervised

[8] N. Quilici, *Origine, sviluppo e insufficienza della borghesia italiana* (Ferrara, 1932), 85-108.

education and filled the most important administrative posts, especially in the papal states, the secular spirit of the Revolution could make little real progress among the Italian people. The material possessions of the clergy might be confiscated, their revenues diverted to lay enterprises, but still their prestige, rooted in popular veneration, would remain all but unassailable. Even in France the Revolution, which had easily abolished the ancient nobility, found it expedient to come to terms with the clergy, though it was able to strip them of political influence. In Italy, where the clerics had assumed much wider political powers, it proved impossible, in the decade of Napoleonic rule, to exclude them from secular affairs or to separate the administration of church and state. The settlement of this problem remained the most crucial issue of Italian politics throughout the nineteenth century, and its persistence explains why to become a liberal in Italy meant almost inevitably to become an anticlerical. The restoration of 1815 proved a reversal of the revolutionary program not primarily because it once again reduced the peninsula to a dozen political fragments, returned exiled princes to their thrones, and resurrected internal tariff barriers, but because it restored many of the monastic foundations, revived an obscurantist censorship, subordinated education to ecclesiastical control, and repaired the shattered intrenchments of clerical privilege.

In the Germanies, as in Italy, the business classes had failed by the eighteenth century to live up to the promises of an earlier emancipation and prosperity. The decline of the Hanseatic League after the sixteenth century, the devastation of the Thirty Years' War in the seventeenth, the political decentralization of the eighteenth, had denied German merchants a merited share in colonial exploitation and in the increasing profits of domestic and foreign trade. By 1800 Italy with a population of 18,000,000 and the Germanies with 21,000,000 were both entitled by strength of numbers to claim a place among the great powers, but political disunity and economic restrictions condemned them to remain pawns in the diplomatic game at a time when Great Britain, with only 11,000,000 inhabitants, was challenging France with impunity. The decentralization of the Germanies, in comparison with France and England, was reflected in the relative size of their leading cities. Paris, in 1800, already exceeded half a million, and London was nearing the million mark, while Berlin, the largest German city, had only 172,000 inhabitants. With heavy and frequent tolls hampering traffic on the German rivers, the jealousy of the free cities and minor states precluding collective initiative, and the privileges of the guilds retarding the introduction of new methods and machinery, German economic life, like German political life, remained narrow, conservative, and particularist in spirit.

Until the development of wider customs unions in the nineteenth century, German industry and commerce submitted to the bondage of these complex and arbitrary restrictions, and the German merchant or manufacturer found himself bounded in his thinking by the limits of the local markets. Under these conditions it was possible to make a moderate living, but difficult to build up a fortune. Lack of imagination and initiative, a spirit of resignation and docile-mindedness, was one common result. Madame de Staël remarked in 1803 and again in 1808 on the subservient attitude of the German burgher towards constituted authority. Reforms introduced from above, as Frederick II and Joseph II had instituted them, satisfied German expectations; not even the example of the gains won by bourgeois aggression in France inspired the middle class across the Rhine to demand a controlling voice in political affairs or a leading position in society.

Confined in his professional aims, denied an opportunity for political activity, the German *Bürger* revenged himself upon fate by deserving a better fortune. Morally and intellectually the German middle class was superior to that of France or England. *Die Gedanken sind zollfrei,* and the pleasures of reflection, pride in respectability, sentimental devotion to the duties of family life and to the demands of friendship were cultivated in German middle-class homes as compensation for adventures denied and riches out of reach.[9] Nowhere else in Europe did the bourgeois *Ethik* find a more intense expression. The heroine of Schiller's *Kabale und Liebe,* who perishes because she will not break her word and repudiate a letter extorted from her by deceit and compulsion, exemplifies an ideal of conduct as exigent as fate itself; indeed, Friedrich Hebbel, in his

[9] G. Huard, *L'évolution de la bourgeoisie allemande* (Paris, 1919), 222-239.

apology for middle-class tragedy, was later to argue that the limitations of the bourgeois character might be equated to the rôle played by fate in the classical drama.[10] In France this spirit of stoic pride was to inspire a Charlotte Corday and a Saint-Just, but in Germany the cult of action languished or was transmuted into the exquisite self-frustration of the romantic revolt. The relative impotence of the German middle class during the revolutionary era and for half a century thereafter cannot be wholly explained on the ground of numerical weakness or political inexperience. It was in part the tragic heritage of an introverted society, prepared intellectually by the *Aufklärung* for an era of opportunity, but denied the leaders or the institutions through which to unlock the future. In their hearts the German burghers of 1800 seem already to be presuffering the rebuffs and failures of 1815 and 1849.

In France and in Belgium, where the middle classes had been freed in fact and in spirit from the shackles of an obsolete feudalism, the end of the revolutionary era found them firmly settled in power. Fortunes acquired in trade, industry, speculation, army contracts and the public services were invested in city residences and country estates. Private coaches and carriages, which had all but disappeared from the streets of Paris under the Jacobin commonwealth, came back into fashion under the Consulate. As all Frenchmen were equal in the emperor's service, the reëstablishment of the court found members of the old nobility, the new nobility, and the as yet untitled *arrivistes* rubbing shoulders. Bonaparte's readiness to ignore the past was appreciated by all factions: what France desired after 1800 was not merely *l'amnistie* but *l'amnésie*. Men who had participated in the furious episodes of the Revolution seldom referred to them and the singing of the *Marseillaise* was forbidden as a threat to public tranquillity. For in the social amalgam of the empire the well-to-do bourgeoisie had become part of the privileged order. In their select circles, to which wealth instead of birth now provided the *entrée*, distrust of popular movements was a ruling passion. The new society might lack the grace and exclusiveness of the old, it might have

[10] C. F. Hebbel, *Werke*, ed. by F. Zinkernagel, 6 vols. (Leipzig, 1913), VI, 99-102; Margarete H. Hill, *Schiller's "Kabale und Liebe" in the light of Hebbel's theory of middle-class tragedy*, Graduate Thesis, New York University, 1932.

"more ceremony and less elegance," but it symbolized for Paris, for France, for all Europe the triumph of bourgeois ambition.

Had the two most powerful and most liberal states of the age, France and Great Britain, united their energies against the institutions of the old régime, the latter could have offered little effective resistance. The decision of the British oligarchy to ally itself instead with the counter-revolutionary forces prolonged the rule of the privileged aristocracies of central Europe and saved Spain and Portugal from social reconstruction. Yet this attitude of Albion, which Jaurès termed decisive,[11] can have been no more than protractive in its ultimate effect. A liberating movement like the French Revolution is not in itself creative; it can clear the ground, but it cannot create a new society where the ground is still historically unprepared or unfertile. Spain, Italy, and eastern Europe could not be revolutionized and aligned socially and economically with France and England by precept or example or bayonets. All Napoleon's efforts would have failed to alter conditions radically even if England had been his ally.

If the years between 1789 and 1815 mark a turning-point in the evolution of European society, this is to be attributed less to the revolutionary reforms than to the economic forces—the active transforming agents—which these reforms quickened and liberated. The principle of absolutism in political affairs was superseded by the principle of contractualism. A governmental decree ceased to be a compulsory ordinance and became in theory an expression of the general will, enforceable by virtue of a contract which bound the state no less firmly than the individual or the corporation. Under a constitutional régime, which was pledged to respect the liberty of the individual and the sanctity of property, business men could compute the gains and risks of an enterprise more confidently, for they were insured against unpredictable interference and arbitrary confiscation. Authority as the product of a legal covenant, limited in its manifestations by legal safeguards, was a conception of government which the bourgeois class could respect and endorse.

More difficult to appraise, but perhaps no less stimulating in its effects, was the reversal in values which installed the materialistic

[11] J, Jaurès, *Histoire socialiste de la Révolution française*, ed. by A. Mathiez, 8 vols. (Paris, 1922-1924), V, 247.

Sixty-two Illustrations
Drawn from Unusual Sources
and Specially Chosen by
the Author

for

EUROPE
AND THE
FRENCH IMPERIUM
1 7 9 9 — 1 8 1 4

by

GEOFFREY BRUUN

1. Napoleon Bonaparte, First Consul.
Painted by Ingres, 1805

2. Napoleon crossing the St⁰Bernard Pass, 1800.
Painted by David

4. The Statesman, Talleyrand, attempting to restrain Napoleon from attacking
John Bull, 1803.
A caricature by Gillray

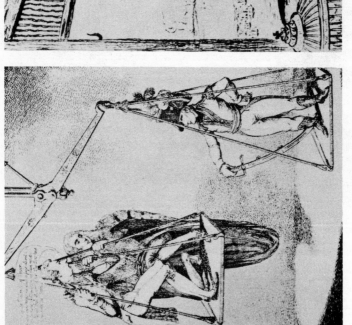

3. The Balance of Power, 1801.
A caricature by C. Ansell

From A. M. Broadley, *Napoleon in Caricature*, John Lane, the Bodley Head, London

5. Pope Pius VII and Cardinal Caprara.
Painted by David, 1805

6. Tsar Alexander I of Russia.
Painted in 1801 by Vigée Lebrun

7. William Pitt the Younger.
Painted by John Hoppner in 1805

Two Statesmen of the Third Coalition

8. Count Kochubei

9. Novossiltsov

10. Prince Adam Czartoryski

11. Count Stroganov

Four of the young friends who encouraged Alexander I in his attempts at reform

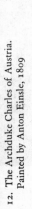

12. The Archduke Charles of Austria.
Painted by Anton Einsle, 1809

13. Lord Nelson.
Painted by John Whichelo, 1805

Two great opponents of Napoleon in 1805

14. The Death of Nelson at Trafalgar.
Painted by J. M. W. Turner in 1808

15. The Glorious Battle of Trafalgar.
From a print published in 1806

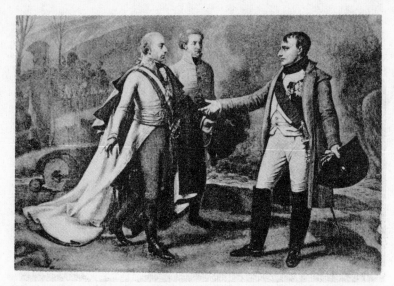

16. Meeting of Napoleon and Francis I of Austria after the battle of Austerlitz.
Part of a larger painting by Gros, 1812

17. The battle of Jena.
From a contemporary picture by J. L. Rugendas

18. Napoleon liberating the Poles.
An English caricature of 1807

19. The famous meeting of Napoleon and Alexander on a raft in the Niemen River.
From a contemporary Russian print

20. The beautiful Queen Louise of Prussia.
From a painting by Grassi, 1802

21. Freiherr vom Stein, reformer of Prussia.
Painted by Lützenkirchen, 1814

22. Count Michael Speranski, the Russian reformer.
From a contemporary portrait

24. Johann Heinrich Pestalozzi, the great Swiss
educational reformer.
From a painting by Schöner, 1808

23. Friedrich Karl von Savigny, the eminent
German jurist.
From a drawing by Schinkel, 1812

26. Schiller in his last years.
From a drawing by Gottfried Schadow, 1804

25. Goethe in the later period.
From a painting by Kügelgen, 1810

27. Beethoven in the period of his maturity.
A portrait by Mähler, 1804-05

28. Ferdinand VII of Spain.
Painted by Goya, about 1807

29. Mass shootings at Madrid by the French.
One of the most striking pictures by Goya

30. The Capitulation of Madrid.
Painted by Gros in 1810

31, 32, & 33. How the Spanish revolt appeared to a great
Spanish artist.
Three scenes from Goya's *The Disasters of War*

35. Andreas Hofer, the Tyrolese leader.
From an anonymous contemporary painting

34. Don José de Palafox, the Spanish leader.
From an English engraving of 1809

36. Prince Michael Barclay de Tolly

37. Prince Michael I. Kutusov

38. Prince Peter I. Bagration

39. Count Leo L. Bennigsen

Four Russian commanders of the War of 1812.
From drawings by Louis de Saint-Aubin, 1812

40. Russian Cossacks of the 1812 campaign.
From a drawing by Gottfried Schadow, 1813

41. A Russian caricature of 1812, picturing Napoleon's flight from Warsaw to Paris. The French eagle is somewhat the worse for wear. Napoleon's famous Mamluk attendant brings up the rear

42. Capture of the British frigate *Java* by the American frigate *Constitution*, December 29, 1812. From an English engraving of 1814

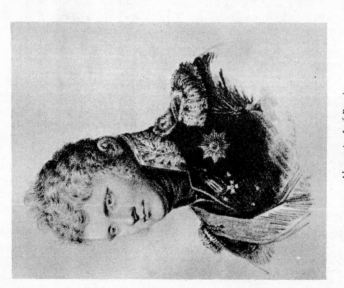

43. Alexander I of Russia.
From a drawing of Louis de Saint-Aubin, 1808

44. Frederick William III of Prussia.
Painted by Gérard, 1814

Two leaders of the Grand Alliance of 1813

45. Metternich, Austrian foreign minister.
From a painting by Gérard, 1808

46. Lord Castlereagh, British foreign secretary.
Painted by Sir Thomas Lawrence, 1810

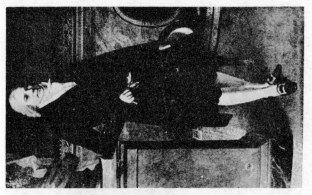

47. Prince Talleyrand.
Painted by Prud'hon, 1809

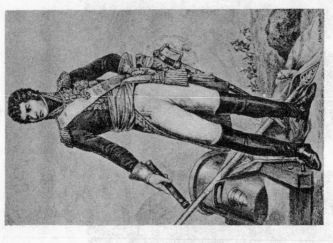

48. Joachim Murat, famous cavalry leader, brother-in-law of Napoleon, King of Naples. From a painting by Gérard. 1800

49. Charles Bernadotte, French general who became crown prince of Sweden and joined Alexander of Russia against Napoleon in 1813. From a painting by François Kinsoen, 1808-09

Two eminent marshals of Napoleon

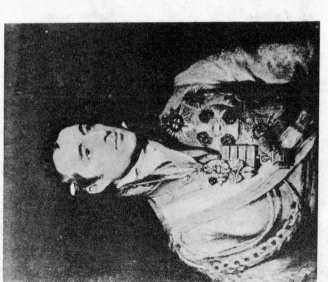

50. The Duke of Wellington.
Painted by Thomas Phillips in 1814

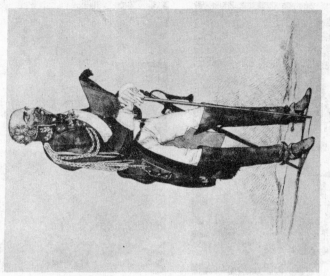

51. The Prussian General Blücher.
From an English print of 1814

Napoleon's most formidable opponents

52. Pin-maker

53. Paper-maker

54. Calico-printer

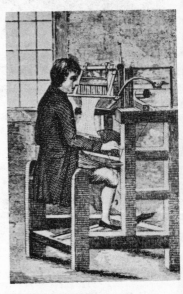

55. Stocking-maker

Early factory workers. English prints, 1805

56 & 57. Soup tureen and candlesticks, by Martin Biennais, *c.* 1810-20.
Probably part of a set given to Prince Borghese by Napoleon

58. The Ruined Monastery of Eldena.
Painted by Caspar David Friedrich in 1807 or 1808

59. An imaginary Gothic Cathedral. Painted by Karl Friedrich Schinkel in 1815
German paintings of the Romantic, Gothic School

60. Pass of St. Gothard, 1802

61. Calais Pier, 1803
Masterpieces of English landscape-painting by J. M. W. Turner

62. Napoleon.
Sketched from life in 1812 by Girodet-Troison

philosophy and counting-house ethics of the merchant class as the religion of the new society. In the opinion of Werner Sombart, this change alone would justify the historian in accepting the French Revolution as marking the transition from the first to the second stage in the evolution of the capitalist economy:

> The evolution of the capitalist spirit still proceeds upon its course, a course in which we can clearly distinguish two phases: until the end of the eighteenth century, and since then to the present day. In the first epoch, which comprised the period of early capitalism, the character of the capitalist genius was essentially restricted and repressed, in the second its expression was essentially free. Its bonds had been the restrictions of a code and a morality riveted by all the Christian catechisms.[12]

Sombart's conclusion is worth emphasizing because the factor which he stresses is at once significant and imponderable. It may well be that, among the many stimuli which the Revolution provided for the encouragement of capitalist enterprise, none was more pervasive in its effect than the substitution of a climate of opinion frankly secular, as an alternative to a social philosophy which had been heavily charged, until the later eighteenth century, with theological preconceptions.

III. EDUCATION AND PUBLIC OPINION

By its confiscation of church property and dissolution of the teaching orders the constituent assembly cleared the way for a national system of education in France. For a decade successive committees on public instruction labored over the project, but lack of funds and lack of teachers circumscribed their efforts. With the law of May 1, 1802, the centralizing tendency characteristic of Napoleonic institutions became recognizable in the sphere of education, and by 1808 the imperial university had acquired a monopoly over all public instruction. Yet the appointment in the latter year of Fontanes as grand master of the university must be counted a victory for the Catholic forces. Under his rule the supervision of the theological seminaries became little more than a formality, and the *frères des écoles chrétiennes*, once more active in primary education, were permitted to evade the oath demanded by the emperor. Napoleon's in-

[12] W. Sombart, *Der Bourgeois* (Munich, 1923), 461.

tention to maintain the supremacy of the lay power in education, but to use the teaching talents of the clerical brethren to consecrate his dynasty, was not easy to execute. Fontanes came more and more under the influence of clerical advisers, whose resources and experience were in general greatly superior to the training of the lay teachers. He consulted the bishops in preference to the prefects when making appointments, and his favoritism towards ecclesiastics and equivocal submission to the emperor's orders sometimes distorted the latter's purposes to a degree which almost squinted at treason.

How adequately the imperial university was serving the educational needs of the French people by the close of the empire is a question not easily answered. Primary education was in the worst state. Relinquished to private initiative or confided to the care of political appointees some of whom were semi-illiterate, it yielded but slowly to the attempts to extend its scope and elevate its standards. Religious orders, as the laws against them were relaxed, reclaimed their leadership in this field, and the *frères des écoles chrétiennes*, one of the most successful teaching groups before 1789, had surpassed their former total of 106 schools by 1806. But it seems doubtful, even on the basis of the most sanguine calculations, that more than one-eighth of the French children of school age could have been accommodated in the 31,000 primary schools mentioned in the *Exposé de la situation de l'Empire* for 1813.[13] Napoleon betrayed no inclination to provide free instruction on a democratic basis for all students; formal education remained a privilege of those classes financially capable of discharging the dues demanded by the private establishments. Secondary education fared somewhat better. France boasted forty-six *lycées* in 1812, in addition to some 510 independent colleges. The colleges remained more popular, and a project instituted in 1811 to increase the number of *lycées* to one hundred by drawing students from the private establishments failed to produce results. Despite all the attempts to enforce state supervision and uniform standards, public instruction in France at the close of the empire remained predominantly a matter of private initiative or clerical enterprise.

An analysis of the enrolment in the institutes of higher learning in

[13] F. A. Aulard, *Napoléon Iᵉʳ et le monopole universitaire* (Paris, 1911), 264.

France for the year 1813 reflects the dominant interest in professional studies. Of a total of 8,859 students, the faculties of law claimed forty-five per cent, medicine twenty-four per cent, letters twenty per cent, theology six per cent and sciences five per cent.[14] The function of the imperial university, in conjunction with the military schools, was to train the civil and military architects of a secular society, and its effect was to indoctrinate the centers of higher instruction in France with the scientific spirit at a time when English universities were still ruled by the ideal of a liberal, and German universities by the ideal of a classical, education. The difficulty of finding subordinates with the technical training to execute his industrial and engineering projects, and the bent of his own genius, led Napoleon to emphasize the training of the scientist as equally important with the training of the scholar, and his efforts helped to make France the home of scientific thought in the early years of the nineteenth century.

The most significant, and in the truest sense the most revolutionary, change in pedagogical practice during this period, best exemplified by the labors of Pestalozzi in Switzerland, affected France little and England not at all. Education for the masses, conceived not only as intellectual instruction but as a harmonious cultivation of the physical, mental, and spiritual faculties, appeared to Pestalozzi an ideal so fraught with possibilities that the born teacher might dedicate himself to it as an artist to his art. The movement spread through the Germanies with remarkable rapidity, and stimulated many of the lesser princes and governments to establish popular schools in the early years of the nineteenth century. In this as in so many other reforms of the revolutionary age the ground had been prepared and public opinion ripened by the labors of the enlightened despots. Frederick the Great had decreed village schools and compulsory education for Prussia as early as 1763, and Joseph II sponsored a popular educational system for Austria between 1770 and 1780. But it required the humane enthusiasm of men like Pestalozzi, Von Fellenberg, Johannes Falk, and Fröbel of Kindergarten fame, to breathe the spirit of life into these well-intentioned edicts.

From the education of children it is but a step, in the mind of the

[14] Aulard, *op. cit.*, 354.

administrator, to the education of adults. Napoleon found three instruments ready to his hand for this second purpose—the priests, the press, and the drama—and he used all three in his determination to guide public opinion. An official *Catéchisme à l'usage de toutes les églises de l'Empire Française* was issued in 1808, and the birthday of the emperor was celebrated on August 15th (the Feast of the Assumption) in a subtle effort to identify the rule of Napoleon with the will of God.[15] Unfortunately, the most independent elements of the populace, the ex-Jacobins and liberals, were the least susceptible to priestly guidance, but a judicious manipulation of the journals went a long way in sparing them contact with inflammatory ideas. Three weeks after the establishment of the consulate sixty of the seventy-three Parisian journals ceased publication, and of the remaining thirteen only nine survived the first year. At what price they survived is evident from their content; the editor whose utterances proved displeasing to the government remained in no doubt of the fact. A communication from Napoleon to Fouché, dated April 22, 1805, suggests the mode of censorship:

Repress the journals a little; make them produce wholesome articles. Let the editor of the *Journal des Débats* and of the *Publiciste* understand that the time is not far distant when, remarking that they are not of service to me, I shall suppress them along with all the rest, and shall conserve a single organ. Let them comprehend . . . that the era of the revolution is closed, that there is now but one party, and that I shall never suffer the journals to say or do anything contrary to my interests. . . .[16]

The single organ which he proposed to retain was of course the *Moniteur*. As the official voice of the government it was closely supervised by the director-general of printing and publishing, and received occasional subsidies, generally of a moderate nature, in the form of paid subscription lists.[17]

That the Parisians endured this curtailment of their intellectual fare without serious objections may be attributed in part to their

[15] H. H. Walsh, *The Concordat of 1801* (New York, 1933), 94-97.
[16] *Correspondance de Napoléon Iᵉʳ*, X, 335-336. No. 8611. For more orders of the same type see L. Lecestre (ed.), *Lettres inédites de Napoléon Iᵉʳ*, 2 vols. (Paris, 1897), I, 58, 342.
[17] G. Vauthier, "La rédaction du Moniteur en 1811," *Revue des études napoléoniennes*, XV (1919), 108-111.

waning interest in politics. They abandoned in these same years their habit of advertising partisan sympathies by the cut of the collar or the color of the cravat, and the trial of Moreau in 1804 seems to have been one of the last occasions when this practice excited comment. It was replaced in large measure by a mania for decorations, which by 1810 had reached a height bordering on absurdity. All mass demonstrations, however, save those of a decorous and semiofficial character, passed out of fashion, and the applause with which audiences in the theaters greeted the dramas, tediously designed to inculcate sound principles, grew increasingly languid as society settled itself under the empire. This absence of enthusiasm seems to have resulted from esthetic disapprobation and not from political resentment, for the theater-going public, drawn predominantly from the bourgeois class, had most reason to support the imperial régime. Even during the Jacobin commonwealth of 1793 and 1794 the most popular play had been *Nicodème dans la lune,* a light-hearted operatic fantasy which celebrated, significantly enough, not the creation of a democratic republic, but the introduction of tolerance and civil equality by a genial and enlightened despot.[18]

The *senatus consultum* of May 18, 1804, the formal constitution of the First Empire, included a clause (section VIII, article 64) which promised that "A commission of seven members, named by the senate and chosen from that body, is charged to watch over the liberty of the press." The authority of the commission was severely limited from the outset by a qualification which excepted journals and periodicals from its jurisdiction, but authors or publishers of other works who found themselves restrained from printing might appeal to it, and the commission, if it judged the liberty of the press had been infringed, could send the minister responsible before the *haute cour impériale.* The fact that the commission never found occasion during the empire to cite a case of infringement cannot be taken as evidence *primâ facie* that no cause existed. Rather it seems probable that the board abstained from action, forewarned by the reception which greeted the protests of its sister council, the *commission séna-*

[18] K. N. McKee, *The evolution of the rôle of the priest on the Parisian stage during the French Revolution,* Graduate thesis, New York University (unpublished), 1937. Chap. One.

toriale de la liberté individuelle. But the tribulations of that board belong to the following section.

IV. THE LIBERTY OF THE INDIVIDUAL

The "crime of arbitrary detention," though specifically forbidden by the constitution of the year VIII (section III, article 46), had been committed repeatedly during the consular period. To reassure public opinion, which was fearful that this abuse of power might increase under an emperor, the *senatus consultum* of 1804 provided that the ministers must submit an account of all arrests to a senatorial commission on individual liberty. If prisoners were not discharged or brought before a court within ten days after arrest, the commission, having failed to secure redress otherwise, might notify the senate that "there was a strong presumption that N—— was detained arbitrarily." The senate, if the occasion appeared to warrant such action, could then cite the minister responsible before the high imperial court. This august tribunal was to consist of sixty senators, the grand dignitaries of the empire, and several other imperial officials, but its exact composition is a matter of no great moment because it never met.

Within a space of four months after its creation the commission on individual liberty received 116 petitions on behalf of prisoners arbitrarily detained. Some forty of these were released after application to the minister of police, but as release frequently meant transfer to a place of surveillance in the interior of France, a condition authorized by no law, from which there was, in consequence, no legal appeal, their condition might still remain an oppressive one. A larger number remained in detention indefinitely on various pretexts, and the commission forbore to catechize the authorities too persistently about them. Its report, submitted the following year, may be read as an expression of its philosophy or as a confession of its impotence. The quintessence of the problem it faced was summed up in a single sentence: "The commission has recognized first of all that, if individual liberty is the primary concern of men in society, the safety of the state is the primary concern of governments. . . ."[19] Four years

---

[19] F. A. Aulard, "La liberté individuelle sous Napoléon," *La Grande Revue,* 11 (1897), 544.

later, still in session, the members received from the emperor a report on the state prisons, which announced that it had been found advisable to authorize the incarceration of political dissidents for a period of one year, or even longer, without trial. The senators acquiesced, persuading themselves, no doubt, that this law on the state prisons would differ in operation from the earlier *lettres de cachet* in that it would be administered without prejudice. In 1814, however, when Bonaparte's star was setting, the senate cited his violation of the constitutional guarantees respecting individual liberty as a justification for demanding his abdication. This belated concern for constitutional guarantees reflects no great credit on the senators, who were themselves, by the authority of that constitution they invoked, the official guardians of its guarantees.

Laws, constitutional or otherwise, arouse the deepest resentment when they confound the innocent with the guilty. The efficiency attained by the ministry of general police under Fouché's ingenious management provided Napoleon with detailed information on the activities of all recognized political agitators, and as the police dealt with such malcontents individually the innocent public was left in tranquillity. The daily police bulletins[20] submitted to the emperor prove how exhaustive yet discreet the police surveillance had become by 1807, when Napoleon decided to attempt a classification of the population in each *département* as a preparation for that gigantic *statistique morale et personelle* which he had conceived. In 1810 Savary, who succeeded Fouché in that year, wrote each of the prefects an explanation of the project. The conclusion of his form letter is amusing in its optimism: "I believe, Sir, that these personal statistics ought to furnish a moral chart of the nation; a deterrent to the wicked; an encouragement to the meritorious; and that they should prove an abundant source of illumination for the government."[21] The results belied his hopes. The project involved too much

[20] A useful abstract of these daily reports has been edited by E. d'Hauterive, with a preface by L. Madelin, under the title, *La police secrète du Premier Empire*, 3 vols. (Paris, 1908-1922). Examples of Napoleon's violation of the guarantees respecting the liberty of the press and the individual can be found in every volume of the officially edited *Correspondance*. For more flagrant cases see L. Lecestre (ed.), *Lettres inédites de Napoléon I*ᵉʳ, 2 vols. (Paris, 1897), I, 58, 65, 72, 293, II, 90-91, and L. de Brotonne, *Lettres inédites de Napoléon I*ᵉʳ (Paris, 1898), 211, 222-223.

[21] L. Deries, "Le régime des fiches sous le premier empire," *Revue des études historiques*, XCII (1926), 160.

labor, depended upon the efforts of too many careless, indifferent, or untrustworthy subordinates, presumed in the cataloguers a mastery of statistical method which too few of them possessed, for it to provide that accurate *tableau moral* which Napoleon anticipated. Even as *dossiers* the thumb-nail biographies lacked precision, being monotonously worded and full of colorless, uncritical phrases. With this world of paper at his disposal Napoleon was no better able to distinguish his friends from his enemies, no surer in his diagnoses of public opinion in 1812 than he had been in 1800. Yet the labor of compilation was not entirely wasted, for the information gathered supplemented that embodied in the departmental annuals, which had been instituted under the Directory by François de Neufchâteau. It is a matter for regret that the preparation of economic statistics covering each *département*, a project which likewise owed its inception (1797) to that same tireless organizer, was interrupted under the empire.

The ceaseless scrutiny of public and private affairs under the consulate and empire wearied the prefects, but it seems to have disquieted the people little, a tribute, one may argue, to their faith in the honesty and impartiality of the government. France, having thrown herself into the arms of a strong man, was content to rest there trustingly. The all but unanimous verdict of the popular plebiscites bears out this impression, and it is noteworthy that few people seemed disposed to challenge their astonishingly one-sided totals. The official figures, 3,009,445 to 1,502 in 1799, 3,568,885 to 8,374 in 1802, and 3,572,329 to 2,579 in 1804, are monotonous in their agreement. The methods of voting and of tabulating the results were open to objection, and the figures very possibly manipulated. Yet there is little reason to doubt that Napoleon could have secured an overwhelming vote of confidence under the most scrupulous secret ballot. The methods that were utilized, the registration of 400,000 votes for the military and 50,000 for the naval forces in the plebiscite of 1804 as unanimously affirmative, and the pressure exerted upon the prefects to secure favorable returns, invalidate the figures as an accurate record of opinion. But it is important to recall that in revolutionary France, still dominated by Rousseau's concept of the general will, the plebiscite was regarded, not so much as a means of demonstrating the division of public opinion, but as a device for advertising its unity. Napoleon was not the first to make shrewd use of this popular obsession with the ideal of unanimity. The constitutions of 1793 and 1795 were both adopted by majorities which were, officially at least, more than twenty to one.

What the modern democrat finds particularly offensive in the consular polls is not the possible tampering with the totals, but the bland assumption on the part of the government that it knew the voter's opinion better than he did himself, and the inartistic crudity of the deceptions practiced upon the electorate. The subtler refinements of the democratic system were still wanting. For political naïveté it is difficult to match, for instance, a letter dispatched from the préfecture of Dyle at Brussels to a communal secretary in 1802: "The interest of the state and the honor of this *arrondissement* demand that we present to the government a satisfactory statement of the public sentiment. It seems to me, therefore, that we need not obsess ourselves unduly with the notion of formal regularity in securing this result." The secretary was advised to register a "yes" for all the individuals in the commune eligible to vote who did not specifically insist upon voting "no."[22] This thoughtful exercise of paternalism no doubt assured to many a perplexed citizen the gratification of finding himself later in complete harmony with the general will.

V. SOCIAL AND FAMILY LIFE

A grating undernote, a mood of restless irascibility, seems in retrospect to have afflicted the life of the Parisian salons during the First Empire and the impression is probably less harsh than the reality. The Revolution destroyed the serenity of the eighteenth century *milieu*, and the social and intellectual graces which embellish an urbane society cannot be transplanted or recultivated at will. Among the former aristocrats who resumed their residence in Paris after the reëstablishment of order very few managed to resist the magnet of the vulgarized court and by 1810 the majority had stooped to solicit

[22] L. Landy, "Comment on votait sous le consulat," *Revue des études napoléoniennes,* XXIII (1924), 76-78.

favors from the Corsican *parvenu*, but their presence soured rather than eased the graceless gatherings.

To have expected little dukes and marquesses whom the Revolution had impoverished to act the part of a Diogenes before such an Alexander was to ask too much of humanity (conceded the Baron de Frenilly). Part of the society in which we mixed—that is, the best society in Paris—had then allowed itself to be allured to the Tuileries. These deserters were none the worse received by us, provided they left off their embroidered court dress before entering our drawing-rooms, appeared to be proud to wear a dress coat again, and rivaled each other in slandering the master whom they had just been flattering. . . .[23]

Between this self-infatuated remnant of the old nobility and the coarse and insolent *élite* of the imperial staff or the dour and resolute functionaries who shared the emperor's administrative labors there could be no affinity. And none of these groups possessed the combination of authority and leisure to establish a new set of social standards. As a consequence, the most vital influence in the higher circles was exerted by the bourgeois *arrivistes*, who corrupted the world of fashion with a flood of innovations.

Families newly rich, yielding to the current mania for the antique and the exotic, crowded their apartments with the spoils of time. "The stairway was of Italian marble, the *foyer* French, the bed Egyptian, the armchairs Greek, the fireplace Prussian, the candelabra Etruscan, the vases from Japan, the tapestry Roman. . . ."[24] Vicissitudes of fortune had transformed many private *hôtels* into family apartment houses, to the further detriment of orderly standards. The first floor was frequently surrendered to shopkeepers, the second to the wealthiest occupants, the third to the well-to-do, the fourth to members of the professional classes, the fifth to artisans and the higher levels to the poorest lodgers. Real estate values fluctuated under the shock of forced sales and the elaborate public works introduced under the empire, and shops invaded precincts traditionally exclusive and immune. The experience was one which the nineteenth century was to make commonplace in most of the cities of Europe,

[23] Baron F. A. de Frenilly, *Recollections*, ed. by A. Chuquet, trans. by F. Lees (New York, 1909), 231.
[24] L. Lanzac de Laborie, *Paris sous Napoléon*, 8 vols. (Paris, 1905-1913), V, 163.

but to the Parisian traditionalist of 1810 it seemed further evidence of the madness of a mad age.

Within the family circle life changed less noticeably. The practice of sending children away from home at a tender age to be raised in the country had fallen into disfavor, in part, no doubt, as a result of Rousseau's preaching, and the relationship between parents and chil dren grew more informal. The Revolution, like all social disruptions, indoctrinated the young with individualist ideals, and hostile critics deplored the impudence, irreverence, and independence of the new generation, declaring that children had come to rule the household, and were growing more rash, moody, and undisciplined with each year. Friendlier observers detected in the generation that came of age under the empire an earlier maturity, a more realistic philosophy of life, and a keener sense of money values than their elders had possessed. There can be little doubt that the relaxation of legal and parental authority, the emphasis upon personal liberty, the electric atmosphere of the early Revolution, and the dissolute society of the Directory turned part of the French youth giddy and set it flaming. The civil code of 1804 reinvested the father with authority over and responsibility for the actions of minor children, and the battle of the generations, which had turned for a decade in favor of youth, reverted to its earlier lines and its traditional deadlock.

Among the working classes, urban and agricultural, the imperial régime remained popular because the price of bread was reasonable and wages in general held firm. They varied from one and a half francs a day to three or four francs for unskilled labor, and as high as ten francs for the most favored trades, but it is extremely difficult to translate the purchasing power and standard of living procurable on these terms into modern equivalents. A safer guide to the status of the laborer and artisan is provided by the record of poor relief; it was neglected with a consistency that would seem not only heartless but dangerous, unless it be assumed that extreme indigence was rare, and avoidable enough to be treated as a crime instead of a misfortune. When, between 1809 and 1812, the average price of wheat doubled, widespread suffering resulted and complaints rose from all quarters of the empire, but there was no threat of serious organized resistance. In 1814, after the upper classes had fallen away, Napoleon could still have called the masses to his support if he had been willing to arm the "jacquerie." After Waterloo, and even after his second abdication, crowds paraded in the Faubourg St. Antoine, cheering for him. To the humblest classes for which he had done least he was still the Son of the Revolution.[25]

25 E. V. Tarlé, *Bonaparte*, trans. by J. Cournos (New York, 1937), 392-393.

Chapter Eight

THE SPREAD OF NATIONALIST REVOLTS AGAINST THE FRENCH DOMINATION (1808-1812)

I. THE AWAKENING OF NATIONALITIES

To QUICKEN national feelings and hasten a day when Europe would be wholly resolved into autonomous nation-states was never Napoleon's intention; it was, in fact, the negation of his imperial aims. Even among his French subjects he preferred to cultivate the sentiment of honor and glory associated with his dynasty rather than the patriotic cult of *la patrie.* As an intermediate step in his evolving plan to disencumber Europe of the wreckage of feudalism and organize the continent in a cosmopolitan empire he did not hesitate to utilize local nationalist sentiments when he believed he could subordinate them to his purpose. But the tradition that he nursed a far-sighted plan to create an independent Italy, a resurrected Poland, a free homeland for the Croats and Slovenes, is part of the Bonapartist legend, not part of the Napoleonic system. His promises to the Poles remained persistently evasive and he refused to restore the word Poland to the political map of Europe even after he ceased to respect Alexander's prejudices on that point. The unification of Italy may have been foreshadowed in the creation of the Italian Kingdom, but the new state was promptly truncated by the annexation of one-third of the peninsula, including Rome, to France. Sections of Croatia, Carniola, and the Dalmatian coast gained a fictitious unity as the Illyrian Provinces, but the unity was strictly administrative, the name was borrowed from a Roman prefecture, and the language favored there was not Croat, was not even Italian or German, but French. Undoubtedly the political reforms which were introduced by the French in Italy and the Germanies, or adopted in imitation of the French methods, helped to shatter the dykes of particularism and clear the way for national institutions. As the most active protagonist of rational reforms Napoleon may be considered the stepfather of Italian and German unification. But to reason, *post hoc, ergo propter hoc,* that he anticipated and sought to hasten a process which might lead to the establishment of two first-class powers on the frontiers of France is to suppose that he worked for the day when France would be stripped of her primacy in Europe.

It was, therefore, contrary to his intentions that his conquests produced a deepening of national passions throughout Europe. Moralists have found a touch of dramatic irony in this dénouement, irony the more apposite because Napoleon himself occasionally took the word nationalism in vain when he needed a recruiting slogan to draw Italians, Poles, or Germans to his standard. To him the sentiment was a serviceable goad and he used it as he used other rivalries which he found latent among men—the vanity of his marshals, the ambition of his ministers, the national pride which stirred the foreign contingents of his international army. But in seeking the loyalty of alien populations he appealed to class, not to regional, prejudices. The largest social group in every state, the peasants, could best be appeased by the abolition of feudal burdens, and the legend that Croat serfs greeted the French invaders with the cry *Galli sumus, liberi sumus,* though it smells of the historian's lamp, is possibly true in substance.[1] For Poland, which had been known as the "Peasants' Hell" in the middle ages and still deserved the title, the introduction of the *code* for the Grand Duchy of Warsaw was a promise and an act of social justice for which Napoleon could claim full credit.[2] But it is significant that he placed at the head of this revived Polish state his ally Frederick Augustus of Saxony, although the gallant Poniatowski had deeper claims on his gratitude and was more popular with the Poles. When Napoleon extended aid he liked it to be and to remain indispensable to the recipient, a fact which may explain why, when Karageorge, successfully engaged in laying the foundations of Serbian independence, appealed to him in 1809 to assist not only the Serbs, but

[1] Dr. Deak, "Les français en Croatie, 1809-1813," *Revue des études napoléoniennes,* XX (1923), 151.

[2] H. J. Grinwasser, "Le code napoléonien dans le duché de Varsovie," *Revue des études napoléoniennes,* XII (1917), 129-170.

also the Bosnians, Hungarians and Bulgars to win freedom, he did not trouble to reply. He had already counseled the sultan three years earlier not to yield to Karageorge's militant demands, and his interest in the national ferment stirring in the Balkans remained frigid. He saw no way of turning it to his own advantage and he distrusted any political change in southeastern Europe because it might open the way for an extension of Russian influence.[3]

No fledgling nationalist hopes could roost confidently beside the imperial eagles. The best proof that Napoleon failed to inspire any sincere trust among the oppressed peoples of Europe who aspired to independence is the fact that none of them (with possibly one exception) attempted to aid him to recover his power in 1815. The exception, if Murat's ill-planned and abortive effort to rouse Italy may be counted an exception, demonstrated how rootless the Napoleonic creations outside of France had been, how lacking in native initiative or vitality. From Milan to Naples Italy fermented in the spring of 1815 as it had fermented on the appearance of Bonaparte twenty years earlier, but the will to live free or die, which had nerved Frenchmen to resist the leagued despots of 1793, was not to be found south of the Alps. The Neapolitans felt no gratitude for the benefits introduced under Joseph Bonaparte or Joachim Murat.[4] The North Italians, who should have been better fitted to comprehend the French reforms, had endured the *code* without enthusiasm and had never foresworn their attachment to the old customs.[5] The natives of the Illyrian Provinces, who had disfigured the period of French rule with several tentative insurrections, likewise betrayed little faith in Napoleon's hints that he might create an independent Yugo-Slav state.[6] In no corner of the shattered French Empire did embattled farmers of 1814 resist the restoration of the old frontiers and institutions with a trace of the ardor which Andreas Hofer and his Tyrolese comrades had shown for the house of Hapsburg in 1809. The outburst of

[3] G. Cassi, "Napoléon, l'Autriche et les nationalités," *Revue des études napoléoniennes,* XV (1919), 38-39.

[4] N. Giacchi, "Napoli durante il decennio francese (1806-1815)," *Rassegna storica del risorgimento,* IX (1930), 52-74.

[5] A. Pingaud, "Le premier royaume d'Italie: le développement du systéme napoléonien," *Revue des études napoléoniennes,* XX (1923), 205.

[6] G. Cassi, "Le popolazioni Giulio-Illiriche durante il dominio napoleonico (1806-1814)," *Rassegna storica del risorgimento,* VIII (1930), 1-70.

nationalism which had been released in France by the Revolution made Napoleon's career possible, but it was unthinkable that beyond the French frontiers the force of national sentiments, once thoroughly awakened, could be made to operate in his favor.

As Napoleon aged he acquired an increasing contempt for all forms of opposition which he could not convert to his uses, a failing which partly explains his inability to recognize the strength of the national resentments which he had excited. That a policy of reason and of progress, such as he conceived his imperial design to embody, could be threatened by a policy shaped by passion and by mystical loyalties he accepted as an irritating fact without attaching overmuch importance to it. All the enlightened despots had learned that even the most beneficial reforms had to surmount an initial opposition due to what today would be termed a cultural lag, and Napoleon himself had dealt with irrational and fanatical opponents in the Vendée and had overcome them by a combination of severity and conciliation. But he was unprepared to acknowledge that men of sound reason, men who had enjoyed a fair opportunity to compare his methods of administration with those illogical customs and inherited absurdities which he sought to supplant, would prefer to see Europe permanently divided and diversified when the continent might be united and well ordered under the rule of reason. Insensate minorities, like anarchists and conspirators, he was prepared to eliminate in the name of progress. Competitors for supreme power, like Alexander of Russia, he hoped to reduce to a subordinate rôle, if possible without too much cost or bitterness. The human emotions, greed, vanity, a sensitive honor, he had learned to play upon for his own purposes. Even with the Roman Church, most evasive and resilient foe of secular absolutism, he had come to terms, without compromising his program. But the new religion of patriotism eluded his calculations. Against its exponents he could invent no argument more subtle than a firing-squad. It was not a very satisfactory nor a final argument, even when it was applicable, as the execution of Palm and Hofer demonstrated, for the new faith, like many before it, was watered by the blood of the martyrs. And it was not an effective argument because the most dangerous of his foes, a Stein, a Stadion, a Castaños, remained outside his reach and beyond his corruption. These men fought with two advantages which Napoleon was losing: they had time on their side and they could raise a standard to which, if not the wise, at least the brave and the honest, would repair. Their cause was the cause of national sovereignty, and when once it joined battle with an imperial tradition two thousand years old the most powerful trend in modern political history prescribed the outcome.

II. THE SPANISH CONFLICT

Of all the western European peoples the Spaniards were the least disposed in 1808 to welcome the revolutionary program of reforms. To the great landowners, jealous of their social and feudal privileges, the French example was anathema. The regular clergy, numerous and richly endowed despite the general poverty of the country, could offer strong opposition to the secularization of their property. The Church and the Inquisition had trained the faithful to regard religious tolerance as little better than heresy and atheism. No large and literate middle class, raised on Rousseau and Montesquieu, clamored for political recognition, and centralizing tendencies in government were not popular in a country where each province clung tenaciously to its peculiar rights. The economic interests of Spain, particularly wool production and colonial commerce, were certain to suffer if the French gained control of the state, for the British would have an added reason for seizing the colonies, and the Spanish sheep-raisers, like those of Italy, would be obliged to market their famous merino fleece in France at a French price. Finally, an inherited conservatism and a fierce pride in their own singularity insulated the Spaniards against alien influences; even in the towns the general dislike of foreigners amounted to xenophobia.

Napoleon's decision to introduce a foreign army into Spain in 1808 was unwise; to seize Madrid and force the Bourbons to abdicate was foolhardy; to divide the French forces and dispatch them against half a dozen scattered objectives was suicidal. The finest divisions of the grand army would have found it extremely difficult to execute the ambitious plan of campaign outlined for the summer of 1808, and the 116,000 French troops assembled in Spain by the end of May were second-rate material, without adequate training or *esprit de corps.* Only one-third of them belonged to reputable units of the regular army, their artillery was inadequate, the equipment defective and insufficient, the generalship mediocre.[7] Their principal asset, the French reputation for invincibility, became a liability after their first defeats.

To argue that the Spanish army was worse equipped, lacked cavalry, and numbered in all probability no more than 86,000 effectives, does not condone Napoleon's blunders; for the disasters of 1808 he could thank his own errors, the fruit of ignorance, of cynical diplomacy, of faulty strategy. Moncey, ordered to seize Valencia with 7,000 men and no siege train, assaulted the city in vain and was fortunate to escape back to Madrid. Dupont, with some 20,000 Swiss and German auxiliaries and conscripts of 1807, marched on Cadiz, was cut off at Baylen by Castaños with 30,000 Spanish regulars, and capitulated on July 22nd. Verdier, checked by the heroic resistance of Palafox and his Aragonese volunteers at Saragossa, abandoned the siege, and Duhesme found himself blockaded in Barcelona. To complete the tale of French reverses Joseph Bonaparte was driven from his new throne in Madrid; and Junot, defeated at Vimeiro by an English and Portuguese army under the future Duke of Wellington, capitulated with 25,000 troops in August. Junot's division was promptly repatriated, but Dupont's ill-fated levies, in defiance of the terms of surrender, were imprisoned by the junta of Seville. In vain the gallant Castaños appealed to his countrymen, "Spaniards, you wish to be good soldiers: learn to respect misfortune." The captives were condemned to die by the score of fever and starvation in a state of misery so abject that British naval officers took pity and sent them what scanty supplies it was possible to spare of medicaments and food.[8]

No disaster so humiliating as Baylen had darkened French military annals since the first years of the Revolution. Napoleon knew by August that it was essential to repair his prestige by a decisive campaign in the Iberian peninsula, but his commitments elsewhere made an immediate move difficult. To withdraw the grand army

[7] C. W. C. Oman, *History of the Peninsular War,* 7 vols. (Oxford, 1902-1930), I, 90, 91.
[8] T. Geisendorf, *Les prisonniers de la guerre au temps du Premier Empire. L'expédition et la captivité d'Andalousie, 1808-1810* (Geneva, 1932), 142-143, 380.

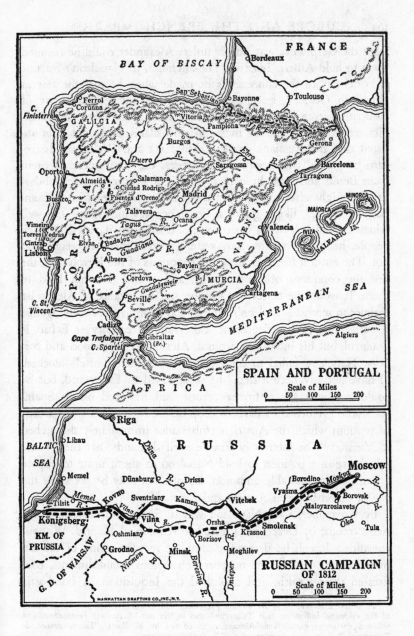

SPAIN AND PORTUGAL

Scale of Miles
0   50   100   150   200

RUSSIAN CAMPAIGN OF 1812

Scale of Miles
0   50   100   150   200

MANHATTAN DRAFTING CO., INC., N.Y.

from the Germanies was unsafe unless Alexander could be counted upon to hold Austria inactive. The alteration in Napoleon's fortune is evident from the concessions he made when he met the tsar at Erfurt in October; he agreed to withdraw the French army of occupation from Prussia and to reduce the unpaid Prussian indemnity, reassured Alexander in regard to Poland, and no longer insisted that the Russians evacuate Moldavia and Wallachia. In return he gained two negative advantages: the banishment of Stein from Berlin and a public demonstration of Franco-Russian solidarity. But night after night, in casual social encounters with Alexander, Talleyrand, like a guileless Penelope, was unraveling the web which he had helped his master weave during the day. The French people, he hinted to the tsar, were civilized, their sovereign was not. The natural frontiers were the conquests of the Revolution, the rest the conquests of the emperor, and France did not hold to them. It would be better for Europe and for France if Alexander forbore to second Napoleon's projects too strongly, especially against Austria. The precise degree of Talleyrand's treachery at Erfurt is doubtful, but his intentions are not. Alexander understood and forbore. Napoleon failed to understand, but he felt himself blocked. "I have not advanced a step," he complained to Talleyrand, but he could not wait for a firmer accord and hastened on to Spain. Talleyrand returned to Paris to drop before Metternich those words of wisdom which the Austrian ambassador immediately dispatched to Vienna: "The interest of France itself demands that the powers which are in a position to hold Napoleon in check unite to oppose a dam to his insatiable ambition. Europe can only be saved by the closest union between Austria and Russia."[9]

By November, 1808, Napoleon was in Spain with 200,000 of his finest troops; by December 4th he had reoccupied Madrid. Without consulting Joseph he decreed a complete reorganization of the administration, reduced the number of religious establishments, confiscated their wealth, and abolished the Inquisition. A bombastic

---

[9] A. Sorel, *L'Europe et la Révolution française,* VII (Paris, 1911), 320. A summary of the evidence, indicating that Talleyrand was in the pay of Austria from 1809, and solicited further rewards from Alexander, is offered by E. Dard, "La vengeance de Talleyrand," *Revue des deux mondes,* XX (1934), 215-229.

proclamation to the Spanish people indicated how little he yet comprehended the reason and the nature of the resistance:

Spaniards, you have been misled by traitors. . . . I have abolished everything that was opposed to your prosperity and grandeur. A liberal constitution offers you a moderate constitutional monarchy in place of absolutism. If all my endeavors are vain, if you do not respond to my confidence, I shall have no alternative but to treat you as conquered provinces. In that case I shall set the crown of Spain on my head and I shall know how to make evildoers respect it, for God has given me the force and the will to surmount all obstacles.[10]

But the thunderbolt missed its effect. A number of minor successes but no echoing victory had befallen his arms, and on December 22nd he started across the Guadarrama Mountains in an attempt to trap a British army of 27,000 men under Sir John Moore, which had advanced into Old Castile from Portugal. Warned in time, Moore beat a successful retreat, and Napoleon, who had announced prematurely the capture of a British army, turned the pursuit over to Soult on January 3rd. When the English finally escaped to sea at Corunna on January 16th, where Moore was killed during the embarkation, the emperor was on his way to Paris. The misery of a winter campaign and the lack of an adequate intelligence system had hampered him more severely than the Spanish resistance. But he knew that his stroke had lacked its intended effect, and Lannes' capture of Saragossa in February, after weeks of the bitterest house-to-house fighting, was a costly Pyrrhic victory which did little to sweeten the knowledge.

The history of the Peninsular War, so ambitiously recounted by Napier and Oman, is a story which French historians, for understandable reasons, have found less attractive.[11] It was a war which violated all the traditions of Napoleonic success; it had opened with French reverses, it persisted after French victories, it was fought by a decentralized and disorganized nation using guerilla tactics,

---

[10] Geoffroy de Grandmaison, *L'Espagne et Napoléon,* 3 vols. (Paris, 1908-1931), I, 402.
[11] Sir W. F. P. Napier, *History of the war in the Peninsula and in the south of France from the year 1807 to the year 1814,* new ed., 6 vols. (London, 1905). C. W. C. Oman, *History of the Peninsular War,* 7 vols. (Oxford, 1902-1930). A comprehensive study in 16 volumes, *La guerre d'Espagne (1807-1813),* was planned under the editorship of A. Grasset, with the assistance of the historical section of the French General Staff. Three volumes have appeared.

it involved long siege operations and the construction of intricate intrenchments, and it saw the emergence of Great Britain as a military power of the first class. To assume that Napoleon largely ignored Spain after 1809 because he affected to do so is to be tricked, as a number of contemporary Europeans were, by the efficacy of the French censorship. In 1810 he concentrated 370,000 men in the peninsula, the largest force he had so far dispatched against a single nation. Organized Spanish resistance was all but crushed by this weight of numbers, but when Masséna attempted to drive Wellington from Portugal he encountered a new type of strategy. He marched to Lisbon through a country stripped of provisions, and he found the city defended by a triple line of fortifications which proved impregnable. From November to March, 1810-1811, the French attempted to maintain a siege, but in the end it was they who were routed by starvation; the Anglo-Portuguese forces had their backs to the friendly sea. From these lines of Torres Vedras Wellington advanced to the frontier of Spain, where the threat of his 50,000 men, added to the persistent revolts of the Spaniards, helped to wear down Marmont's and Soult's divisions. In 1813, when the war with Russia had compelled Napoleon to reduce the forces in Spain, the Anglo-Portuguese and Anglo-Spanish detachments resumed the offensive, and by 1814 Wellington was able to march on Bordeaux and Toulouse.

III. THE AUSTRIAN WAR OF 1809

For the Austrian ministers of state 1808 was a year of anxiety that hardened slowly into desperation. If Napoleon could dethrone a monarch as pliant as Charles IV, what hope remained for Francis I, who had refused to recognize Murat as King of Naples or Joseph as King of Spain, and had permitted his subjects the luxury of planning a war of revenge. Philip Stadion, minister of foreign affairs, frankly allied himself with the war party. The Archduke Charles was laboring patiently to refashion the army and make good the defects revealed during the campaign of 1805. Archduke John, the most patriotically German member of the ruling house, communicated with Andreas Hofer and kept alive the loyalty of the Tyrolese, who had been placed under Bavarian sovereignty by the Treaty of Pressburg. The empress, Maria Ludovica, third wife of Francis I, presented standards to the new regiments of Viennese *Landwehr*, or citizen militia, the creation of which in 1808 was itself a gesture of defiance towards France. All Austrian men between eighteen and forty-five who could bear arms were bidden to the defense of the fatherland in a decree reminiscent of the *levée-en-masse* of 1793. Patriotic proclamations, poems, and plays fired the populace to enthusiastic demonstrations, the uprising of the Spanish people was applauded as an omen and an example, and poets invoked the shade of Arminius to defend German liberty against "the new Romans." The French *chargé d'affaires* at Vienna noted with amazement the rapidity with which zeal for a national war spread to all classes. "In 1805," he wrote to Paris, "the war spirit was alive in the government but not in the army or the people. In 1809 the war is popular with the administration, the army, and the populace."[12] The parallel with the foolhardy Prussian challenge of 1806 was obvious to many, for Austria too had a hesitant and pacifistic monarch, a young and enthusiastic consort whose name was also Louise, a war party intoxicated with notions of honor and revenge, and an army that burned to redeem its reputation.

But the Austrian leaders in 1809 believed that they possessed advantages which the Prussians had lacked before Jena. Unless the Anglo-Spanish resistance collapsed very suddenly, half of Napoleon's forces would be detained in the peninsula. The French people had grown weary of war and further conscription might bring the discontent to a head. Metternich, Austrian ambassador to Paris, had assured Stadion in September, 1808, that elements in France opposed to Napoleon were gaining ground.

Two parties exist in France, as much opposed one to the other as the interests of Europe are to the individual ideas of the emperor.

At the head of one of these parties is the emperor with all the military men. . . . The other party is composed of the great mass of the nation, an inert and unpliable mass, like the residuum of an extinct volcano. At the head of this mass are the most eminent persons of the

[12] W. C. Langsam, *The Napoleonic Wars and German Nationalism in Austria*, Columbia Studies in History, Economics, and Public Law (New York, 1930), 31.

state, and principally M. de Talleyrand, the minister of police (Fouché), and all those who have fortunes to preserve, who can feel no stability in institutions founded on ruins, which the restless genius of the emperor only surrounds with new ruins.[13]

With discord at home, and disasters like the capitulations of Baylen and Cintra dogging his armies abroad, Napoleon seemed about to waver in the saddle, and Stadion believed that Austria might never find a more favorable moment to save herself. The Archduke Charles recognized the gravity of the risk but accepted it, and the Empress Maria Ludovica feared nothing except the thought of peace.[14] On February 8, 1809, an imperial council presided over by the emperor in person decided for war.

It still remained in the power of the Russian tsar to restrain Austria by a word, but that word was never uttered. In response to Napoleon's interrogation Alexander replied with feigned regret that his conflicts with Sweden and Turkey left him no reserves for a demonstration against Austria. To satisfy appearances he recalled his representative at Vienna, but he assured Francis through other channels that he would do everything humanly possible to keep their respective armies from a hostile collision.[15] The Austrians asked nothing more; they had flung down the gage to Napoleon on April 12th by invading Bavaria; on the 14th an Anglo-Austrian convention brought them the promise of a subsidy and a British military diversion against Holland; the Prussian court was waiting, jealous of the emotion which the Archduke Charles had excited in German hearts through his proclmations, ready to join in a war of liberation when the call grew loud enough, as it was all but certain to do at the news of an Austrian victory. In Paris the consolidated bonds were sagging on the exchange. Talleyrand, whose plotting had cost him his post of grand chamberlain in January, was beguiling his retirement with women and whist; and Fouché, whose disgrace had been postponed a year, was rehearsing his rôle for that moment of silence which soon or late would follow Napoleon's fall.

[13] *Memoirs of Prince Metternich, 1773-1815*, ed. by Prince Richard Metternich, trans. by A. Napier, 2 vols. (New York, 1880), II, 283-284.
[14] Langsam, *op. cit.*, 34.
[15] A. Sorel, *L'Europe et la Révolution française*, VII (Paris, 1911), 350-351.

It is easy to criticize the Austrian plans in the campaign of 1809. Offensives were attempted on too many fronts, in Galicia, in northern Italy, and in Bavaria. It is still easier to deplore the lethargic marches which carried the Archduke Charles forward less than fifty miles in the week between April 11th and 17th. When Napoleon arrived at Donauwörth on the latter date he decided to concentrate his scattered divisions at Abensberg, a plan conceived in ignorance of the enemy's dispositions, which exposed Davout to a flank attack by the major Austrian forces as he hastened southwest up the Danube from Regensburg. But Austrian irresolution and French daring permitted him to escape, and by the 19th Napoleon was ready to take the offensive. In four days of rapid fighting the Austrian center was broken before Abensberg, the left rolled south to Landshut on the Isar, and the right, after a dogged struggle at Eckmühl, escaped across the Danube at Regensburg to the protection of the Böhmer Wald. The French, following up their victories with their customary speed, swept down the Danube Valley at twenty miles a day and entered Vienna on May 13th.

Reverses so sudden and so staggering might well have broken the Austrian fighting spirit. But Napoleon had scarcely established himself in the palace of Schönbrunn when the archduke took up a position opposite Vienna with his divisions reunited and reorganized. To attack him the French had to cross to the left bank. Gaining a foothold at Aspern and Essling, they held out against heavy attacks, but the difficulty of bringing up reinforcements and the collapse of their military bridges forced them to withdraw after losing 20,000 men in two days of desperate engagements. The Austrians had lost even more heavily, but they had the consolation of a victory achieved against Napoleon in person. For seven weeks the campaign remained at a standstill while both sides sought reinforcements. Then on July 5-6th the French crossed the Danube a second time, attacked the Austrians with superior numbers at Wagram, and gained a costly but not a wholly decisive victory. The archduke drew off his forces in good order, and although he asked for an armistice a week later, the Austrian army continued to be a factor throughout the ensuing negotiations.

Francis I was ready to abandon the struggle. He accepted Stadion's resignation, permitted Charles likewise to retire, and agreed to cede territory to Bavaria, to the Duchy of Warsaw, and to the Illyrian Provinces, in all a loss of 3,500,000 subjects. In addition Austria assumed an indemnity of 85,000,000 francs and the Austrian army was reduced to 150,000 men. This Peace of Schönbrunn was concluded October 14th; five months later, on March 11, 1810, the Archduchess Marie Louise, daughter of Francis I, was betrothed to Napoleon at Vienna, the Archduke Charles acting as proxy for the absent Corsican. In this dynastic alliance with a house which he had four times humiliated, some biographers of Napoleon have professed to find a deep design. It was a rebuke to Tsar Alexander for his double-dealing, a recognition of the fighting qualities of the refashioned Austrian battalions, a public announcement of a new international policy which was to align Europe around the Paris-Vienna axis. More than ever, a permanent ally had become necessary to Napoleon's designs, but no understanding which he had hitherto formed with a European power had held firm when he relied upon it. What hopes could he repose, therefore, in a marriage alliance dictated to a defeated foe, and disfigured in the same week that it was proposed by the execution of the Tyrolese patriot, Andreas Hofer, whose heroic defense of Innsbruck against the French and Bavarians had finally been crushed. Yet when the Emperor Francis interceded with Napoleon in the name of their newly proclaimed friendship to reprieve the patriotic innkeeper, the petition was refused. Napoleon remained insensible to the fitness of a generous gesture at such a moment, and blind to the hatred nursed against him in Austria, which Hofer's death intensified. He still considered opposition, like vice, an individual phenomenon, to be punished as such, and was so far from comprehending the force of a collective hatred that after three months' occupation of Vienna the previous summer he had invited the Viennese to celebrate his birthday on August 15th. The obedient burghers placed candles in their windows, but not even the presence of 100,000 French soldiers could suppress their malice. Among many subtly impertinent placards displayed for the occasion perhaps the most ingenious was an acrostic on the word compulsion, *Zur Weihe An Napoleons Geburt-stag*.[16]

IV. THE FERMENT IN THE GERMANIES

The appeal sent forth from Vienna in 1809 for a united effort against the French had failed to rouse the Germanies. But it had not fallen entirely upon deaf ears. In the Kingdom of Westphalia, where Jerome Bonaparte's extravagance had disgusted his subjects, Baron von Dornberg headed a Hessian revolt in April which was suppressed with difficulty. The same month a Prussian officer, Frederick von Schill, hoping to compromise his government and rouse it to action, invaded Jerome's domains and defeated the French in several minor engagements before he was overtaken and slain at Stralsund.[17] Duke Frederick William of Brunswick-Oels led a force from Bohemia to Dresden, repulsed the troops dispatched against him, and, more fortunate than Schill, succeeded in reaching the Weser, where his contingent escaped on English ships. Had the British government landed a well-equipped army in North Germany in the summer of 1809 it might have stimulated a formidable uprising, but political calculations induced the cabinet to favor an invasion of the Low Countries instead. Forty thousand men were disembarked on the island of Walcheren in July, and Flushing captured in August, but fever and mismanagement crippled the operations and the troops were finally withdrawn in December without achieving any results commensurate with their losses or the cost of the enterprise. Once again the divided aims of the allied governments had saved the French from serious danger.

With the Treaty of Schönbrunn, followed so shortly by the marriage alliance with Napoleon, Francis I forfeited his chance to reassert the ancient formula *Kaiser und Reich*. The Austrian effort had come both too early and too late: too early because the ferment in the Germanies had not quite reached the boiling point, too late because the military campaign, once opened, had been pressed so tardily that the initiative passed to the French after the first week.

[16] W. C. Langsam, *The Napoleonic Wars and German Nationalism in Austria*, Columbia Studies in History, Economics and Public Law (New York, 1930), 134.
[17] J. H. Rose, *Life of Napoleon I*, 6th ed., II (London, 1913), 193.

Compelled once again to recognize their fatal lack of a national will, the German people turned from Francis to other leaders who were striving more unequivocally to indoctrinate them with a *Nationalgeist*, and Prussia succeeded Austria as the center of reform and the focus of national aspiration.

Denied the reality of political, religious, economic, or even territorial uniformity, the Germans in their will to unity learned to emphasize those few elements of nationhood they did possess in common: a common speech, a common history, a common soul. The foremost apostle of the ideal of cultural unity was Johann Gottfried Herder. Turning against the popular cosmopolitanism of the eighteenth century, Herder rebuked his compatriots for their uncritical admiration and imitation of foreign models. "We are working in Germany as in the confusion of Babel," he protested, and pleaded for a deeper veneration of German literature, of the German past, of the unique flower that was German culture.[18] A son of his century in his sanguine faith in a natural order, he wove· this concept into his philosophy by insisting that each nation is a separate species in the garden of humanity, that "a nationality is a plant of nature."[19] Rousseau's axiom that the individual could best develop his potentialities through an unfettered assertion of his personal values Herder extended to the national group. For him the fetters to be broken were the false and alien standards, particularly the Gallomania, which had too long constricted the German mind and heart. Like many of the earlier romanticists he was inclined to transfer his land of heart's desire from classical Greece to the middle ages; he venerated German *Volkslieder* above the neoclassical *Kunstlieder* of his time, an enthusiasm which he communicated to Goethe, and he was planning further collections of folk songs when he died in 1803.

The patriotic note which Herder sought to stress in German culture as a whole was sounded more specifically in philosophy and education by Johann Gottlieb Fichte. Fichte's demand that philosophy justify itself not only as a "system of knowledge," but as a

[18] R. R. Ergang, *Herder and the foundations of German nationalism*, Columbia University Studies in History, Economics and Public Law (New York, 1931), 115.
[19] *Ibid.*, 95.

mode of action, signalized a transition in the German mood from the ideal and abstract to the pragmatic and real. In the hour of Prussia's deepest humiliation after Jena, Fichte dared to impute the late disasters to a failure of morale, and he urged a new system of education which would transmute subjects into citizens. His moral earnestness lent force to his argument that the true aim of philosophy is not to raise doubts, but to resolve them, to instill that sense of absolute conviction without which men remain hesitant and cowardly. Had the French officers swaggering about Berlin in the winter of 1807-1808 comprehended the inner sense of his *Reden an die deutsche Nation* he might have swelled the list of German martyrs. His advocacy of educational reform marked him out for a leading position in the new university established at Berlin in 1810, that *alma mater* whose first sons were to complete their training in civic duty upon the battlefields of the War of Liberation. On February 19, 1813, Fichte terminated his lecture with the memorable words, "This course will be suspended until the close of the campaign, when we will resume it in a free fatherland or reconquer our liberty by death."

Credit for the more practical side of the reform program, for the administrative and military reorganization which reinvigorated Prussia in the years 1807-1814, is more difficult to assign. The Prussian school of historians long preferred to view it as a self-instituted and self-executed regeneration which demonstrated again the innate superiority of the Prussian character and Prussian institutions, but most of the outstanding leaders who forced it through—Stein, Hardenberg, Scharnhorst, Gneisenau, Blücher—entered the Prussian service from other states, and the program itself was conditioned by the French example. Yet German patriots have history on their side when they claim that the ideas of administrative reform which agitated the later eighteenth century were an international bequest, and that the Prussian revolution in its aims and methods fulfilled the program of the *philosophes* more obediently than the French upheaval had done. Hardenberg, in the suggestions which he submitted to Frederick William III in September, 1807, comprehended the situation with a clarity which later historians might envy:

The French Revolution [he wrote], of which the current wars are an extension, has brought the French people a wholly new vigor, despite all their turmoil and bloodshed. All their sleeping energies have awakened; their miseries and languors, their obsolete prejudices and infirmities, have been extinguished, inclusively, let us admit it freely, with much that was good. Those who stood in the path of the torrent, those who were overborne, have been swept away. . . .

It is an illusion to think that we can resist the Revolution effectively by clinging more closely to the old order, by proscribing the new principles without pity. This has been precisely the course which has favored the Revolution and facilitated its development. The force of these principles is such, their attraction and diffusion is so universal, that the State which refuses to acknowledge them will be condemned to submit or to perish. . . .

Thus our objective, our guiding principle, must be a revolution in the better sense, a revolution leading directly to the great goal, the elevation of humanity through the wisdom of those in authority and not through a violent impulse from within or without. Democratic rules of conduct in a monarchical administration, such is the formula, it appears to me, which will conform most perfectly to the spirit of the age.[20]

A month after Hardenberg wrote this clairvoyant appeal the first fruits of the new policy appeared, the edict of emancipation of October 14, 1807. Caste barriers which had excluded nobles from bourgeois professions and peasants from the vocations reserved for their social superiors were swept away by royal decree, together with serfdom and the personal obligations surviving from feudal days. Prussian farmers gained a clear title to the greater part of the land they worked despite strong protests from the landlords. Fortunately, Baron vom Stein, who bore the chief responsibility for carrying out this decree, was a man of unflinching patriotism and determination. His primary objective was administrative efficiency; he labored like a true son of the Enlightenment to break the paralyzing hold of a privileged officialdom, to abolish outmoded class distinctions, to build up a unified and harmonious bureaucratic machine under royal authority. The strength and inflexibility of his character, the blend of traditional and progressive ideals in his

[20] *Denkwürdigkeiten des Staatskanzlers Hardenberg,* ed. by L. von Ranke, 5 vols. (Leipzig, 1877), IV, appendix, 7-9.

philosophy, have made him an historic symbol of the spirit of Prussia in a former hour of humiliation and redemption. He remains, in the phrase of a recent eulogist, *ein Denkmal: ein Ende und ein Beginn*.[21] Hardenberg, who carried on the work of reform after Napoleon forced Stein from the ministry in 1808, has never captured the German imagination to the same extent. He had more vision and more tact, but he did not personify Prussia so well as he personified the French Revolution in Prussia, and his convocation of an assembly of notables in 1812, although it proved a harmless experiment in *Scheinparlamentarismus*, struck a slightly discordant note in that authoritarian symphony.[22]

The collapse of Prussia in 1806 had exposed the abuses of the existing system so relentlessly that the conservative forces could offer little effective resistance to bureaucratic reforms. In the army the opposition of the old guard was somewhat better organized, but Frederick William III had less reverence than his subjects for the Frederician system, and himself took the lead in recommending reforms. The men who carried through the task of military reorganization, Scharnhorst, Gneisenau, Boyen, had the penetration to recognize that at Jena an army of serfs and mercenaries commanded by nobles had gone down ignominiously before an army of freemen led by officers chosen on the sole basis of audacity and talent. To promote the linesman's self-respect, the more barbarous and shameful punishments current in the Prussian regiments were abolished, and military service extolled as a patriotic duty incumbent upon able-bodied men of all classes. Napoleon's objection to the creation of a *Landwehr* and his mandate limiting the Prussian army to 42,000 men did not prevent a systematic enrolment and transference of trained soldiers to the reserve, and this *Krümpersystem* enabled Prussia to put 270,000 men in the field by 1814.[23] Furthermore, the forced retirement of a number of incompetent officers and promotion of others on a basis of merit definitely introduced the principle of equality of rights. With the introduction

[21] A. Berney, "Reichstradition und Nationalstaatsgedanke, 1789-1815," *Historische Zeitschrift*, CXL (1929), 86.

[22] J. M. E. G. Cavaignac, *La formation de la Prusse contemporaine*, 2nd ed., 2 vols. (Paris, 1897-1898), II, 110.

[23] G. S. Ford, "Boyen's Military Law," *American Historical Review*, XX (1915), 534.

of universal compulsory military training in 1814 the Prussian army regained full strength and efficiency, and in the campaigns of 1813-1814 it recaptured its prestige. Brains had superseded brutality, and patriotic ardor supplied the quickening impulse formerly provided by the corporal's cane.[24]

To liberate and utilize neglected assets, moral and material, to release the enthusiasm of the individual and direct it effectively towards a collective aim, was the central purpose of the reform movement. The principle evil to be eradicated, as Fichte pointed out, was the spirit of indolence and obscurantism which led men to cling to outworn formulas and to resist beneficent progress. Only the strength that flowed from magnanimous impulses could overcome such apathy and egotism. Wherever the gospel of the Revolution had penetrated it brought its converts a sense of joyful strength, *Kraft durch Freude*. But the Prussians added a characteristic reservation to the general formula—*und durch Ordnung*.

V. THE DEFECTION OF THE BELGIANS, THE DUTCH, AND THE SWEDES

In the first year of the consulate the peoples of the Belgian Provinces were penetrated by a sentiment of deep and genuine admiration for Napoleon. They felt confident that after the restoration of peace he would permit them to organize a United States of Belgium, an independent state allied with France and under French protection. But ten years of protracted subordination, trade restriction, and military conscription alienated their loyalty despite the benefits conferred by the rule of honest and energetic French prefects. Firmly attached to the Catholic faith, the Belgians resented the coercion of the clergy in the interest of secular policies, and Napoleon's breach with the Pope in 1809, followed by the virtual imprisonment of Pius VII at Savona, further strained their allegiance. Weary of the emperor's endless wars, from which they drew no patriotic gratification, of the blockade which had paralyzed their ports, of the exactions in men and money for aims to which they were indifferent, the Belgian people were ripe by 1812 for invasion

---

[24] M. Lehrmann, *Scharnhorst und die preussische Heeresreform* (Berlin, 1935). Reprinted from his *Scharnhorst*, Vol. II (Leipzig, 1887), 67-126.

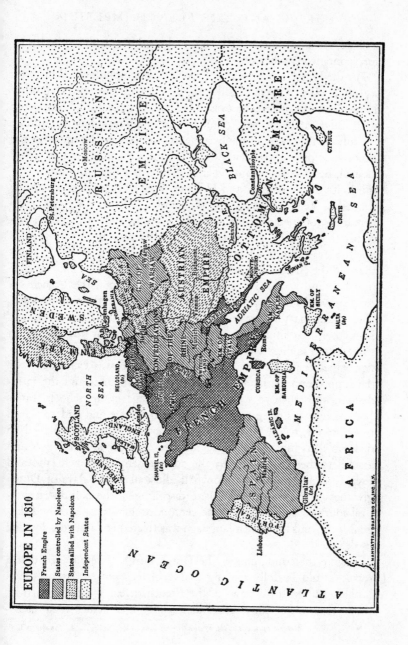

EUROPE IN 1810

French Empire
States controlled by Napoleon
States allied with Napoleon
Independent States

ATLANTIC OCEAN

AFRICA

MEDITERRANEAN SEA

RUSSIAN EMPIRE

OTTOMAN EMPIRE

AUSTRIAN EMPIRE

FRENCH EMPIRE

SPAIN

PORTUGAL

SWEDEN

DENMARK

NORTH SEA

SCOTLAND

ENGLAND

IRELAND

WALES

FINLAND

BLACK SEA

ADRIATIC SEA

BALTIC SEA

CONFEDERATION OF THE RHINE

GRAND DUCHY OF WARSAW

Moscow
St.Petersburg
Constantinople
Copenhagen
Berlin
Warsaw
Budapest
Vienna
London
Madrid
Lisbon
Rome
Naples

CORSICA
KM. OF SARDINIA
BALEARIC IS.
EM. OF SICILY
MALTA (Br.)
CRETE
CYPRUS
IONIAN IS.
MONTE NEGRO
HELGOLAND (Br.)
CHANNEL IS. (Br.)
Gibraltar (Br.)

KM. OF ITALY

MANHATTAN DRAFTING CO.,INC. N.Y.

and deliverance, though they lacked the spirit and the opportunity for spontaneous rebellion.

For the Dutch the burden of French domination doubled in severity after 1810. Angered at the supple recalcitrance of his brother Louis, and the persistent evasion of his decrees forbidding trade with England, Napoleon goaded Louis into resigning his throne on July 1, 1810, and formally annexed the Dutch Provinces to the French Empire a week later. The urbane Lebrun, erstwhile Third Consul, became lieutenant-general, Amsterdam was proclaimed the third city of the empire, and Holland received representation in the council of state, the senate and the legislative body. As partial compensation for their moribund maritime trade, restricted more stringently than ever by the vigilance of new French customs inspectors, the business classes of Holland were promised a more generous share in the French markets, but a rigid application of the conscription law and a tax rate double that imposed upon the French *départements* chilled any sentiment of gratitude for these concessions. The years 1811-1813 proved the darkest the Dutch had yet known. Java, their last important colony, was captured by the British in 1811; 15,000 soldiers were drawn from the Netherlands for the Russian expedition in 1812; and their local pride was exacerbated by the suppression of the ancient provincial boundaries and the introduction of French as a compulsory language in the schools. Louis Bonaparte had striven to learn the Dutch tongue and had displayed pride in the native literature, but Napoleon scarcely troubled to dissemble his intention to denationalize the new *départements* and assimilate them to France by the enforcement of French laws and French standards of education. All allusions to the days of Dutch greatness and independence were discouraged, the half-dozen political journals authorized by the censors could appear only in bilingual form, and the Dutch language was treated as "a dialect doomed to death."[25]

Despite their indignation, the Dutch burghers recognized that a revolt would be folly so long as Napoleon's power remained unbroken. But with the news of the French defeat at Leipzig in 1813 they prepared to throw aside their caution. Whether their libera-

[25] P. J. Blok, *History of the People of the Netherlands*, V (New York, 1912), 378.

tion was a result of their own initiative or was due to the advance of the Prussian and Russian forces long remained a disputed historical question. A Dutch historian has offered the acute suggestion that the real emancipators were not the Dutch, the Prussians, or the Russians, but the French, who resolved a dubious situation by running away. The Dutch had the presence of mind promptly to declare themselves free under their legitimate king, and by this shrewd move regained both their dignity and their independence.[26] William, Prince of Orange, who had fought against Napoleon at Jena and at Wagram, returned to Holland in November, 1813, to rally the nationalists, and while the swift final scenes of the Napoleonic drama were played out from Mainz to Fontainebleau, a Dutch commission was at work composing a constitution for the Kingdom of the Netherlands, to which the victorious allies shortly added the Belgian Provinces.[27] It is an ironic commentary on Napoleon's statecraft that under his rule the institutions of the Netherlands were modernized and centralized for the ultimate benefit of a king hostile to France, and the Dutch citizens driven to embrace as friends and liberators the nation which for fifteen years had been plundering their colonial empire.[28]

In the Scandinavian countries the repercussions of the revolutionary era resulted in extensive changes, but these followed no orthodox pattern. The peripheral location of Denmark-Norway, Sweden and Finland, though it protected them from the march of the Napoleonic armies, exposed them none the less to the implacable pressure of British sea power from the west and the bear-like caresses of Russia on the east. Neutrality was the easiest course they could adopt but the most difficult to maintain. Denmark suffered two destructive attacks by the British fleet, the first (1801) as a penalty for joining the Tsar Paul's League of Armed Neutrality, and the second (1807) because the British cabinet feared the Danish navy might be used to further the Franco-Russian designs formed at Tilsit. For Sweden the accord fostered between Alexander and

[26] G. J. Renier, *Great Britain and the establishment of the Kingdom of the Netherlands* (London, 1930), 118-119.

[27] H. T. Colenbrander, *Vestiging van het koninkrijk* (Amsterdam, 1927), 48-92. The articles covering the union of Belgium and Holland are printed on pp. 181-182.

[28] A. Sorel, *L'Europe et la Révolution française*, VII (Paris, 1911), 473.

Napoleon at this famous interview in 1807 promised even worse results. The Swedish government had long leaned on France for aid and subsidies in maintaining itself against Russia, and suspected that it was about to be betrayed. The proof came promptly: a Russian army invaded and occupied the Duchy of Finland, almost the last remnant of Sweden's trans-Baltic empire, in 1808, and the Swedes, furious in their impotence, dethroned their monarch, the unlucky Gustavus IV Adolphus, in favor of his uncle, Charles XIII. As Charles was a feeble and childless old man, the Swedish estates then solicited the advice of the Emperor of the French in selecting a successor to the throne and, under the misapprehension that Napoleon favored the choice, they offered Marshal Bernadotte the position of heir-presumptive.

Though Bernadotte had risen to the rank of a marshal of the empire and Prince of Ponte Corvo by grace of Napoleon, the independent Gascon felt little gratitude or loyalty towards his imperial master. Before leaving for Sweden he firmly refused to bind himself never to bear arms against France, and Napoleon reluctantly yielded. "Go, then," the emperor dismissed him, "and let our destinies be accomplished."[29] At Stockholm, where he took up his new responsibilities in 1810, Bernadotte achieved immediate popularity and surprising influence. "I gambled," old Charles XIII confessed after their first interview, "and I think that I have won." Tackling the raveled skein of Swedish foreign relations, the crown prince decided upon a dramatic reversal of policy involving a dissolution of the traditional tie with France and a *rapprochement* with Russia, for he divined a Franco-Russian conflict impending. When Napoleon insisted upon a breach with England, Sweden "declared a war with her fingers crossed and fought it with her arms folded,"[30] while Bernadotte's agents at London and St. Petersburg bargained for permission to annex Norway as compensation for renouncing Finland. The French occupation of Swedish Pomerania in January, 1812, must be counted among Napoleon's major blunders, for it induced the indignant Swedish patriots to embrace the pro-Russian

[29] Sir D. P. Barton, *Bernadotte and Napoleon* (London, 1921), 307.
[30] F. D. Scott, *Bernadotte and the Fall of Napoleon,* Harvard Historical Monographs, No. VII (Cambridge, Mass., 1935), 12.

policy of their prince, which hitherto they had viewed with misgiving. Bernadotte's reward for his farsightedness in allying himself with Russia *before* Napoleon's march on Moscow brought him the crown of Norway[31] as well as that of Sweden, and preserved his position in the general collapse which overtook the other revolutionary dynasties. With this he had to rest content, for his ambitious dream of replacing Napoleon on the French throne had been compromised when he bore arms against his native land and it never had more than a shadowy chance of realization.[32]

[31] The crowns of Norway and Denmark had been united since 1397. When Frederick VI of Denmark ceded Norway to Sweden by the Treaty of Kiel (1814), Norwegian patriots attempted to proclaim the independence of their country, but subsequently accepted a union with Sweden. The terms of the accord, signed August 14, 1814, may be found in Martens, *Nouveau recueil des traités,* II, 62-65. For a penetrating analysis of Norwegian national feeling, still incompletely crystallized at this time, see O. J. Falnes, *National Romanticism in Norway*, Columbia University Studies in History, Economics and Public Law (New York, 1933), especially pp. 21-34. The sentiment of the Finns in the first two decades of the nineteenth century is lucidly discussed by J. H. Wuorinen, *Nationalism in Modern Finland* (New York, 1931), chaps. I and II.

[32] F. D. Scott, "Propaganda activities of Bernadotte, 1813-1814," *Essays in the history of modern Europe,* ed. by D. C. McKay (New York, 1936), 29-30.

Chapter Nine

EUROPE CASTS OFF THE FRENCH HEGEMONY

I. THE ORIENTAL MIRAGE

Napoleon's preoccupation with the eastern Mediterranean, his projects for the dismemberment of the Ottoman Empire and for the revival of French influence in India, provide a colorful and fantastic fringe to the pattern of his European exploits. To suppose that the heir of Cæsar and Charlemagne aspired also to be a second Alexander conforms to the popular impression of his invincible egotism, and fable has not failed to exploit the notion that he regarded himself as an "exile in the Occident" denied a chance to play the rôle of conqueror on the ampler Asiatic stage. Within the mists of this fantasy are to be found sober elements of truth which help to clarify the long duel which Napoleon waged with both England and Russia. As a native of Corsica he had been familiar from boyhood with the traditions, stretching back to the crusades, which associated French commercial enterprises and colonizing projects with Egypt and Syria. The expedition of 1798, though advertised as a grandiose gesture against English power in the east, was organized as a practical colonizing venture. "Egypt was a province of the Roman Republic; it should become a province of the French Republic," Talleyrand wrote in his memoir on the subject, and the possibility that France might acquire an empire in the east as compensation for recent losses in the western hemisphere appeased French pride.[1]

The Battle of the Nile, and the final surrender of the French army of occupation in Egypt (1801) closed this first chapter of French trans-Mediterranean conquest. The general project, however, though halted temporarily, was by no means abandoned. The Treaty of Campoformio had given France the Ionian Islands and,

[1] F. J. Charles-Roux, *Bonaparte, gouverneur d'Egypte* (Paris, 1936), 2.

although these stepping-stones to the east were lost in 1799, France acquired a title to Istria and Dalmatia by the Peace of Pressburg (December, 1805), while the Neapolitan Kingdom passed under French control a few months later. Despite his lack of naval support Napoleon seemed capable of building a land bridge to the Bosporus, and Tsar Alexander revealed his apprehension by seizing Cattaro on the Dalmatian coast before the French could garrison it. At Constantinople the adroit Sebastiani made French diplomatic influence paramount in the summer of 1806. Subsequent Anglo-Russian attempts to overawe the sultan failed, and British demonstrations against Constantinople and Alexandria were repulsed. The prestige of France was steadily rising in the Mohammedan world, and in May, 1807, Persia, like Turkey, succumbed to French diplomacy and accepted a treaty of alliance.

The diplomatic revolution effected at Tilsit compelled Napoleon to modify his Near Eastern policy, but he did not relinquish his aims. Deserting the Porte, he plunged into discussions with Alexander which forecast a division of the sultan's inheritance between them. This betrayal of the Turks, who had been drawn into war with Great Britain and Russia by the assurance of French aid, could be the more conveniently glossed over because a revolutionary upheaval at Constantinople dethroned Selim III in May, 1807, and the Ottoman empire appeared on the point of dissolution. Egypt was half-detached, Syria insubordinate, Ali Pasha ruled Albania like a sovereign prince, the Montenegrins had won acknowledgment of their independence, and the Serbians were in rebellion. In these circumstances it was a tribute to the firmness and ability of Mahmud II, who was raised to power in 1808, that he was able to restore some measure of internal order. The murder of Selim III and Mustapha IV (who followed him briefly) in the disorders of 1807-1808 made Mahmud the last survivor of his dynasty. Forced to temporize with the privileged and insubordinate Janissary corps, which opposed all enlightened reforms, he quietly prepared to consolidate his power and build up a military force on modern lines, a program which was to culminate two decades later in the destruction of the Janissaries. During the first years of his reign, however, Mahmud owed his survival largely to the favors of fortune. His empire held together because more important matters prevented the great powers from speeding its dismemberment. Had Alexander and Napoleon concurred in pressing the partition, not even the British, who made peace with Mahmud in 1809, could have protected his dominions from invasion.

The cordial friendship which the two emperors cemented at Tilsit and renewed at Erfurt failed to dissipate the clouds which veiled their conflicting eastern policies. Napoleon declined, through Caulaincourt, to concede the tsar's claim to Constantinople; if, as a final gesture of friendship, he should yield the city, he insisted that France would have to hold the Dardanelles. But that, as the Russian minister Rumiantsev pointed out urbanely in 1808, would be giving the key of the house to a stranger, so he offered France Egypt and Syria instead. The offer, at least, was safe enough while the British patrolled the Mediterranean, and Napoleon let further discussions lag for the moment. He was awaiting the outcome of his Spanish venture, confident that, with Spain in his possession, he could bargain to better advantage. "No one," he was later to insist, "saw in my Spanish war the mastery of the Mediterranean." But the ill-success of the peninsular campaigns and the distraction of the Austrian war of 1809 delayed the drive to the east.

The delay, however, could not be mistaken for a withdrawal. In 1807 France had regained the Ionian Islands and Cattaro with the consent of Russia. The Peace of Schönbrunn two years later added Carinthia and Carniola to the Illyrian Provinces, with the ports of Trieste and Fiume. These conquests, coupled with the decline of Austria, made France a Balkan power. The French outposts in the Ionian Islands were almost as close to Constantinople on the west as the Russian forces on the Dnieper to the north, and Alexander's understanding with the Serbian patriots was countered by Napoleon's alliance with Ali Pasha of Janina. The only effective check imposed upon the French in the eastern Mediterranean during these years was administered by the British, who reft the Ionian Islands away from them at the close of 1809. The stroke helped to remind Alexander where his true interests lay. For if Great Britain collapsed under the pressure of the economic blockade which

Napoleon was urging the Russians to tighten, Egypt, Syria, even the Dardanelles, would be laid bare to French attack.

The Russo-Turkish War, stirred up by Napoleon in 1806, dragged on for five years. But the need to keep his forces available for action elsewhere deterred the tsar from pressing hostilities to a ruthless conclusion, and a desire to free his hands for the duel with Napoleon which he saw approaching moved him to abandon hostilities with the Porte after 1811. By a treaty signed at Bucharest (May 28, 1812), Russia retained all conquests east of the Pruth but relinquished Moldavia and Wallachia. The sultan promised an amnesty to the rebellious Serbs, though he insisted that Turkish garrisons must reoccupy the country, a betrayal which the Serbians found it difficult to forgive the tsar, who had encouraged their rebellion and courted their assistance. On the withdrawal of the Russians, the sultan's forces subdued Serbia once more and the gallant Karageorge, who had led his people in their fight for freedom, was driven into exile.

II. THE INVASION OF RUSSIA

By 1811 France and Russia were drifting towards war as if caught in the current of an inflexible destiny. When Caulaincourt returned in June from his embassy to St. Petersburg he noted with despair how completely Napoleon had embraced the prospect of hostilities. "Once an idea which he considered expedient lodged itself in his head, the emperor became his own dupe. He adopted it, caressed it, impregnated himself with it; he distilled it, as it were, through all his pores. . . . When he sought to seduce you he had already seduced himself." Caulaincourt insisted courageously that Alexander was acting in good faith; he even ventured Cassandra-like prophecies regarding the hazards of a campaign in Russia; but he found himself silenced with the taunt, "M. de Caulaincourt has become a Russian."[2] For Napoleon had other sources of information concerning Alexander's military preparations and knew that they had been going forward since 1810. The Austrian marriage of that year had left the tsar without illusions, and he countered it

---

[2] *Mémoires de Général de Caulaincourt*, ed. by J. Hanoteau, 3 vols. (Paris, 1933), I, 309-315.

in December by the *ukas* wherein he abandoned the continental system and admitted British commerce into the Russian Empire. Such an action, coming in the same month that Napoleon pushed the system to its limit by annexing the German coastline to the Elbe (thereby dispossessing the tsar's uncle, the Duke of Oldenburg) was a public announcement that the friendship formed at Tilsit and proclaimed at Erfurt was dead. Napoleon confessed as much to his ally the King of Württemberg three months later:

If the tsar desires war the inclination of the public spirit is conformable to his intention; if he does not wish it and does not arrest the current promptly he will be swept away next year against his volition, and war will come in spite of me, in spite of the Emperor Alexander, in spite of the interests of France and of Russia. I have already seen this thing happen so often that my experience in the past enables me to read the future. All this is a scene from an opera and the English are pulling the strings.[3]

The one logical mode of escape from the fateful situation, the negotiation of a truce between France and England, had been tried and had failed. Without committing himself officially, Napoleon authorized his brother Louis to sound the British cabinet in the spring of 1810, and found it polite but unresponsive. The severity of the commercial war had softened a little for the English with the prospect of military successes in Spain and diplomatic successes in Russia. Concurrently, Fouché and the Parisian speculator Ouvrard attempted secret negotiations with London and met the same rebuff. Napoleon's discovery of these unauthorized overtures brought dismissal for Fouché and imprisonment for Ouvrard by decrees of June 3rd. To cover his discomfiture Napoleon then intensified his campaign against Great Britain, the motto at Paris became once more *delenda est Carthago*, and the annexation of Holland and the North German coast followed before the end of the year.

As the estrangement between France and Russia ripened towards war the attitude of Austria and Prussia acquired a vital significance: throughout 1811 Vienna and Berlin experienced the half-forgotten privilege of balancing competitive offers. The ostensible victory in the diplomatic duel went to Napoleon, who wooed with threats

[3] *Correspondance de Napoléon I*er*, XXII, 16. No. 17553.

while Alexander wooed with promises. On February 24, 1812, Frederick William concluded an offensive and defensive alliance with France, promising 20,000 Prussian soldiers for a war against Russia. Vienna came to terms on March 14th, promising 30,000 men in return for a pact establishing union, alliance, and mutual guarantee of existing territories between France and Austria. Evidence recently assembled indicates that Napoleon secretly subsidized Austria to the extent of 1,000,000 francs to defray the upkeep of these auxiliary divisions which their commander, Prince Schwarzenberg, had already promised Tsar Alexander he would never see in action.[4] At the same time Metternich was privately assuring Hardenberg that the Austro-French accord was nothing but an "imitation alliance," and the courts of Vienna and Berlin were both protesting secretly to the tsar that they would never lend their aid for an attack on Russia, and were reminding him that all three powers were united by the necessity of opposing the reconstitution of the Polish kingdom which they had dismembered. Nothing is so binding as a debt of dishonor: "The truth is that in 1812, despite Tilsit and the Austrian marriage, Napoleon had never really separated the three powers which were co-partitioners of Poland and opponents by definition of the French Revolution and of everything which could extend its principles in Europe."[5]

Alexander was already freeing his hands for the impending conflict. The time for playing at domestic reform on the French model was past: the liberal minister, Speranski, fell from office on March 29, 1812. Hostilities between Russia and Sweden were superseded by an offensive and defensive alliance signed April 5th. The Russo-Turkish War was terminated by the Treaty of Bucharest of May 28, and negotiations with England crystallized in a treaty of alliance concluded July 2nd. Russian agents were circulating through Poland proclaiming Alexander's intention to recreate a unified Polish state under Russian protection. The Poles preferred to rest their hopes on a French victory, but Napoleon let slip the chance to rouse and utilize their national aspirations effectively. No sin-

---

[4] P. Marmottan, "A propos du traité d'alliance défensive du 14 mars, 1812, entre la France et l'Autriche: la défection autrichienne," *Revue des études historiques*, XCII (1926), 431-442.

[5] Marmottan, *op. cit.*, 438.

cere understanding, no real accord or adjustment of interests, had been worked out between France and Poland, and Jerome Bonaparte, dispatched to the Grand Duchy of Warsaw in April, 1812, without a clear program of action, chilled instead of firing the ardor of the Polish patriots. The failure to evoke a Polish national rising by a frank appeal to the Poles of White Russia and Lithuania is to be counted as one more opportunity lost by Napoleon.[6]

At no point in the Russian campaign does Napoleon's genius shine forth at its best. The mania for numbers which led him to assemble half a million men for the invasion of a country in which it was impossible to maintain adequate supply convoys or live by foraging was itself a catastrophic blunder. And once the campaign had opened, his hours of indecision multiplied, his concept of the scope and purpose of the war wavered with each week. Contempt for the Russian generals altered to reluctant admiration as they continued to evade his enveloping movements. After storming Smolensk on August 17th-18th he declared the year's campaign at an end, then reversed his decision and pressed on a hundred and fifty miles to Borodino. Weariness, a head cold, and stomach pains combined to dull his mind as he made his dispositions for battle on September 7th, for that decisive battle he had been seeking for three months.[7] It proved a second Eylau on a vaster scale; the Russians fought at a numerical disadvantage, 120,000 against 135,-000, but with desperate tenacity, and both sides called the day's slaughter a victory. Napoleon had lost one-fourth of his men, Kutusov one-third of his, including the valorous Bagration. But the way to Moscow was open and the French entered the all but deserted city on September 16th, only to see it consumed in flames, as Smolensk had been, by order of the Russian commander.[8]

Of the five weeks wasted in the half-ruined city, the abortive overtures to Alexander, the reluctant order to retreat finally issued

[6] A. Mansuy, *Jérôme Napoléon et la Pologne en 1812* (Paris, 1931), 653-658.

[7] *Napoleon's letters to Marie Louise,* ed. by Charles de la Roncière (New York, 1935), 88-89.

[8] The responsibility for the burning of Moscow will probably never be settled with certainty, but there is a strong presumption that it rested with the military governor, Rostopchin, though he later denied it. Incendiary fires were started almost simultaneously at several points, particularly among the grain magazines. See M. de la Fuye, "Rostopchine et Koutousov, Moscou, 1812," *Revue des questions historiques,* LXIV (1936), 184-204.

on October 19th, enough has been written. The demon of indecision had one more trick to play, for at Maloyaroslavets the Russians blocked the way, and after pondering the map for an hour Napoleon reverted to the devastated route by which he had advanced, unaware that Kutusov had decided not to risk a further engagement if he had pressed forward. It was, as Rose notes ironically, almost the only time that Napoleon erred through excess of prudence.[9] With the advent of Generals November and December the French losses multiplied horribly and the straggling divisions lost all semblance of discipline. Of the 430,000 men who had marched into Russia perhaps 50,000 found their way back and 100,000 remained as prisoners; but over 100,000 had died in battles and skirmishes, and nearly twice as many had perished of disease, cold, and famine.[10]

On December 5th at Smorgoni Napoleon turned over command of the phantom army to Murat and set out for Paris. Disturbing news had reached him; the conspirator Malet had barely missed success on October 23rd by spreading a report of Napoleon's capture and attempting a *coup d'état*. Caulaincourt, who accompanied the emperor in that twelve-day dash across Poland, Germany, and France, found him animated and serene in spirit, his brain already busy with plans for regilding his slightly tarnished prestige. The idea of compromise remained as unthinkable as ever. "In this world," he assured his companion with tranquil certitude, "there are only two alternatives: to command or to obey. The conduct displayed towards France by all the cabinets has proven to me that France has nothing to depend upon except her prestige and consequently her might."[11] Three weeks after his arrival in Paris he presented his account to the senate, with a demand for more men, and the senate approved a draft calling for 350,000 new recruits.

III. THE WAR OF LIBERATION

As the *débris* of the grand army fell back, between December, 1812, and March, 1813, from the Niemen to the Vistula, the Vistula

[9] J. H. Rose, *The Life of Napoleon I*, 6th ed. rev. (London, 1913), II, 260.
[10] G. Bodart, *Losses of life in modern wars* (Oxford, 1916), 120-130.
[11] *Mémoires de Général de Caulaincourt*, ed. by J. Hanoteau, 3 vols. (Paris, 1933), II, 230.

to the Oder, the Oder to the Elbe and the Saale, the peoples of the Germanies realized with amazement that the hour of liberation had struck sooner than they had believed possible. On December 30th General Yorck, commanding the Prussian division which had been assigned the responsibility of guarding the French left, signed a truce with the Russians on his own initiative. A month later the Austrian auxiliary corps commanded by Schwarzenberg was immobilized through an analogous pact. This Convention of Zeycz was for the French a more ominous betrayal, for it was approved by the Austrian government in defiance of treaty obligations and it compelled the unprotected French right to retreat to the borders of Saxony. In January it had been a question whether Napoleon could continue to hold the Germanies in subjection; by March it had become a question whether he could reconquer them.

Two major problems still occupied the emperor's attention in Paris. The first was a reconciliation with the Pope, now a prisoner-guest at Fontainebleau. To reassure Catholic consciences, Napoleon yielded his claim that he should have authority to nominate some of the cardinals and granted an amnesty to his most active clerical foes. But when he published this preliminary compromise as a definitive reconciliation (February 13th) Pius repudiated it, and the schism remained unhealed. The second project, the enrolment of a new army, proceeded more successfully. On April 16th he left for Mainz and Erfurt, master once more of forces which totaled over 200,000 men. But he lacked cavalry, cannon, ammunition, *matériel* of all classes. The levies could be raised, but they could not be equipped, for the manufacturers, wise enough now to produce only for cash, could at best supply no more than 30,000 small arms a month.[12] It was not the quarter of a million men whose bodies were scattered from Vilna to Moscow that were irreplaceable, it was the 500 cannon, the 10,000 wagons, the 200,000 muskets or bayonets or sabers.

The military initiative remained to Napoleon, but all else had passed out of his hands. In Prussia an irresistible popular pressure swept the ever-hesitant Frederick William into decided action at

[12] Lefebvre de Béhaine, "Le crépuscule de l'empire," *Revue des questions historiques*, CXVI (1932), 147.

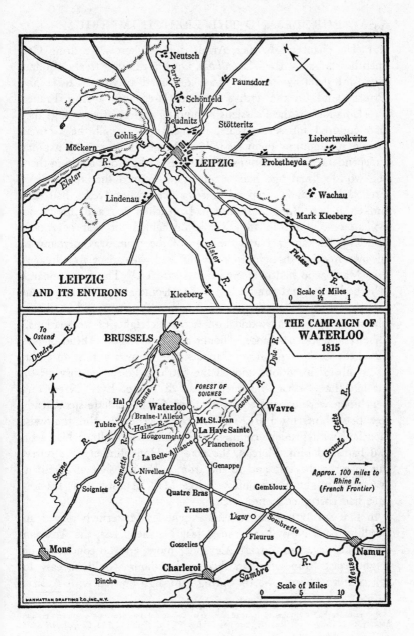

LEIPZIG AND ITS ENVIRONS

Neutsch
Paunsdorf
Partha R.
Schönfeld
Reudnitz
Stötteritz
Liebertwolkwitz
Gohlis
Möckern
Elster R.
LEIPZIG
Probstheyda
Lindenau
Wachau
Elster R.
Mark Kleeberg
Pleisse R.
Kleeberg

Scale of Miles
0   ½   1

THE CAMPAIGN OF WATERLOO 1815

To Ostend
Dendre R.
BRUSSELS
Dyle R.
N
FOREST OF SOIGNES
Lasne R.
Hal
Senne R.
Waterloo
Wavre
Tubize
Braine-l'Alleud
Mt.St.Jean
Hain R.
La Haye Sainte
Grande Gette R.
Hougoumont
Planchenoit
Sennette R.
La Belle-Alliance
Nivelles
Genappe
Soignies
Senne R.
Approx. 100 miles to Rhine R. (French Frontier)
Quatre Bras
Gembloux
Frasnes
Ligny
Sombreffe
Mons
Fleurus
Namur
Gosselies
Meuse R.
Binche
Charleroi
Sambre R.
R.

Scale of Miles
0   5   10

MANHATTAN DRAFTING CO.,INC., N.Y.

The 1st Volks Krieg

last. The chants of Körner, Arndt, and Rückert were firing German hearts like a new *Marseillaise*. On March 1st, a treaty of offensive and defensive alliance was concluded between Russia and Prussia, and on the 17th Prussia declared war against France. Proclamations to the Prussians reminding them of the wrongs they had endured for seven years, proclamations to all the German people summoning them to follow Prussia in a war of national independence, proclamations to the nations of Europe assuring them the world's great age had begun anew, proved that the spell of French propaganda, preponderant for over twenty years, had been broken at last. "In 1792 France had preached war and the cosmopolitan revolution; in 1813 Russia unchained the war of nationalities."[13] Alexander I was the man of the hour, was, perhaps, in his own mystical thought, so lately suffused with apocalyptic images, "the Man" who had overcome the Antichrist.[14] The first monarch who had faced and vanquished a Napoleonic army, he entered the Germanies in 1813 as the avatar of nationalism wrapped in cloudy phrases, "the hereditary and imprescriptible rights of free nations," "liberty and independence," "honor and fatherland." Ahead of him flitted the Greek republican, Capodistrias; on his right, as an augur of his liberal intentions, moved the patriotic Pole, Czartoryski; on his left the Corsican refugee, Pozzo di Borgo. Even Napoleon's henchmen were passing to his standard, for Bernadotte stood ready to support him (for a price) with 15,000 Swedes; Jomini, the Swiss tactician, with prudent counsel. From America, whither Napoleon had banished him, Moreau, the hero of Hohenlinden, was hurrying to serve the tsar and to die from a French shot at Dresden. Napoleon might have confessed, like Mark Antony, that his fortune had corrupted honest men.

In that springtime sown with treacheries Metternich played an excelling part. Now that he need fear Napoleon less, the Austrian chancellor began to distrust Alexander more, and no concession he might exact from either in their critical hour would be easy to collect from a victor. So the spring campaign opened with Austria

---

[13] A. Sorel, *L'Europe et la Révolution française*, VIII (Paris, 1912), 69.
[14] Alexander had commenced to read the New Testament the previous summer and the apocalyptic passages particularly fascinated him. W. A. Phillips, *The Confederation of Europe* (London, 1920), 56-57.

waiting to sell her mediation dearly. At Lützen on May 2nd Napoleon met the Prussians and Russians in a bloody and indecisive engagement which he counted a victory. On May 20th he repeated the stroke at Bautzen. Germany was half reconquered, but his losses had been extravagant and had to be replaced if he was to continue. On June 4th he acceded to an armistice which was to last until July 28th, and was afterwards extended to August 10th. Metternich, reading the omens carefully, went over to the Allies on June 24th. The last coalition had crystallized, for Great Britain joined on June 15th, assuring subsidies, and a renewal of the fighting would find France at an unenviable disadvantage. It seems doubtful if Napoleon's acceptance of any of the several projects proposed could have prevented further hostilities. On the expiration of the truce Austria declared war despite Napoleon's attempts to buy her neutrality, and for the first time in his military career he faced four great powers simultaneously. For the first time, too, he allowed political considerations to corrupt military strategy. His plan of attack, hastily formulated, involved a drive against Bernadotte's divisions, 120,000 strong, which blocked the road to Berlin, although the main Allied army was concentrating in Bohemia under Austrian command. The hope that the Austrian forces would remain passive unless he forced a fight upon them apparently diverted him from his logical objective, the destruction of the enemy's strongest force.

Fighting recommenced in the middle of August, when the Allies concerted their efforts in a general but highly cautious offensive. By common accord they were to avoid battle where Napoleon commanded in person, while harassing his subordinates and defeating them piecemeal. Oudinot, obeying his master's order to advance on Berlin with 70,000 men, divided his columns, and they were badly mangled by Bernadotte and Bülow at Blankenfelde and Grossbeeren (August 22nd-23rd) when almost in sight of their goal. The Allied army in Silesia, 100,000 Russians and Prussians under Blücher, held its own against an equal French force under Macdonald until Napoleon suddenly joined Macdonald on August 21st. Divining immediately that he had a stronger antagonist, Blücher fell back from the Bober to the Katzbach, preserving his army with difficulty, but remembering to lure the emperor on so that Schwarzenberg, debouching from the Erz Gebirge fifty miles to his rear, could threaten Dresden with the army of Bohemia. But Schwarzenberg, timid and ill-informed, delayed his advance on Dresden, where St. Cyr had only 30,000 defenders. On the 23rd, Napoleon received an urgent warning from St. Cyr that the Austrians were approaching in force and he started back from Görlitz with the imperial guard. Macdonald, left to follow Blücher's exhausted divisions, blundered the pursuit, and was hurled across the swollen Katzbach with 18,000 casualties. But Napoleon and the guard, splashing fifty miles through the Lusatian mud in forty-eight hours, arrived in time to relieve Dresden.

The fortunes of war had now brought Napoleon the chance which he had neglected to seek: he was in the presence of the enemy's main army of 200,000 men with his own forces raised to 120,000 by two days of that centripetal concentration at which the French excelled. When the Austrians and Russians launched their tardy assault against Dresden on August 26th-27th they were repulsed with losses exceeding 35,000 men. Split into bewildered fragments, the army of Bohemia streamed back through the passes of the Erz Gebirge. Napoleon ordered a merciless pursuit; but the Russians were always dangerous in retreat, and the Austrians and Prussians were no longer sheep to be gathered in by Murat's cavalry after a single beating. On the 29th, Vandamme's command, losing contact with the other French columns in its impetuous advance, was cut off at Kulm by Kleist's Prussian corps, and overwhelmed with losses of 35,000. The victory of Dresden had been cancelled.

One last lunge Napoleon made in the first week of September, racing back to Görlitz with a division of the imperial cavalry in an effort to trap Blücher. But again that cunning old wolf eluded him. Then the iron ring began to close in. Ney, replacing Oudinot in the north, lost 20,000 of his best men at Dennewitz (September 6th). Davout, with 35,000 more, was shut up in Hamburg. For a month the Allies felt their way forward while Napoleon tested their lines for a weak link, drafting audacious plans only to discard them. On October 14th he returned to Leipzig. Schwarzenberg was approaching the city from the south, Blücher from the north, but he could still have hurled 150,000 men against either if he had acted with the old decision. By the 16th it was too late. When the Allies opened their attack on that gray October morning they had already 200,000 men available against 170,000. A day of bloody struggle ended with the lines much the same, but the odds were shifting. An additional 40,000 Russians under Bennigsen and 60,000 Prussians and Swedes under Bernadotte were due on the morrow, whereas the French had no more than 150,000 effectives with which to continue the battle. Yet Napoleon waited irresolutely through the 17th, when the alternative was clearly to attack or to retreat, and on the 18th he resumed the struggle against forces now double his own. Another 50,000 casualties about evenly divided were the result. In the north the attackers had fought their way into the suburbs of the beleaguered city, and 3,000 Saxon troops deserted to them in the midst of the fighting. Yorck's Prussians, who had captured Möckern on the 16th, were less than a mile from the western route through Lindenau, the only safe line of retreat.

At nightfall Napoleon ordered a general retirement, and by dawn of the 19th the western gate was jammed with fugitives. But no extra spans had been thrown across the Pleisse and the Elster, the single bridge was soon blocked with a slow-moving horde, and to crown a day of disaster the engineer in charge blew up this causeway prematurely, leaving 35,000 veterans of the rearguard no choice but to lay down their arms. A bare 40,000 survivors fought their way to the Rhine early in November, with typhus thinning their depleted ranks. Nearly 200,000 French troops remained behind in the Germanies, dead, wounded, or prisoners.

The campaign in France, from November, 1813, to March, 1814, is logically and dramatically the completion of the Napoleonic epic. Historians, dazzled by the wizardry of the defense tactics, have in general failed to note that the Allies were impeded chiefly by their own ineptitude and lack of coöperation, and that they dared not advance too rashly into French territory for fear of exciting a national resistance. Prudence suggested that a nation which had lately sent its soldiers through all the capitals of Europe might have resources of defiance and a capacity for guerilla warfare equal at least to that displayed by the Spaniards. The most remarkable thing

ut the campaign of 1814 was not the skill Napoleon showed in
ttling his dwindling divisions back and forth, but the apathy
of the French populace. The campaign was a war of movement
by professional forces. The defenders made little attempt to throw
up earthworks or to resort to that stubborn house-to-house fighting,
the effectiveness of which had been demonstrated in Spain. No
spirit of heroism moved Parisians to mount the breach and face a
siege in 1814 as they did in 1870. When the Allied soldiers entered
the capital on March 31st the citizens lined the streets to watch
them parade, and displayed so little evidence of political sentiment
that Alexander, who sincerely desired to assure France a government that might prove popular and permanent, was at a loss to
surmise whether that government had best be monarchical or republican, despotic or democratic. No institutions existed which
could be said to represent French opinion except the senate and the
legislative body, and these had never received a direct popular mandate. No more striking proof exists of the thoroughness with which
Bonaparte had disciplined the Revolution, and paralyzed the volition of the French people, than the inertia which held them motion-
less in the face of this national crisis.

It was the hour for which Talleyrand and many other notables
had waited. Convening the senators on April 2nd he presented
them with a solution which would placate their sharpest fears. A
provisory government was his proposal, accompanied by guarantees
that senators should retain their rank, army officers their grades,
owners of national lands their titles, bondholders their investments,
and the people their liberty of conscience. France was declared ab-
solved from its allegiance to the Bonaparte dynasty, and a majority of the sixty-four senators in attendance invoked the restoration
of the Bourbons. Alexander was astonished to note among the list
of advocates the names of several ex-regicides.[15] Even so, he hesitated until Marmont rallied to the provisory government with his
division, and thereby demonstrated that even the army was deserting its chief. On April 4th Napoleon yielded to the persuasions of

[15] Sorel, *L'Europe et la Révolution française*, VIII (Paris, 1912), 319. For a lucid
analysis of the events and negotiations which culminated in the restoration of the
Bourbon, see E. J. Knapton, "Some aspects of the Bourbon restoration of 1814,"
Journal of Modern History, VI (1934), 405-424.

his marshals at Fontainebleau and abdicated in favor of his son.
Two days later the senate formally decreed the restoration of Louis
XVIII.

IV. THE BOURBON RESTORATION AND THE HUNDRED DAYS

The charter of 1814, which the returning monarch offered the
French people, provided for a parliamentary government as liberal in
appearance as any then functioning in Europe. The king was to rule
through his ministers and with the aid of a bicameral legislature,
consisting of a house of peers nominated by the monarch and an
assembly chosen by electors who paid 300 francs a year in direct
taxes. Purchasers of national lands retained their titles, civil liberty
was guaranteed, and the bureaucracy and institutions of the empire
continued to function with few alterations. Members of the upper
middle class were disposed to regard with complacency a settlement
which left the voting of taxes and laws to a conservative legislature
and denied the populace a vote, while the masses accepted their
exclusion from political influence with resignation.

If, within a year, powerful groups and individuals ranged themselves against this restoration government, the explanation is that it
proved to be less a government than a régime. There was no cabinet
responsibility; ministers reported separately to the king and often
ignored the chambers; returned courtiers crowded the anterooms of
the Tuileries, while Napoleonic officers were retired on half-pay; and
émigrés, priests, and nobles pressed for the restoration of their
former privileges. The ultra-royalists openly derided the charter as a
temporary device soon to be discarded for a frank absolutism, and
the king's laxity and neglect of state business made it seem highly
probable that the ultras would have their way. Ex-soldiers of the
imperial forces found peace and civilian rule particularly obnoxious,
and several officers were already plotting a revolt when Napoleon,
weary of his exile on Elba, disembarked in the Gulf of Jouan on
March 1, 1815. Three weeks later he reached Paris, as he had prophe-
sied he would do, "without firing a shot," and the Bourbons were
in flight.

The French nation, humiliated by defeat and apprehensive of the
reactionary tendencies of the restoration government, had not been

able to resist the heady sensation of defying Europe once again. But only two classes, the peasants and the ex-soldiers, sincerely welcomed Napoleon's return. The rich distrusted the reviving clamor of the Jacobin elements, the sober-minded quailed at the certainty of renewed war. For the British parliament voted to resist a Bonaparte restoration with all available resources, while the Allied governments declared Napoleon an outlaw and pledged their faith to destroy him. All his efforts to rally France to his support, his promises of a liberal régime, his renunciation of further conquests, could not cancel the verdict that stood recorded against him: his own past. The army which he assembled in desperate haste numbered scarcely 160,000, and of these 30,000 were diverted to subdue an outbreak in the Vendée. Against him the Allies could marshal 700,000. Blücher with 120,000 Prussians and Wellington with 95,000 troops of mixed nationality, Belgian, Dutch, German, and British, were already in Belgium. His peace overtures failing, Napoleon left Paris on June 12th to try his fortunes on the battlefield for the last time. He needed a victory that would electrify France and paralyze the coalition.

Neither Blücher nor Wellington anticipated an early attack. The French advance on June 16th split the Prussian center before Ligny, while Ney held Wellington at bay ten miles to the northwest at Quatre Bras. Well pleased with the day's work, Napoleon ordered Grouchy on the 17th to follow the retreating Prussians to Gembloux, reserving to himself the destruction of Wellington's force. But Wellington had evacuated Quatre Bras and was falling back towards Brussels; it was evening before a crash of artillery checked the French pursuit with the realization that the army they were so eager to overtake was waiting for them on the ridge of Waterloo. When the rainy dawn of the 18th showed the enemy still there, Napoleon prepared his assault, counting the day already won. But the French attacks, infantry and cavalry, were poorly concerted; Wellington's dispositions permitted him to feed his battered lines with reinforcements from behind the shelter of the crest; and the arrival of Prussian detachments (which had evaded Grouchy) on the extreme French right turned a deadlock into a disaster for Napoleon's exhausted divisions. In the fading light a scant half of the 73,000 French troops which had swung into action at noon fled from the field in undisciplined panic. The reverse was irretrievable, and four days later Napoleon acknowledged the fact by a second abdication. Unable to secure passage to America, he surrendered himself voluntarily on July 15th to the captain of H.M.S. *Bellerophon*, which was cruising off La Rochelle.

This last flight of the eagle cost the French almost all the remnants of their revolutionary conquests still remaining: Philippeville, Marienburg, Saarlouis, Landau, and a portion of Savoy. It cost them in addition an indemnity of 700,000,000 francs, and military occupation of seventeen fortresses at French expense for three years. More than ever the restored Bourbons had come to symbolize the national humiliation and the reversal of the revolutionary achievements. Yet the historian cannot but regret that Louis XVIII failed in 1815, as he had failed in 1814, to risk a national plebiscite as a test of French opinion. Such a move, though contrary to monarchical precedents, might have destroyed at the outset the hardy legend that the nation had yielded only to force in 1814, and welcomed Napoleon's return a year later with rejoicing. It is significant that the elections which the returned emperor ordered in May, 1815, show only thirty-four per cent of the eligible voters responding, and the result was a radical, almost a Jacobin, chamber. The disinherited classes, for which Napoleon had done least, were still the most devoted to him, or perhaps it would be more true to say, were still the most strongly opposed to the Bourbons. But the old aristocracy remained in hiding, and of the imperial notables only a minority rallied to his support during the Hundred Days. After Waterloo the same electorate, with seventy-two per cent voting instead of thirty-four, chose the famous *chambre introuvable*, giving a sixteen-to-one victory to the conservative forces. Despite the criticism of liberal historians, this election of August, 1815, was perhaps the freest of any held in France between 1814 and 1848.[16] If its verdict may be taken as representative (and there is no more authoritative expression of public opinion available) a majority of the French people at the close of 1815 had little sympathy for Jacobinism and even less for Napoleon. For them, as for Europe, the campaigns of 1813-1815 had been a war of liberation

---

[16] E. P. Dean, "Elections in France: the election of August, 1814," *Essays in the History of Modern Europe*, ed. by D. C. McKay (New York, 1936), 31-47.

against the rule of the military. The trial of Marshal Ney before the chamber of peers in November, 1815, on the charge that his desertion to Napoleon the previous March constituted treason against the state, offers further striking proof of the hostility felt, even in France, against the military clique which Napoleon had so long favored and rewarded. Many of the peers had risen to office under the empire; most of them were civilians; all of them no doubt had some reason for wishing to strengthen their position under the restored dynasty. But the vote by which they found Ney guilty, a vote of 157 to 1, cannot be attributed entirely to Bourbon pressure. It reflects a revulsion in the French mind against the fire-eaters, and against the misfortunes which an arrogant and irresponsible military dictatorship had brought upon France.

V. THE VIENNA SETTLEMENT

Security against French aggression, the aim which had ruled the councils of the successive coalitions for twenty years, was realized with the overthrow of the empire and Napoleon's abdication. Europe could now be restored to the relative order and stability which had characterized the relationships of the great powers in the eighteenth century. The cynical and often quoted observation of Friedrich von Gentz that the real purpose of the Congress of Vienna (to which he acted as secretary) was to divide among the victors the spoils taken from the vanquished, missed the more essential truth that the real purpose of a peace conference is to make peace, a task at which the Vienna Congress succeeded better than most. It is an interesting comment upon the subjectivity of historical writing that it required another general European war, and another peace conference, to persuade students of history to think less reverently of Napoleon's generalship by demonstrating the chronic ineptitude of coalitions, and to think more highly of the diplomats who framed the Vienna settlement by revealing anew the perils and perplexities of peace-making.

Three major projects conditioned the thinking of the Allied statesmen in 1814: the restoration of security, which they sought by reëstablishing a balance of power and by interposing checks upon France; the restoration of social stability through the convenient formula of legitimacy; and the distribution of rewards and compensations to those states which had earned them by sacrifices made in the common cause. In pursuit of the first aim, "the assurance of European tranquillity by the establishment of a just equilibrium," as the general treaty of alliance concluded at Chaumont on March 10, 1814, had defined it, the four powers, Britain, Russia, Austria, and Prussia reclaimed for themselves the prestige and approximate mutual status which they had enjoyed before the era of French preponderance, while France, reduced to the limits of 1792, formed a fifth power in a balanced system. To discourage a future eruption of French energy and lust for conquest, the cordon of states on the borders of France was strengthened. Belgium and Holland, united as the Kingdom of the Netherlands, guarded the northeast frontier; Prussia, invested with a stretch of Rhenish territory including Cologne and Coblenz, could maintain a watch on the Rhine; Switzerland was neutralized; and from Switzerland to the Mediterranean the passes into Italy were confided to the Sardinian Kingdom, which was reconstituted and strengthened by the addition of Genoa.[17]

The restoration of internal order and stability in states disorganized by the revolutionary convulsion was a more complex problem. But the Dutch had set an example by their promptitude in rallying to the house of Orange, and the French senate emphasized it by recalling the Bourbons. As a counter-revolutionary argument legitimacy had some pragmatic virtues, but it was an obnoxious principle that set Ferdinand VII on the throne of Spain and Ferdinand I on that of the Two Sicilies. The force of dynastic polity likewise restored Portugal to the house of Braganza and Hanover to the rule of George III. Pius VII, who had been released by Napoleon in January, 1814, was reinvested with his theocratic powers over the affairs of the Papal States, although Metternich himself was to confess that "the papal government cannot govern." Victor Emmanuel I returned to Turin as monarch of an enlarged Kingdom of Sardinia; Tuscany, Parma, Lucca, and lesser Italian duchies reverted to Hapsburg or Bourbon pretenders. But the benefits of legitimacy applied only to dynastic claims, and were invoked in vain on behalf of the ancient Italian

[17] The Treaty of Chaumont may be found in G. F. Martens, *Nouveau recueil de traités*, II (Göttingen, 1887), 683-684; the final "Acte du Congrès de Vienne" on pp. 379-431.

republics. Venetia remained an Austrian province, while the Genoese realm was absorbed into the Kingdom of Sardinia.

Only on the subject of territorial compensations did the debates at Vienna reveal an opposition of interests sharp enough to threaten a rupture of the conference. The extravagance of the Russian claims to Poland and the Prussian claims to Saxony drove Britain, Austria, and France into a secret treaty of resistance (January 3, 1815). In the outcome, Russia received about four-fifths of the area which had comprised the Kingdom of Poland before 1772, while Prussia kept two-fifths of Saxony and added Swedish Pomerania. Of the continental states, Russia profited most generously in the revolutionary era, retaining Finland, Congress Poland, and Bessarabia. The Hapsburgs reclaimed their former possessions and received Lombardy and Venetia in exchange for the former Austrian Netherlands. Great Britain added Malta, Ceylon, the Cape of Good Hope, and some lesser colonial territories to her empire. The ancient diplomatic tenet of reciprocal compensation, so charily practiced by Napoleon, had returned to rule the international councils of Europe, and the results, however unscrupulous in detail, were collectively beneficial, at least to the extent of promoting a thirty-nine year period unmarred by war between the great powers.

For the masses in most European countries these political and dynastic adjustments seem to have held as little interest as a croupier's accounting in a game grown stale and meaningless. A spirit of disillusionment, febrile and confused, succeeded the high certainties of the Age of Reason and the expectations voiced in the revolutionary creed. The philosophy of the Restoration was for many a thing of shreds and patches after the stark and glittering mirror-world the *philosophes* had held before the gaze of humanity, and the reversion to traditional pretensions, petty policies, checks and balances and compromises, though it might mark a return to sanity and repose, still left behind a despairing conviction that humanity had failed itself.

Not all the magnanimous sentiments of the Revolution, however, perished with its ideology. Humanitarianism was one tenet of the rationalist creed which pietists, reactionaries, and romantics could adopt with equal ardor, and two acts of the Vienna statesmen testify to its continued vigor. The first was the abolition of the trade in negro slaves. Slavery had been abolished in the French colonies by a decree of the national convention (1794) and had been restored by Napoleon (1802). Great Britain after 1806 and the United States after 1808 repudiated the traffic, and largely through British efforts a clause was added to the Final Act of the Vienna Treaty prohibiting it, but leaving to the discretion of the signatory powers the time and manner in which the prohibition should be enforced.[18] The second and more famous testimonial to the belief in human brotherhood, drafted during the Vienna deliberations, was the Holy Alliance. Alexander's initiative in calling upon his fellow monarchs "to take for their sole guide the precepts of the Holy Religion, namely, the precepts of Justice, Christian Charity, and Peace," proved that he at least among the statesmen of the restoration had the intuition to respond to the profound aspiration for a better world still animating European society.[19] Cooler-headed colleagues shaped the Quadruple Alliance as a more practical instrument for the resolution of international strife, but Alexander preferred the vision of a world transformed by the miracle of a mystical conversion. In this flight from reality he retraced on a vaster stage the drama of his domestic policy which had been in such large measure a tragedy of good intentions. "Your character, Sire, is a constitution," Madame de Staël flattered him when he regretted his frustrated plans for national reconstruction. In 1815 Madame de Krüdener consoled him with the same generous suggestion, and with the same negative results.[20]

VI. THE REBUKE TO NATIONAL AND LIBERAL ASPIRATIONS

To defeat Napoleon, "the Revolution incarnate" as Metternich styled him, the Allied nations had adopted revolutionary reforms

---

[18] G. F. Martens, op. cit., II, 432-434. Great Britain and the United States had agreed jointly to abolish the traffic by Article X of the Treaty of Ghent, December 27, 1814. Ibid., 84.

[19] Alexander's halo of liberalism still shone brightly enough in 1814 to excite admiration even in the United States. See W. P. Cresson, The Holy Alliance (New York, 1922), 48-49.

[20] R. Kayser, "Zar Alexander I und die deutsche Erweckung," Theologische Studien und Kritiken, CIV (1932), 160-185. For the relationship between Alexander's conceptions and the Christian utopias of Adam Müller and Franz von Baader consult H. Schaeder, Die Dritte Koalition und die Heilige Allianz (Königsberg, 1934), 58-71. The literature on Mme. de Krüdener is extensive but an admirable critical list of the most significant items is given by E. J. Knapton, "An unpublished letter of Mme. de Krüdener," The Journal of Modern History, IX (1937), 483-492.

and utilized the magic of revolutionary phrases. French military strategy, the organization of an army in corps and divisions, the transformation of serfs into citizens and citizens into soldiers, the awakening of the people to a sense of their rights, the deflection of their indignation outwards against a foreign oppressor, all these formulas which had stimulated the passion and the energy of revolutionary France in its struggle to survive had been borrowed by the Allies in their struggle to defeat it. With Napoleon's fall "kings crept out again to feel the sun," and the diplomats hastened to Vienna to prepare an international audit and strike off a balance sheet for the epoch. The settlement which they devised excited widespread disappointment in their own day and passed into history as an example of princely perfidy, a Machiavellian betrayal of Europe's millions who had made the triumph of the monarchs possible.

Under this "conspiracy theory," so long popularized by the liberal historians, the Vienna assembly appears a cynical cabal of liberticides. Distrust of all national and liberal sentiments supposedly led the delegates into a series of oppressive acts which had later to be rectified by spasms of that revolutionary violence which they vowed it their chief purpose to avoid. The restored Bourbons were driven from France by a second revolution in 1830; the union of Catholic Belgium and Protestant Holland likewise dissolved in violence after fifteen years. The union of the crowns of Norway and Sweden, never satisfactory, ended more happily with a peaceful separation in 1905. Spain, where Ferdinand VII celebrated his return in 1814 by repudiating the doctrinaire constitution concocted in his absence and by imprisoning the most prominent liberals in the kingdom, sank into a melancholy state of alternate ferment and stagnation. The Poles, wronged in the eighteenth century, appealed in vain for national liberty and unity in the nineteenth.[21] But the most shameful provisions of the Vienna Treaty, in the opinion of its detractors, were those concerning Italy and Germany, where liberal and national aspirations were deliberately stifled for half a century.

It is impossible to deny that in rearranging German and Italian affairs the congress looked backward instead of forward. The loose Germanic Confederation of thirty-eight states, flimsily constructed to replace the defunct Holy Roman Empire, brought German unity no nearer, and the diet of princes' delegates which symbolized it became a convenient instrument for furthering policies of repression. Yet it is not easy to see how the obstacles to German unification, the *Grossdeutsch vs. Kleindeutsch* issue, the Austro-Prussian rivalry, the opposition between the concepts of a *Staatenbund* and a *Bundesstaat*, could have been solved before the later nineteenth century in any case.[22] In 1815 these problems had received no more than superficial diagnosis, and any attempt to disentangle the elements of a modern, national territorial state from the wreckage of the medieval feudal empire must have failed then even more ignominiously than it failed in 1848-1849. German patriots who dreamed of abolishing feudalism and particularism as the French had done, by a series of formal decrees, overlooked the fact that France already possessed a tradition of centralized administration in 1789 and the revolutionists made use of this in executing their reforms. In Prussia a similar but less turbulent reorganization was effected by royal decree between 1807 and 1814. But no central authority yet existed which could undertake the reorganization of the Germanies as a whole, or crush the local resistance which a program of hasty unification would have excited.[23]

For the Italians the restoration of the princely despots meant a partial return to the petty politics and obscurantism of the eighteenth century. French books, dress, manners, schools, and laws suddenly passed out of favor. The return of Pius VII to Rome, the reëstablishment of the Society of Jesus, and the revival of clerical influence in education ended the brief supremacy of the secular spirit.[24] Italy in 1814 was probably no better prepared than Germany for national political unity,[25] but the Congress of Vienna dealt the national

---

[22] For the solution found for these issues at a later date consult the volume in this series by R. C. Binkley, *Realism and Nationalism* (New York, 1935), chaps. XI and XII.

[23] The nebulous state of German thought on the problems of national unification in the early years of the nineteenth century has been analyzed by A. Berney, "Reichstradition und Nationalstaatsgedanke," *Historische Zeitschrift*, CXL (1929), 57-86.

[24] The decrees reëstablishing the States of the Church and the Jesuit Order can be found in C. Mirbt, ed., *Quellen zur Geschichte des Papsttums und des Römischen Katholizismus*, 4th ed. (Tübingen, 1924), 424-426.

[25] A project instituted by a small group of patriots to offer the throne of a united Italy to the House of Savoy in 1814 won very slight support from the Italians and was discouraged at Allied headquarters. See D. Spadoni, "Carlo Comelli di Stuckenfeld e il trono de' Cesari offerto a Casa Savoja nel 1814," *Rassegna storica del risorgimento*, XIV (1927), 593-656.

cause of the Italian patriots a far more crippling blow. For the settlement not only dismembered the Italian Kingdom constructed by Napoleon and restored the provincial divisions of the old régime, it readmitted into the peninsula two powerful conservative institutions, the Papal government and the Austrian army. As the power of the Pope and of Austria was fortified by the grant of important territorial possessions (the temporal domains and Lombardy-Venetia), the spirit of Italian nationalism could not triumph completely without dispossessing both. The Roman question was a logical if troublesome heritage of Italian politics, though it might have been simplified at this juncture by restoring the Pope to Rome without restoring the States of the Church to theocratic rule. But the admission of Austrian garrisons into Lombardy-Venetia, a step which ultimately proved almost as fatal to Austria as it threatened to prove to Italy, must be laid to the charge of Hapsburg ambition and to diplomatic blindness.

There was one European country, long subject to all the miseries of military repression, religious discrimination, social inequality and political mismanagement for which the congress did and could do nothing. Ireland had gained a separate legislature in 1782, though Roman Catholics (and three-fourths of the Irish were of that faith) could not sit in it, or even vote for members until 1793. But the contagion of the French Revolution, and the promise of French aid, intensified the demand of the Irish for genuine independence. Fortunately for the British, ill-luck and ill-management thwarted the French expeditionary forces of 1796 and 1798, and the revolts incited by the United Irishmen ended in defeat and the death of Wolfe Tone, Robert Emmet, and other leaders. An Act of Union designed to reconcile Irish and English sentiments by giving Ireland a hundred representatives in the British parliament was passed in 1800. Pitt intended to follow it by further legislation permitting Roman Catholics to hold office, commuting the tithe which Irish Catholics paid for the support of the Anglican clergy, and providing an income for the Irish priests. But the obstinacy of George III blocked all attempts to improve the status of the Catholics and Pitt resigned (February, 1801). Discontent continued though violence declined after 1803, and the French failure to come to the aid of the Irish patriots with men and materials spared the British government a war which might have devoured its reserves as implacably as the Spanish conflict drained Napoleon's resources. With the defeat of the French in 1814 the hope of Irish independence definitely waned, and Ireland settled into a century of subjugation which crippled its agriculture and industry, poisoned its politics, and reduced its population. The injustice, so vehemently denounced, of which Poland remained the victim in 1815 was perpetrated by three governments, but the responsibility for the continued subjugation of Ireland rested with one.

It is no more than just, in passing judgment upon the work of the Vienna Congress, to ponder how many European provinces affected by its decisions were in reality as remote from its jurisdiction as Ireland or as insusceptible to an impartial collective decision as Poland. And it is easy to forget that, like the Paris Peace Conference of 1919, the older congress found all its major cases had been anticipated and prejudiced by preëxisting treaties. As early as 1798 the general outlines of the settlement had been framed: union of Belgium and Holland, compensation of Austria in Lombardy, compensation for Prussia in northern Germany, restoration of the Kingdom of Sardinia, guarantees for the independence of Switzerland, and the reduction of France to the limits of 1789 or even less. All the subsequent coalition treaties propounded the same general aims: they are to be found, avowed or implicit, in the Anglo-Russian alliance of 1805 which formed the basis of the Third Coalition; the Anglo-Austrian negotiations of 1809; the engagements concluded by Austria, Prussia and Russia at Töplitz in September, 1813; the grand alliance of Chaumont of March, 1814; the treaties arranged with a defeated France two months later and consummated in the Final Act signed at Vienna on June 9, 1815—all invoked the same general settlement, the restoration of equilibrium in Europe, the adjustment of the border states to "contain" France, the compensations so insistently claimed by the victors. Even the secondary questions, the return of Naples, the Papal States, and Spain to their "legitimate" rulers, the annexation of Finland to Russia, and the union of Norway and Sweden had been the subject of independent accords before the congress accepted them. What force of arms had achieved, diplomacy validated. The delegates who signed the Vienna protocol amended little and initiated less. Their chief labor consisted in devising compromises where previous agreements conflicted. Their decisions were recognized as constituting, in form and substance, a rebuke to the aspirations of nationalists throughout Europe, but they were hardly the authors of that rebuke. It would be more just to call them its instruments.

What doomed the liberal reform movement for a decade after 1814 was not betrayal but bankruptcy. The twin impulses which had carried it forward as part of the war effort suddenly slipped their yoke. In sponsoring reforms and appealing for popular support the Prussian, Russian, Austrian, and Spanish governments had been motivated by an immediate aim: the defeat of Napoleon. Their political, social, and military programs were conditioned to that aim, and were almost as inconceivable apart from it as their unprecedented but transitory coöperation in external affairs. Success doomed the domestic as it doomed the foreign policy. With the abdication of Napoleon the Quadruple Alliance lost its *raison d'être* and the reform measures lost their spurious momentum. Lacking any clear-cut alternative program of reform, and unwilling to proceed further with the revolutionary innovations which they had adopted from calculation rather than conviction, the European monarchs and statesmen reverted to the ideal of the *status quo ante*, that is to a policy of immobility. It is, of all political principles, the least inspiring, but it sufficed because Europe was avid for peace, and the active reform party, now in a minority, had no more persuasive principle to oppose to it. Twenty-five years earlier all Europe had been ready to celebrate the marriage of politics and philosophy, but the children of that stormy union had been the Jacobin commonwealth and the Napoleonic creations, and moderate-minded men everywhere had reached the conclusion that it was time to divorce the ill-mated pair. By 1814 the philosophy of Voltaire had fallen into disrepute, the eighteenth-century Utopia no longer beckoned so clearly, the old certitudes had dissolved. Nothing better illustrates the change of mood than the fate of the political theorist under the Restoration. Princes no longer invited *philosophes* to their courts, they set their police to harry them. Both revolutionaries and reactionaries, in the vacant aftermath which followed the War of Liberation, found themselves without an adequate principle to which they could appeal, but the despots had Talleyrand's formula of legitimacy, and if it lacked any profound historical or philosophical validity, it had enough pragmatic value to overcome the half-hearted resistance of the disillusioned liberals.[26]

[26] See, on this subject, the succeeding volume in this series, F. B. Artz, *Reaction and Revolution* (New York, 1934), chap. III, "The search for a principle of authority."

Chapter Ten

EUROPEAN THOUGHT AND CULTURE IN THE NAPOLEONIC ERA

I. THE REVOLT AGAINST THE PHILOSOPHY OF REASON

THE shallow and optimistic faith in the perfectability of man, a doctrine which won such wide acceptance in the later eighteenth century, depended for its foundation and authority upon the "philosophy of reason." Baldly stated, the tenets of rationalism as popularly conceived taught that all reality is intellectually knowable, that right reason could reduce society to a harmonious pattern ordained by Nature or by Nature's God, and that humanity, having accepted this revelation, stood on the threshold of a golden age to which the legislator held the key. By 1814 Europe had studied the fruits of this philosophy and found them to be discord, violence, and disillusionment. The result was an intellectual war of liberation, a deliberate campaign fought to turn back the march of those certitudes which had seemed so deceptively clear, so self-evident, to the generation of 1789. German thinkers, never profoundly convinced by the arguments of this school of thought, were the first to challenge and reject them.[1] Even in France "the philosophy of reason" lost much of its vogue after 1800. A narrowing group, ridiculed by Bonaparte as *idéologues*, intrenched themselves in the Institute, and continued to press their conclusions in the old doctrinaire fashion as if society were a branch of physics, but their stronghold, the *Académie des Sciences morales et politiques*, was suppressed in 1808. This group of social scientists, representing the persistence of the Cartesian and Newtonian traditions, had numbered in the first generation such honored names as Condillac, Turgot, and Condorcet. The second generation, headed by Cabanis and Destutt de Tracy, narrowed

[1] The degree to which this faith affected German thinkers, and their reaction to it, has been well analyzed by A. Stern, *Der Einfluss der Französischen Revolution auf das deutsche Geistesleben* (Stuttgart, 1928).

their emphasis to psycho-physical problems and laid the foundations for a positivist study of the mind. With the third generation, so rapid was the disintegration of the naturalistic, sensualistic, and mechanistic philosophy of the eighteenth century, the ideologists tended to lose themselves in Christian metaphysics.[2] The frustration and ridicule which overtook this group at a time when their colleagues in the physical sciences, Monge, Berthollet, and especially that French Newton, Laplace, were marching forward to fresh triumphs, is highly instructive. The Revolution had exposed the fallacy of their thinking, the fallacy of supposing that it was possible to conquer sciences of classification with a technique which yielded universal mathematical formulas only when it was applied to sciences of measurement. Their failure epitomizes in this respect the failure of the revolutionary philosophy.

But the *idéologues* were not the only victims. All along the intellectual front other rationalists found themselves attacked after 1800. Faith in pure democratic dogmas had already succumbed. No one after the reign of terror found it easy to defend the naïve belief embodied in the Jacobin motto that the force of reason and the force of the people are the same thing. But faith in reason as the one authoritative guide in social and political legislation was too fundamental a concept of the revolutionary philosophy to be easily repudiated; it was in fact the essence of the revolutionary philosophy, and Napoleon might claim to exemplify the principle where Robespierre had failed. Logically to challenge the Revolution, it was necessary to deny that reason itself was an adequate guide, to refute, for instance, the rational argument that the affairs of Europe could be more intelligently and more efficiently administered if Napoleonic institutions were imposed upon the continent as a whole, if the relics of feudalism were everywhere abolished, and the metric system, the prefectoral system and the French codes extended from Lisbon to Moscow. Under its older, more familiar formula of enlightened despotism the Revolution won more astounding victories in Europe after 1800 than it had before. Those who sought to resist its triumphant progress realized that they must turn their attack upon its

[2] F. Picavet, *Les idéologues, essai sur l'histoire des idées et des théories scientifiques, philosophiques, religieuses, etc., en France depuis 1789* (Paris, 1891), has traced the work of this group with remarkable breadth and clarity.

basic postulate, the proposition, namely, that only the customs, beliefs and institutions which could justify themselves before the bar of reason had a right to exist. This postulate had, in theory, sustained the whole fabric of revolutionary jurisprudence, and the opposition won its first resounding victory against jusnaturalism when Savigny published his critical attack, *On the Vocation of our Age for Legislation and Jurisprudence* (1814).

A true legislator, in the optimistic view of the *philosophes*, like a true geometrician or physicist, did not make laws, he discovered them, or discovered at least the natural principles which underlay and validated all civil legislation. Savigny summarized this legal philosophy with contemptuous brevity: "Men sought new codes, which would assure by their completeness a mechanical certainty in the administration of justice. The judge, spared the exercise of private opinion, was to be limited to a stark and literal interpretation. At the same time the codes were to be delivered from all historical variations, and to possess equal utility for all nations and all ages."[3] But, as Savigny objected, the times might not be ripe for a general codification of the law, and in his opinion were not ripe, particularly in Germany. An intelligent study of jurisprudence had been too long neglected, the German language was not yet mature, the historical background and evolution of existing laws were too little understood, and the arrogant superficiality of the rationalist philosophy was still too powerful. Not even the widespread adoption of the French civil code impressed this critical founder of the historical school of jurisprudence. He condemned the Napoleonic legislation as "a legal system which does not rest upon a firm foundation of historical knowledge and serves no loftier purpose than that of recording the practice of the courts."[4] Only after an exhaustive study of national institutions, he insisted, in the light of their historical origins and development, would jurists be competent to abridge and unify the laws of a state or draft a constitution.

It is doubtful, of course, whether the arguments advanced by Savigny (and by Burke before him) to prove that the revolutionary program violated the historical rules of proportion and continuity

[3] F. K. Savigny, *Vom Beruf unsrer Zeit für Gesetzgebung und Rechtswissenschaft* (Heidelberg, 1840), 5. This edition is a reproduction of the original essay.
[4] Savigny, *op. cit.*, 78-79.

converted people not already disposed to respect those rules. A much larger audience, even an illiterate audience, could be reached by the simpler affirmation that the philosophy of reason was wrong because it was amoral. Reason, which dissolved the foundations of religious faith, could offer no substitute sanction for moral behavior which proved equally satisfying. In nature there are neither rewards nor punishments, there are only consequences, and the society of the *civitas humana*, resting on Nature's laws, possessed no clear justification for a sense of moral obligation. This problem had haunted many of the eighteenth century *philosophes*, themselves anxious to be esteemed men of virtue, and had more than once cast a cloud over their confident speculations: "It is as if, at high noon of the Enlightenment, at the hour of the siesta when everything seems so quiet and secure all about, one were suddenly aware of a short, sharp slipping of the foundations, a faint far-off tremor running underneath the solid ground of common sense."[5] Immanuel Kant, in the quiet of his Königsberg study, rightly recognized that the formulation of a rational foundation for a science of ethics was the most challenging philosophical issue of the revolutionary age and dedicated the profoundest speculations of his closing years to its solution. But he failed to find a sanction for morality in the phenomenal world, and was driven to predicate in each individual the existence of an intuitive ethical sense as well as an element of "radical evil," and to presuppose the existence of God and the immortality of the soul as unprovable but indispensable postulates. Metaphysics, so consistently scorned by the *philosophes*, was taking its revenge upon rationalism.[6]

In a second important respect German idealism demonstrated its capacity to liberate the European mind from the constrictive axioms of the rationalists. The reverence which the latter preserved towards the physical and mathematical sciences had inclined them to seek as the pattern of the perfect society a formula essentially static, a ground-plan from which social principles could be deduced by reason as Euclid demonstrated the relationships of a triangle.[7] German

[5] C. L. Becker, *The Heavenly City of the Eighteenth Century Philosophers* (New Haven, 1932), 68-69.

[6] The *Rechtslehre* and the *Tugendlehre* in which Kant developed his final conclusions on the ethical problem both appeared in 1797.

[7] In this connection the reader may consult with profit the thoughtful essay of A. Lewkowitz, *Die klassische Rechts- und Staatsphilosophie, Montesquieu bis Hegel* (Breslau, 1914).

thinkers, even when they turned to probe the physical sciences, were not so completely fascinated by the invariability of the laws deduced that they ignored the problem of origins, as Kant indicated by his speculations on the genesis of the planetary system, in which he anticipated Laplace by fifty years. Several of the post-Kantian idealists, notably Schelling, approached the concept of a general theory of evolution, and Hegel's vast influence, though contradictory in this as in most aspects, served to popularize the notion that social development had been a progressive evolution from a simpler to a more complex state. His defense of the state as the expression of a moral idea and a demonstration of God's increasing purpose in the world is the antithesis of the mechanistic view of society and helped to displace it; but a secondary tendency in his thought, the reverence for enlightened authority and its energizing function in political administration, which led him to hail Napoleon as an embodiment of the World Spirit and prompted his later admiration for the Prussian bureaucracy, stems from the *Aufklärung* and the faith in benevolent despotism. Hegel's thought is, indeed, a solvent for, rather than a system of, ideas. But the credit may justly be claimed for him that with the publication of his *Phänomenologie des Geistes* (1807) he projected for the first time in recognizable form the central task of nineteenth-century philosophy, the explanation of how the universe and man came to be what they are in the fullness of time. If his solution, the first comprehensive answer proposed for this emerging challenge, proved unsatisfactory, the fault is attributable to his idealist predilections which led him to postulate the Absolute as Mind and infuse into the world-machine the concept of immanent spirit, which ordains the progress recognized as history under a law of inherent necessity, a sort of "prophetic soul of this wide world dreaming on things to come." Half a century later Herbert Spencer undertook the same challenging task from a positivist approach, with a degree of success which would have gratified a Condorcet or a Cabanis. For Spencer had the benefit of Utilitarian and Darwinian speculations to provide a genealogy of morals without reference to a transcendental sanction.[8] The revolutionary philosophy thus received an answer to

---

[8] J. T. Merz, *A History of European Thought in the Nineteenth Century*, 4 vols. (Edinburgh, 1914), IV, 529-535.

its most troublesome problem, and closed a major breach in its defense, but the resolution came nearly a century too late and found the European mind still unprepared to accept it.

A third characteristic of German philosophy in the early nineteenth century, in which it differed from the philosophy of reason, was the emphasis it placed upon effort as more important than ultimate achievement. The mechanically perfect society, vaguely suggestive of an idealized and enduring China, which the *philosophes* delighted to paint, had a quality reminiscent of More's *Utopia* in that the citizens could not fail to be happy because they "could not choose but be good." Yet it was by no means certain, as Burke pointed out, that man was made for happiness; it seemed, on the contrary, almost indubitable that he was born to trouble as the sparks fly upward. Toil and conflict were the salutary conditions of his existence. "Human history," Hegel observed, "is not a garden of felicity. The periods of good fortune form its emptiest pages." This conviction that all creation labored and that man obeyed his duty and his destiny by living strenuously, a theme to be amplified subsequently by Schopenhauer and Nietzsche, darkly mirrored the grim encouragement later to be drawn from the doctrine of the survival of the fittest. But the ideal, as formulated by German thinkers in the first years of the century, was endowed with their inevitable ethical implications. "Nature," affirmed Novalis, with his customary flair for incisive generalization, "ought not to be expounded as a state of immobility, but as an active progression towards morality."[9] It would be difficult to find a phrase that sums up more succinctly the divergence between the French and the German, the rationalist and the idealist schools of this period.

II. CLASSICAL AND ROMANTIC INFLUENCES IN LITERATURE AND ART

In France the last decade of the eighteenth century saw the classical standards in literature hold firm, while political and social institutions dissolved. But few French works of outstanding merit were written during the revolutionary stress, if one excepts the poems of

[9] E. Spenlé, *Novalis: essai sur l'idéalisme romantique en Allemagne* (Paris, 1904), 216.

André Chénier.[10] German writers, better able to cultivate the leisure necessary for creative labors, endeavored to reconcile the divergent tendencies of the time into a harmonious and artistic formula. The violence of the *Sturm und Drang* movement had spent its force before 1789, the wave of romantic and patriotic emotionalism which swept the nation in the early years of the nineteenth century had not yet broken. In the interval, the best German minds sought to bring the awakening passion for social justice and the romantic yearning for the ideal within the bounds of decorum, and to preserve those standards of moderation and harmonious self-development which they respected as the noblest expression of the classical discipline. Schiller, though honored with French citizenship by the revolutionaries who admired the democratic sentiments of *Die Räuber*, turned against the Jacobin madness after 1792. Sobered by his historical studies, he revealed in his later dramas, particularly in the *Wallenstein* trilogy (1799) and *Die Braut von Messina* (1803) a growing preoccupation with classical formulas and the problem of the moral regeneration of the individual. His last drama, *Wilhelm Tell* (1804), which celebrated Tell's patriotic defiance of foreign oppression, was prophetic of the nationalistic passion which was to inflame the Germans ten years later in their war of liberation against Napoleon.

In 1799 Schiller moved to Weimar to be nearer Goethe, and the two dominated the culminating period of the "Weimar School." Goethe's admiration for classical forms had been intensified by his Italian journey (1786-1788), and in 1798 the author of *Die Leiden des jungen Werther* produced *Hermann und Dorothea*, his most "classic" poem. A deeper veneration for the virtues of objectivity and discipline had given him a saner and more earnest view of life, already perceptible in *Wilhelm Meisters Lehrjahre* (1795-1796), but his attempts at classical drama struck a cold and formal note amid the mounting chorus of the romantic revolt. The best evidence that Goethe's protean genius comprehended the contemporary reversion from the rigidity and abstraction of classical forms, and from the static ideals of the rationalists to the infinite aspirations of the

---

[10] For a survey and analysis of the progress of the fine arts and literature in Europe during the last years of the eighteenth century the reader may consult the preceding volume in this series, C. Brinton, *A Decade of Revolution, 1789-1799* (New York, 1934), 246-259.

romanticists, may be found (as what may not?) in his *Faust*, the first part of which appeared in 1808. Defeated in the search for ultimate truth by the limitations of natural science, Faust turns, as the idealist school was turning, to necromancy and to transcendental inspiration. The final wisdom which rewards his quest may perhaps be taken as Goethe's judgment on the hopes of the revolutionary age, for Faust concludes that surety is unattainable, that the best any man can ask or procure is freedom for active labor, and that only those deserve such freedom who each day conquer it anew:

> *Nur der verdient sich Freiheit wie das Leben*
> *Der täglich sie erobern muss.*

But few of the romanticists possessed Goethe's classical admixture of moderation and balance, and fewer still could view the drama of human frustration with his Olympian calm. The Romantic School of the early nineteenth century was a lost generation that died young or lived on the memory of a withered ecstasy. Even the sober Wordsworth, remembering the visions which had dazzled his French friends in 1791, could confess that it was bliss in those days to be alive and that to be young was very heaven. But with the fading of the "vision splendid" Wordsworth learned to cultivate a sense of duty for support and espoused a mild Anglicanism. "His *Ecclesiastical Sonnets* are the Anglican counterpart, on a much narrower basis, of Chateaubriand's *Génie du Christianisme*."[11] With Chateaubriand the search for a city of the soul, wherein he could find certainty after disillusionment, and serenity after spiritual anguish, was a more urgent quest than Goethe or Wordsworth knew, and it drove him into the arms of the church. Resigning his post in the French diplomatic service after the execution of the Duc d'Enghien, he started on a journey to Jerusalem (1806). It was a symbolic pilgrimage and *Les Martyrs*, which he published after his return, reflected his concept of the clash between pagan and Christian standards, a conflict of which his whole generation were the modern victims.

The persistent and lyrical *Weltschmerz* of the romanticists was the symptom of an inner disharmony, though it was clearly aggravated for the more liberal-minded by the political reaction after 1815.

[11] *Cambridge History of English Literature*, XI (Cambridge, 1914), 108.

It was a favorite affectation of theirs, not wholly unfounded, that tragedy had marked them for her own. Coleridge and De Quincy were victims of the opium habit, Byron and Shelley were exiles from conventional society, Keats and Novalis were consumptives, Heinrich von Kleist's haunted days ended in suicide, Hölderlin's in madness. The malady of the spirit which affected all but the sanest of the school lent to their work its unachieved quality; their insistent theme was frustration, their inspirations moved them to lyric protests of excelling beauty, but they lacked the architectonic sense required for sustained dramas. Their extreme subjectivism remained in large degree an escapist phenomenon and they created ideal poetic worlds because in practical activities they encountered an unendurable feeling of limitation, of abdication. When a whole generation responds to such a mood it becomes a challenge to the historian, and Georg Brandes has offered the interesting explanation that the Revolution, by throwing down social barriers, left superior and sensitive youths without the traditional consolations when they failed (as most of them were doomed to fail) in the quest for fame.[12] As compensation they identified themselves with the heroes of the current romances, those superb and tragic rebels who bruised themselves against the world's incomprehension or stung their souls to death with blasphemies. In support of Brandes' theory it may be urged that romantic literature appealed most strongly to the ambitious middle classes and its popularity reflects the triumph of bourgeois tastes. But it is probable, too, that the romantic spirit, so subtly compounded of ennui and revolt, so insistently preoccupied with far times and places and with exotic lore, was the after effect of a dawn vision flashed upon receptive minds and too suddenly withdrawn. For those who had sipped the heady brew distilled by the *philosophes* the mundane world became insupportable and fantasy a necessary drug. *Die Poesie ist das echt absolut Reelle,* Novalis proclaimed dogmatically; but he also added the half-nostalgic confession, *Der Geist der Poesie ist das Morgenlicht.*[13]

Elements of romanticism can be found in every age and the roots of the Romantic Revolt have been traced far back into the eight-

[12] G. Brandes, *Main Currents of Nineteenth Century Literature,* 6 vols. (London, 1923), I, 39-42.
[13] E. Spenlé, *op. cit.,* 2.

eenth century and before, but the sudden exotic flowering of that movement is a phenomenon difficult to account for without reference to the intellectual mood at the turn of the century. The year 1798, memorable in literary annals, saw the collaboration of Wordsworth and Coleridge bear fruit in *Lyrical Ballads*, while in Berlin Ludwig Tieck, the brothers Schlegel, and Novalis (Friedrich von Hardenberg) provided the German Romantic School with an independent organ in the *Athenäum*. At the same time Chateaubriand was exploring the romantic possibilities of French prose in his *Atala* (1800) and Madame de Staël in her *Delphine* (1802). Scott had already translated Goethe's *Götz von Berlichingen*, and was collecting material for his *Border Minstrelsy*. Romanticism, in its most intense and characteristic expression, was born with the century, and despite the lively interest many of its exponents showed in each other's efforts, an interest which transcended linguistic and political barriers, the universality of the movement cannot be accounted for on the ground of literary imitation. The misanthropic De Sénancour, for instance, in his Swiss retreat, yielded to the same melancholy and struck the same notes as the German romanticists whom he had not read, and his *Obermann*, published unostentatiously in 1804, remains perhaps the most individual, most personal, and at the same time most typical expression of the *maladie du siècle*.

Nor is it fortuitous that in these same years Beethoven was shattering the "classical" forms of Haydn and Mozart with his titanic originalities, which paralleled the innovations of Bonaparte (he was one year younger), in the political sphere. By 1800 he had composed the *First Symphony* and essayed the field of the drama and oratorio; the *Eroica*, completed in 1804, he first dedicated to Napoleon, but withdrew his homage when he saw the Prometheus transformed into a despot. In his final period, after 1814, domestic worries and increasing deafness fretted his genius, and it may well be that the fading of the revolutionary vision helped to darken his spirit. His attempt to celebrate the Allied victories with a *Battle Symphony* resulted in a work of confused inspiration which he rightly considered *eine Dummheit*, and the years 1815 and 1816 were among the least productive in his career. The *Ninth Sym-*

phony, over which he labored from 1817 to 1823, proved the most unreal, the most subjective in spirit, of his major works. When his compositions are considered as a whole, however, their originality of structure and instrumentation, freshness of approach, beauty of form, and power of suggestion justify the veneration which has been paid to his memory as the founder of modern music.

Beethoven's younger contemporary, Carl Maria von Weber, shares with him the honor of opening the vast storehouse of romantic music, for under his inspiration the romantic opera liberated itself from the affectations and the conventionality of the Italian models. In 1800 his first opera, *Das Waldmädchen,* revealed those gifts of imagination, warmth, and color which enabled him to enthrall his generation. His fame has eclipsed that of several able composers, Joseph Weigl, Friedrich Heinrich Himmel, Ignaz von Seyfried, who anticipated him, and others, such as Ludwig Spohr and Heinrich Marschner, who were his equals, if not in talent, at least in their enthusiastic attachment to the new operatic form.

In Italy at the opening of the nineteenth century, the opera, ever responsive to the demands of the audience, had tended to become vapid or sensational save in the hands of composers with exceptional force and originality. Not a few of these found that their greatest reward and stimulus lay north of the Alps, and it was such expatriates who first learned to fuse the melodious Italian style with the more powerful harmonies of the German composers. Ferdinando Paër, after five years at Vienna, where he became acquainted with the methods of Mozart and Beethoven, went to Dresden as choirmaster in 1802, and was later invited to Paris by Napoleon. Gasparo Spontini, who likewise betook himself to Paris (1803), initiated a new style with his historical operas *Milton* and *La Vestale.* The greatest Italian composer who emerged in this period, Gioachino Rossini, achieved a European reputation by his technical skill, versatility, and vivacity before he, too, moved to Vienna (1822) and later to Paris. His later work, as well as that of his fellow countrymen, Gaetano Donizetti and Vincenzo Bellini, fell in the period after 1815, when the revived Italian opera acquired an influence which lasted until the middle of the century. Although Paris enjoyed unique prestige under the Empire as a center where both the *opéra comique* and grand opera were encouraged and appreciated, and both these forms as developed there acquired a spirit and distinction peculiarly French, the most successful composers were not Frenchmen. This is the more surprising in view of the official patronage. As head of the newly created *Conservatoire de musique*, Bernard Sarrette disposed of a liberal subsidy for the training of talented pupils and the *Prix de Rome* was established in 1803.

In the representative arts the pantheism of the nature poets found a reflection in the *beseelte Landschaften* of the romantic painters. Of these the most typical was perhaps Caspar David Friedrich, the friend of Heinrich von Kleist and Ludwig Tieck, whose canvases celebrate so seductively the mystic love of Nature and the fatherland. Ruined monasteries, hoary oaks, the magic of moonrise or the immensity of the sea are his recurrent themes, and, despite a spiritual affinity with contemporary English masters of the romantic landscape, Friedrich reveals moods more profound than those of Constable and conceptions less fantastic than those of Turner. With him, but expressive of the south rather than of the north German spirit, may be linked Wilhelm von Kobell, whose reproductions of the scenery about Munich set the spirit free with their lifted horizons. To pass from the soul-infused nature-world of Friedrich and Kobell to the "heroic landscapes" of Joseph Anton Koch, each formally organized as a stage for allegorical figures after the style of the Nazarene School, and thence to the balanced compositions and statuesque forms of Louis Joseph David, is to traverse the distance separating the romantic and the classical traditions. For at Paris classicism was still triumphant. David sketched his characters as nude athletes before he clothed them; and his pupils, immortalizing the glories of the First Empire with heroic battle scenes or epochal ceremonies, never seemed able to forget that they were portraying a people which was acting its dream, not dreaming its actions. The official empire style, precise without subtlety, ornamental without imagination, bespeaks the strength and the limitations of the French spirit in these years as surely as Lawrence's classic portraits perpetuate the arrogant assurance of the English ruling classes in the same period. To place Gros' *Meeting of Napoleon and the Emperor of Austria*

beside the stark and horrible canvases on which Goya pictured
incidents from the Peninsular War or the *Sehnsucht* of Friedrich's
Moonrise over the Sea is to comprehend, at least in some small
measure, the imperious conviction of the French in these years
that the First Empire, like the ancient Roman Empire, was an
island of noonday clarity and order environed by an irrational
twilight world where the shadows of fanaticism, superstition, and
mysticism had not yet been lifted.

In the fields of sculpture and architecture neo-classicism, which
had revealed its strength before 1789 in the *Panthéon* and the colon-
nades of the Place de la Concorde, preserved an almost unchal-
lenged sway. Antonio Canova, founder of the modern classical
school in sculpture, alternated between Rome and Paris during
the Empire; the Dane, Thorwaldsen, drawn irresistibly to the
capital of the ancient world, surpassed the native Italians in his
ability to imitate the power and serenity of the antique monuments. The classical tradition dominated the style of the First
Empire so powerfully that even errant Egyptian influences were
subdued to it;[14] the conception of the triumphal arches and of the
Vendôme Column was designed to unite Napoleon's fame with
that of the Cæsars, and the *Madeleine Church* is a pagan temple
dedicated to Christian worship. Architecture yields but slowly to
new influences and the neo-classic style remained dominant even
in Germany until far into the nineteenth century. At its best it
inspired such compact and symmetrical buildings as *Die Wache,*
designed by Karl Friedrich Schinkel in 1816, and the *Munich Pro-
phylaea* with its strong combination of Greek and Egyptian forms,
the work of Leo von Klenze. But neo-classical architecture, even
in the hands of the masters, betrayed an alien origin in its in-
tractable externality which resisted adaptation to current needs.
The *Schauspielhaus* at Berlin might be mistaken for anything except a theater, and the *Nikolai-Kirche* at Potsdam, though it has
been much admired, fails to induce the desired sense of strength
and unity because it is a temple rather than a church, and the

[14] Egyptian *motifs* had already acquired a minor vogue in Paris before 1798 when
Bonaparte's expedition to the east popularized them. Illustrations of their adaptation to the
classical trend, particularly in furniture and interior decorating, may be found in
P. Marmottan, *Le style empire*, 4 vols. (Paris, 1920-1927).

massive dome dwarfs the beautiful colonnaded porch and makes it appear an afterthought. Almost all the neo-classical edifices retain the power to impress, but they are likely to trouble the observer with an obstinate suggestion of incongruity, like a seashell, perfect in design, which is found on closer scrutiny to be empty of life, or to house an extraneous organism.

III. THE SCIENCES

Napoleon stands almost alone among the rulers of his day in his appreciation of the scope and utility of the current scientific investigations.[15] The report submitted to him in 1808 by Delambre and Cuvier *On the Progress of the Mathematical and Physical Sciences since 1789* demonstrates how conclusively France might then claim to be the true home of the scientific spirit. Between 1799 and 1814 Laplace, in the first four volumes of his *Mécanique céleste*, dispelled the last doubts that had been urged against Newton's principle of gravitation as an adequate explanation of the mechanics of the solar system. Monge, head of the newly established *École Polytechnique*, founded the science of descriptive geometry through his application of graphical methods to mathematical problems. Chemistry, already transformed into an exact science by the researches of Lavoisier, before the guillotine terminated his experiments in 1794, had been drafted into the service of the state, and Berthollet at the *École Normale* made new discoveries yearly on the extraction of needed salts or the casting of better cannon. At the same time Gay-Lussac in his laboratory was pressing less practical but no less momentous researches which he published in 1809 as the law of combining proportions for gases.

Pride in their own achievements, however, did not blind French scientists to the discoveries made in other lands. William Herschel's

[15] Napoleon has often been criticized for a lack of scientific imagination because of his failure to utilize Fulton's plans for a steamboat and a submarine, but the blame rests chiefly upon the committee of investigation. An account af the tests conducted by the French ministry of marine can be found in H. W. Dickinson, *Robert Fulton, Engineer and Artist* (London, 1913), and W. B. Parsons, *Robert Fulton and the Submarine* (New York, 1922). The first steamboat which Fulton launched on the Seine sank immediately, and negotiations regarding the submarine were apparently delayed by the inventor's insistence that he must have letters guaranteeing him against the possible penalties of piracy. For some interesting documents hitherto overlooked in this connection see H. Furber, "Fulton and Napoleon in 1800, new light on the submarine *Nautilus*," *American Historical Review*, XXXIX (1934), 489-494.

calculation of the motion of the solar system in space (1783) and his demonstration that the law of gravitation applied to the fixed stars (1802), Dalton's atomic theory made public in his *New System of Chemical Philosophy* (1808), and Avogadro's brilliant conjecture that, under the same conditions of temperature and pressure, equal volumes of different gases must contain the same number of molecules, were accepted as striking proofs that the mechanism of the universe had been laid bare. If atoms could be taken as the ultimate building-blocks of matter and laws formulated for them as invariable as those which Laplace and Herschel found everywhere in space, the day seemed near at hand when the entire realm of matter would be reduced to an intelligible order. Laplace was moved to a prophecy which expressed in all its grandeur the dream inspiring the mathematical physicist: "A mind which for a given moment apprehends all the forces animating Nature and the reciprocal impulses from which they arise, and subjects these data to mathematical analysis, could include in the same formula the movements of the largest celestial bodies and the smallest atoms. Past and future would be one in its sight."[16]

Carried away by the same vision of a calculable universe composed of indestructible units, Dalton affirmed the principle of the conservation of matter with dogmatic assurance, asserting that the chemist could no more create or destroy an atom than he could add or subtract a planet in the solar system. The successive triumphs in physics, astrophysics and mathematics were sweeping the more enthusiastic materialists towards an impasse. They might well have recalled Napoleon's common-sense rebuke when he was accused of desiring absolute power: the position of God Almighty, he objected, *c'est un cul-de-sac*. Fortunately for the advancement of knowledge the German idealists were propounding at the same moment the salutary truth that to recognize the finite is to transcend it; and investigators in other fields of science had already indicated the corridors by which the European mind was to escape the prison of the mechanistic hypothesis.

In mathematics itself Gauss published before 1815 his concep-

[16] F. Dannemann, *Die Naturwissenschaften in ihrer Entwicklung und in ihrem Zusammenhange,* 4 vols. (Leipzig, 1920-1923), III, 128.

tions of the continuous and the infinite, conceptions which, developed by Cauchy, were to open the door to the most notable developments of subsequent mathematical thought. Rumford and Sadi-Carnot were preparing the way for an enunciation of the law of the conservation of energy through their researches on the mechanical equivalent of heat. Volta, who announced his voltaic pile in 1800, Ampère, and others had presented the young century with their investigations into the nature of electricity and magnetism. Thomas Young, Humphry Davy and Malus, experimenting with light rays and their polarization, forecast the substitution of the wave for the corpuscular theory of transmission. These investigations were prophetic of the prominent place the concept of energy, as distinguished from the concept of mass, was to assume in nineteenth-century thought. No serious effort seems to have been made at this time, however, to challenge the Newtonian definition of mass as an absolute constant. It remained for the twentieth century and the theory of relativity to provide the conclusion that mass is a function that varies with velocity. This and other dramatic reversals of principle in the past century have made modern physicists less dogmatic in their claims, and it is instructive to contrast the implicit assumption of the more arrogant rationalists of the eighteenth century, that everything in the universe was revealing itself as rationally as man's irrational mind could comprehend, with the quaint warning recently offered by Nils Bohr that everything in the universe seems to be behaving as oddly as it can, or at any rate as oddly as our orderly minds will allow it to.

The most notable achievement of nineteenth-century thought, the theory of biological evolution, had faint foreshadowings as early as 1800, particularly in the speculations of Lamarck and Geoffroy Saint-Hilaire in France, and the theories of Schelling, Goethe, and Oken in Germany. But the extraordinary prestige of Cuvier, whose *Leçons d'anatomie comparée* appeared between 1800 and 1805, to be followed by his comprehensive *Règne animal distribué d'après son organisation* in 1817, discredited the search for a common genetic origin for all organic forms. So long as the biblical chronology, which limited the age of the earth to a few thousand years, or the faith in catastrophism, which ascribed its conformation to a series of epochal upheavals, continued to dominate the field, the eons of unbroken development required for a differentiation of species could not be predicated. Cuvier himself insisted repeatedly that no force now active in shaping the surface of the globe could account for the successive geological formations or the extinct species of terrestrial life which investigation had revealed. Saint-Hilaire justly accused him, in their celebrated controversy, of pursuing in his great task of classification the *distinctions* which characterize organic forms while neglecting the more challenging problem of the *analogies* to be noted in them, analogies which might provide the clue to a uniform theory of biological development. Cuvier's habits of thought reflect both the strength and the weakness of the French scientific school with its emphasis upon exact observation, systematic analysis and patient classification. Had he speculated more imaginatively, as Buffon had done before him, on the possibility of the mutability of species and the causes that would account for it, he might have developed further the theory of evolutionary descent suggested by his colleague Lamarck in his *Philosophie zoölogique* (1809). But he missed, despite his enormous labors, the single integrating principle he had hoped to find, and the biological sciences had to wait for the clues provided by the geologists.

It fell to a Scotsman, James Hutton, to offer the first adequate arguments that would sustain a "uniformitarian" explanation of geologic processes. Hutton published his speculations in 1785 in his *Theory of the Earth*, but they attracted little attention until 1802 when another Scotsman, John Playfair, defended them in his *Illustrations of the Huttonian Theory of the Earth*, and they did not receive their full vindication until yet a third Scotsman, Charles Lyell, presented the classical defense for the uniformitarian theory in his *Principles of Geology* (1830-1833). But Hutton had divined the central principle that the slow agencies still observable at work altering the earth's face might be held to explain all past geologic changes, without invoking special acts of God or catastrophic interventions. The extraordinary lapse of time required for these changes, whether effected by the agency of water as the Neptunists pretended, or by fire as the Vulcanists assumed, remained a major objection, but even this difficulty had been attacked by 1808 through the researches of a German geologist, Leopold von Buch. After two years spent in analyzing the rocks of the Scandinavian Peninsula, Buch decided that some of them were older than the greatest age credited to the earth, a conclusion which suggested, as Goethe observed with irony, that the children were more ancient than the parent.

The steps whereby Charles Darwin applied the principle of uniform natural agencies to explain developments in the organic realm lies outside the period under discussion. But it is of interest to note how shrewdly, in their revolt against the philosophy of reason, the German thinkers had invoked half-intuitively and half-emotionally the one principle which could successfully join battle with the rationalist *système d'analyse*. Both the historical and the transcendental school of anti-rationalists found a vicarious vindication in the later conquests won by the genetic view of nature, to which even French thought, belatedly and with reluctance, was forced to bow after 1860.

IV. THE RELIGIOUS REVIVAL

As if stricken nerveless by Voltaire's battle-cry *écrasez l'infâme*, the champions of the Church Militant no longer rode forth to battle in the eighteenth century, and the forts of orthodoxy, once so prompt to discharge their thunders, remained curiously mute. The Society of Jesus, erstwhile spearhead of the Catholic Reformation, and exemplar of that discipline which was the strength and glory of the church, *religionis et ecclesiae catholicae splendor et columen,* disintegrated under the rationalist assault and was dissolved in 1773.[17] The spread of religious toleration, deism, and agnosticism vitiated those dogmatic distinctions for which men had shed their blood a century earlier, and the rationalists, always overeager to identify religion with ritual and superstition, fell into the error of supposing that the religious impulse itself had spent its force. To support this view they pointed to the moribund condition of the

[17] The brief of Clement XIV dissolving the order can be found in C. Mirbt, ed., *Quellen zur Geschichte des Papsttums und des Römischen Katholizismus,* 4th ed. (Tübingen, 1924), 404-411.

established churches, Catholic, Anglican, and Lutheran, in which a spirit of formalism reigned that sometimes degenerated into apathy. Elements of the population, especially in Protestant countries, which still yearned for a faith that was fervent and heart-warming, turned to the evangelical sects. In England and Germany the pietist movements grew rapidly throughout the revolutionary era, and the emphasis they set upon religion as a matter of inward emotion rather than outward observance, a personal quest for God instead of a belief in a body of doctrine, is closely related in mood to the romantic revolt in literature and the transcendental currents in philosophy.

In the speculations of such German theosophists as Franz von Baader and Adam Müller the religious spirit assumed the function which the rationalists ascribed to reason: it appears as the clarifying and unifying principle which should inspire the formulas of good government and regulate the social relations of men.[18] Not the imposition from without of enlightened decrees, but the inner, spiritual rebirth of the individual citizen was the miracle which, according to these mystics, must precede the establishment of peace on earth and goodwill towards men. How deeply these doctrines influenced Alexander of Russia in his later years is still a matter of dispute, but there is no doubt that he was strongly attracted to them.[19] German mysticism, because of its subtle invasion of all contemporary fields of thought, exerted an effect not easy to calculate. Apparently it aided Alexander to recognize one grave shortcoming of the political philosophy of the Enlightenment, the tendency, namely, to "atomize" society, a defect which Napoleon also criticized and sought to repair. The attractions and repulsions which swayed the members of a social group could not safely be regarded as analogous to the laws which prevailed in mechanics or kinetics, for men possessed and were bound by loyalties which knit them into organic rather than mechanical aggregates. Hence the

[18] For the religious and political ideas of the German theosophists the reader may consult D. Baumgart, *Franz von Baader und die philosophische Romantik* (Halle, 1927); J. Baxa, *Adam Müller, ein Lebensbild aus den Befreiungskriegen und aus der deutschen Restauration* (Jena, 1930); and H. Schaeder, *Die dritten Koalition und die Heilige Allianz* (Königsberg, 1934).

[19] R. Kayser, "Zar Alexander I und die deutsche Erweckung," *Theologische Studien und Kritiken,* CIV (1932), 160-185.

failure of Reason to provide, for instance, a satisfactory justification for national sentiments, a limitation from which many German patriots escaped by resting their cause with God. "A Nation," Fichte protested, "is no fortuitous society of individuals within the mechanism of a state, but a unique and autochthonous species created by the Eternal." If plants and animals could retain their independent form through countless generations, he insisted that nations no less might be considered as "seedlings of the Godhead."[20]

But if society were indeed held together by mystical bonds which the reason could not justify, it followed that these vital bonds could only be sanctioned and preserved through traditional observance and a mystic reverence. Hence, as Kant decided in his old age, positive or statutory religion was useful to a society because it could impress upon the unthinking those ethical imperatives which were engraved, however obscurely, in every soul.[21] Eight years later Bonaparte proved that he had reached the same pragmatic conclusion when he restored the Catholic faith in France as a social preservative against the inroads of anarchy. "The godless man," he commented, "I have watched him at work since 1793. One does not govern such a man, one shoots him. I have had enough of his breed."[22] An established cult provided the simplest and most effective means of training the ignorant and imperceptient to respect those rules of moral decency and civic obedience without which they were a menace to their neighbors. All sects were equal in the eyes of an enlightened administrator, in so far as they contributed to this end. Napoleon secured a working arrangement with the Protestant churches in France, and encouraged the organization of consistories (1808) to provide for a more systematic control over the Jewish citizens of the Empire.[23] Priests, pastors and rabbis

[20] A. Lewkowitz, *Die klassische Rechts- und Staatsphilosophie, Montesquieu bis Hegel* (Breslau, 1914), 88.

[21] Kant's *Religion innerhalb der Grenzen der blossen Vernunft* (1793), in which he attempted to show that valuable ethical truths are buried in the doctrines of the Christian sects, brought him, ironically enough, into difficulties with orthodox minds, and he received a warning from the court to keep within the bounds of philosophy.

[22] G. Hanotaux, "Du consulat à l'empire: issue napoléonienne de la Révolution," *Revue des deux mondes*, XXVI (1925), 102.

[23] The general opinion that the reform program of the later eighteenth century offered unmixed advantages to the Jews is only partly justified. The emphasis set by the reformers upon toleration and civil equality could hardly fail to improve the lot of a class which had endured so many legal and political disadvantages. But the rationalists were in some respects scarcely less hostile to Jewish customs and religious practices than the

were expected to justify the ways of the emperor towards his subjects as part of their mission, and were at the same time cautioned against the temptation to indulge in political criticism or to excite undue religious enthusiasm. The mild revival of Catholic sentiment in France under the Consulate and Empire was a phenomenon which progressed independently of the official program, and the growing influence and assurance of the priesthood would almost certainly have become a matter of concern to Napoleon had he reigned another decade.

The temper and the policy of the imperial régime remained severely secular and rational despite the concordat with the church. Napoleon was too intelligent to make martyrs of the clergy as the revolutionary assemblies had done, but he had no intention of making them masters again even in their own house: in that he was true to the traditions of the Enlightenment. Lamennais, one of the most profound social thinkers of his generation, recognized that the struggle between the revolutionary and the counter-revolutionary forces was at bottom a war of conflicting evangels; that in the prophets of the rationalist school the Roman Catholic Church was fighting not atheists, but heresiarchs; and that any accord which it might reach with them on their own ground would be a pact with death. "They adore *Science* under the name of human reason," he wrote with his flying pen. "Science, for certain minds, is the God of the universe. They have no faith save in this God, they hope for nothing save through him; his wisdom and his power shall replenish the earth, and by rapid advances elevate man to a degree of felicity and perfection that transcends his imagination."[24] The aftermath of such a vain Utopian dream is certain to be a winter of discontent, and Lamennais wrote his *Essai sur l'indifférence en matière de religion* in the midst of it. "Who can say what are the doctrines of the governments, what the beliefs of the peoples?" he

Christian dogmatists had been. See H. Brunschwig, "La lutte d'Aufklärung contre les orthodoxes juifs en Prusse à la fin du dix-huitième siècle," *Annales historiques de la Révolution française*, No. 77 (1936), 436-459. Napoleon's attempt to assimilate the Jewish minority into French society, by restricting their commercial activities and forbidding exemption from military service to Jewish youths, dismayed the objects of it and met with small success. It has been admirably discussed by R. Anchel, *Napoléon et les juifs* (Paris, 1928), 353-411.

[24] H. F. de Lamennais, *Essai sur l'indifférence en matière de religion* (Paris, 1859), II, 15. The *essai* was first published between 1817 and 1820.

asked in 1820. "One sees nothing but a chaos of irreconcilable ideas, and in the people a violence, and in the sovereigns an irresolution that is ominous of sinister tomorrows."[25] The remedy, as he saw it, was to reëstablish a true principle of authority. Reaso.: had failed her devotees, the generation which came of age after 1810 were children of disillusionment, and as they felt the philosophical foundations of the *civitas humana* failing beneath their feet they might be persuaded to lift their eyes to the *civitas Dei*. But the true gospel must be able to offer them certainties as vigorous, conquests as glorious as the false had done, must find a way to capture and convert to noble uses that passion for social justice which inflamed the age. Lamennais was a revolutionary reformer within the Roman Catholic Church and he suffered the fate that frequently befalls such spirits: he died outside it.

For the religious revival which followed the French Revolution remained in its official aspects a pragmatic program, not a moral or a humanitarian crusade. Too many churchmen were preoccupied, like the returning *émigrés*, with the quest for lost privileges and emoluments, too few with the question of their own function in post-revolutionary society. Restoration monarchs, who labored to wrap the tendrils of tradition about their shaken thrones and to resurrect the altar as a bulwark against revolution, often entertained towards religion itself a sentiment no more sincere and no less pragmatic than Napoleon himself had displayed. The ancient schism dividing church and state had not been healed, it had been widened by the Revolution, and the statesmen of 1815, however much they might extol the alliance of altar and throne, had no intention of reviving papal absolutism on medieval lines. A philosophy which founded all legitimate powers of government upon a theocratic basis was no more friendly in its premises to the arrogant pretensions of the national monarchies than Bonaparte's imperium based upon right reason had been. Hence the caution shown by the secular governments in their endorsement of traditionalist doctrines. De Bonald, who had defended the divine origin and constitution of society as early as 1796, in his *Théorie du pouvoir politique et religieux dans la société civilisée*, may be considered the systematizer

[25] Lamennais, *op. cit.*, II, 12.

of the new traditionalist creed. But De Bonald's logic, while it fortified the authority of consecrated monarchs, fortified still more effectively the superior prerogatives of the Roman pontiff. With Joseph de Maistre this doctrine of papal supremacy emerged as the central dogma of the traditionalist testament, and De Maistre's treatise, *Du Pape* (1817), became a charter for the ultramontane school. The dichotomy thus manifested in all attempts made at this time to derive lay and ecclesiastical domination from a common source, and to express the terms of that derivation in a formula acceptable to prelates and princes, doomed the effort to construct a consistent philosophy of reaction. Into the breach which could not be closed the spirit of positivism, recovering its vigor, soon forced its way; and jurisprudence, which De Bonald had sought to make the servant of morality, became with the disciples of Jeremy Bentham the servant of utility.

Chapter Eleven

THE REVOLUTIONARY TESTAMENT

I. THE REPUBLICAN TRADITION

To THE political thinkers of the nineteenth century the French Revolution bequeathed a legacy of ambiguities. The oracle had spoken, and with a voice of thunder, but seekers after truth were deafened or disconcerted by its message. Traditionalists, monarchists, republicans, socialists, and anarchists all appealed to its turbulent annals for confirmation of their creeds, but the answers which they extracted agreed on one point only: the Revolution had been a failure. No two schools were in precise accord, however, as to the reason for that failure. The Saint-Simonians saw it as a result of irresolute half-measures; the revolutionists had abolished social privilege without daring to attack economic privilege. To Edgar Quinet the inability of the Revolution to cut itself wholly free from the spirit and dogma of the Roman Catholic Church and to maintain that separation represented the fatal error. To Louis Blanc and Alphonse de Lamartine it was the collapse of the First French Republic that doomed the movement to defeat and tarnished the glorious visions of 1793.[1] This last exegesis, which idealized the revolutionary program in its essential aspects as a republican and democratic program, won the widest acceptance in liberal circles throughout Europe. As the retrospect lengthened and the legends coalesced the revolutionary tradition tended to become, more and more exclusively, a republican tradition. The spirit of the Revolution in its purest expression was symbolized by the superb challenge of '93, republican France throwing down the gauntlet to the leagued tyrants of Europe.

Pragmatically such a view had value for the malcontents in

[1] G. P. Gooch, *History and Historians in the Nineteenth Century* (London, 1913), 181-184.

many countries who plotted to disturb the Restoration settlement, and for the revolutionaries of 1848-1849 who dotted the European map with their short-lived republics. But as an historical interpretation it is open to question. For the great French Revolution had not been, in its inception or its conclusion, a republican (in the sense of an anti-monarchical) movement. "It was no part of the philosophical program of the eighteenth century to regenerate humanity by hoisting the republican flag over the capitals of Europe."[2] The general *cahiers* of 1789, the most comprehensive body of source material surviving on the state of public opinion in France at the close of the old régime, were "well-nigh universal" in their expressions of confidence in the king. The force of the American example no doubt served in some measure to prepare French opinion for the idea of a republic but the effect of such extrinsic influences can be very easily over-rated.[3] Similarly, though a reading of the classics had acquainted most of the revolutionary leaders with the republican ideals of antiquity, their subsequent careers proved them guilty of much more classical plagiarism in their oratory than in their politics.[4] The establishment of the First Republic was largely an unplanned deviation, forced upon France by the pressure of circumstances and the ambitions of a small but well-organized minority, and this sudden transition to an unfamiliar form of government obscured the earlier and more fundamental aims of the reform program.[5]

Of all the great issues which the French Revolution left undecided this question of the best *form* of government remained the most confusing, and possibly in its false emphasis the most pernicious. Between 1789 and 1814 France had become successively a constitutional monarchy, a democratic republic, a bourgeois republic, an enlightened despotism, and finally an hereditary liberal monarchy. Had any one of these forms triumphed permanently over its rivals, had the republic endured through the complete collapse of monarchism, or Cæsarism won a clear popular vindication over repub-

[2] H. A. L. Fisher, *The Republican Tradition in Europe* (New York, 1911), 65.
[3] There is no direct allusion to the United States to be found in any of the general *cahiers.* B. F. Hyslop, *A Guide to the General Cahiers of 1789* (New York, 1936), 77.
[4] H. T. Parker, *The Cult of Antiquity and the French Revolutionaries* (Chicago, 1937), 113-115.
[5] Fisher, *op. cit.*, 64.

licanism, the lesson might have been appreciated much earlier that the abuses and the injustices which the reform program had been intended to rectify did not derive necessarily from the form of government at all.[6] But the vicissitudes through which France had passed, and the tendency to divide the phases of the Revolution by political formulas, obscured this lesson. Throughout the nineteenth century liberal historians continued to measure political progress, during the Revolution and since, almost exclusively in terms of the extension or curtailment of the franchise, and the substitution of elective for hereditary or irresponsible officials. It came to be confidently believed that once all European states achieved democratic republican governments, resting upon a universal franchise, all internal tensions and external conflicts would find a harmonious solution. The concept of majority rule replaced the more doctrinaire concept of the General Will, and the total electorate became a lowest common multiple in which all minority groups and selfish interests were somehow to be assimilated.

Such an exaltation and such an implementation of the democratic and republican ideal represented a wide deviation from the political teaching of the *philosophes*. It represented an equally wide deviation from the institutions of the Revolution as these were consolidated and perpetuated by Napoleon. And, judged by the pragmatic test, it met but indifferently the political requirements of the more enlightened European peoples in the nineteenth century. The inadequacy of the pure republican-democratic tradition was manifested in the mid-century revolutions. No example, no impulse ever flashed across Europe more impetuously than that provided by the Paris revolutionists of 1848; the spontaneity of the liberal demonstrations in Italy, in Austria, in southern and western Germany, paralyzed the conservative governments. Yet the concessions to the democratic principle won in the panic of the early months were nearly all annulled at the first opportunity, and not one of the republics proclaimed by the revolutionists survived the reactionary wave which gathered in 1849. The republican ideal of government was so swiftly and so widely discredited that it lost its

[6] R. Soltau, *French Political Thought in the Nineteenth Century* (New Haven, 1931), Intro., xxi.

glamour, and neither the Third French Republic, so diffidently and haphazardly established after 1870, nor the turbulent and short-lived Spanish Republic of 1873 excited European liberals in other lands to enthusiasm or imitation.

Thus, if the republican and democratic ideals of 1793 are taken to represent the basic aims of the Revolution, the conclusion would seem to be that after these ideals had been fermenting in Europe for half a century the European peoples, even the French, were unprepared for them. But this may be a superficial interpretation, and it raises the question: what were the ideals, or, more specifically, the aims, of the revolutionary program? If the primary motivation for the Revolution was the will to establish democracy and republicanism, that will scored but a questionable triumph, for although democracy made considerable progress in the nineteenth century, republicanism paused, and in the twentieth century both have lost ground before dictatorships. But if the major objective of the revolutionary effort is taken to have been (as manifested in France so strikingly between 1799 and 1814) the creation of an efficient centralized nation-state, the coördination of national energies for the enhancement of national prestige, and the development of the secular spirit in government and society, then the influence of the Revolution has continued to work with increasing effect up to the present time, and has seldom been more active than in the fourth decade of the twentieth century. It was this practical mandate of the revolutionary program that Napoleon chose to execute, at the expense of the more idealistic and humanitarian elements, and posterity, while sighing for the still-born Utopia, has generally endorsed his interpretation of the revolutionary testament in preference to the codicils of the Saint-Simons and the Mazzinis.

II. THE SECULAR SOCIETY

"Every attempt to make science serviceable to the world," wrote a German journalist in 1834, "every union of science and statecraft, implies immediate unity with France."[7] The union of science and

---

[7] From Arnold Ruge's *Deutsche-Französische Jahrbücher*, quoted in H. A. L. Fisher, *The Republican Tradition in Europe* (New York, 1911), 256. See also, for the intimate relation of the revolutionary and scientific spirit, E. Castelar y Ripoll, *Storia de movimiento republicano*. 2 vols. (Madrid, 1873-1874). I, 20-20.

statecraft expresses, perhaps as nearly as a single phrase can do, the spirit which had inspired French administrators from the opening of the states general to the fall of the Empire. No society theretofore had striven with such consistent and single-minded devotion to promote the general welfare of its members by an intelligent application of the methods, laws and discoveries which modern science has placed at the disposal of modern man.

It is surprising that the historian of ideas, quick to note the charm which the republican ideals of antiquity exercised over the mind of a Saint-Just or a Desmoulins, should have neglected to stress another quality which rendered the ancient climate of opinion attractive to eighteenth-century liberals. It was not alone the republican austerity celebrated by Livy or Tacitus which seduced them, but the secular-mindedness that breathes in Cicero or Lucretius. Like the classical students of the Italian Renaissance they required the pure serene of the *litterae humaniores* to fortify them for their conflict with sanctified prejudices and a moral code invested with supernatural authority. The radical thinkers of the Enlightenment were rebels against an ecclesiastical tradition fifteen centuries old, a tradition which insisted that man is a sinful creature, living in hourly danger of death and an after-judgment, and powerless to save himself without the assistance of divine grace and intervention. To substitute for this view the more pagan and more rational concept that the virtue of an act depends upon its consequences implied a revolution in ethical thought, for it made reason, not conscience or tradition or revelation, the supreme authority in moral decisions.

When the Revolution broke out the long-maturing hostility between the theologian and the rationalist came into the open. Financial exigencies provided the excuse for the confiscation of the church property, but the justification for the act, in the minds of many advanced thinkers, lay in the conviction that Catholicism was a superannuated cult which must soon be supplanted by a civic religion, a worship of Reason, perhaps, or of the Fatherland. But it is not easy to convert a habitually religious people to a secular philosophy by legislative decree. No issue throughout the course of the Revolution provoked such bitter controversy as the relation of church and state. The "civil constitution of the clergy" raised more difficulties than it settled. The concordat of 1801, extorted from the Pope by pressure, forced through the legislative chambers by bribery and chicanery, remained a realistic compromise on an irreconcilable schism. Napoleon's solution of the problem was frankly Erastian, but it provided a workable precedent for later governments. The organic articles subjected the established churches to police supervision, set a limit to the number of seminaries and the growth of monastic orders in France, and left the people free, through the neutral attitude of the civil magistrates, to attend any church or none, to make contributions only if it pleased them, and to observe Sundays and fast days at their own option. The provisions for civil marriage and divorce in the code, the relegation to the local *mairie* of the registers of births, marriages, and deaths, and the development of a secular school system, left organized religion only a minor rôle to play in the affairs of the nation. So widespread had the spirit of indifference become by 1805, so inconsiderable were the voluntary contributions of the populace, that Napoleon found it advisable to grant national subsidies to the churches to cover their operating expenses, and in 1810 the communes were ordered to assume part of the burden. Napoleon recognized and was eager to utilize the talents of the French clergy, but his purpose can hardly be read as a determination to restore the authority of the clerical spirit: it was a desire to transform an educated and disciplined group of public servants into "spiritual gendarmes." But the Catholic sympathies of influential ministers like Portalis and Fontanes, and the dignified and intelligent labors of many churchmen in seconding the imperial program for the stabilization of French society, won for the bishops a steadily increasing prestige and influence. In some cases where an anticlerical prefect quarreled persistently with the bishop of his *département* it was the prefect who was removed, and the resurrection of clericalism as a force in French politics, usually considered a phenomenon of the Restoration, had already become discernible in the later years of the Empire. It was a development contrary to Napoleon's expectations or intentions, and it provides one more illustration, not merely of the quiet struggle for supremacy still going on between the rational and the re-

ligious camps, but of the manner in which Napoleon could be subdued by the tools with which he worked.

The march of the revolutionary principles after 1815 might be
gauged not inaccurately by the conquests of the secular spirit in
social theory and practice. Anti-clericalism, and particularly anti-
Catholicism, was a powerful element in the radical faith, and fused
itself readily with an idealized republicanism, especially in the Latin
countries. In the fields of jurisprudence and sociology the spread
of the secular spirit is particularly interesting to trace. Sociology as
a science struck its first roots, as might be expected, in France, and
its program and method were foreshadowed in Comte's *Plan of
the Scientific Operations necessary for the Reorganization of Society*
published in 1822.[8] In the dispute over social aims and social control the conflict between the devotees of religion and of science
tended to become more and more a conflict between a static and a
dynamic interpretation of history. The theologians guarded a moral
code for the governance of men which, in theory at least, was
adequate, absolute, and unchanging.[9] But the adequacy of these
"innate and original morals of mankind," validated by appeals to
revelation, became in the revolutionary and post-revolutionary decades the object of an insistent and increasingly critical attack. The
response of the Roman Catholic Church, historically speaking, to
the challenge so confidently flung down by the revolutionary reformers, is to be found in the *Syllabus of Errors* issued by Pius IX
in 1864.[10] There the notion that the human reason is itself a sufficient judge of good and evil and can find the remedies for social
problems unaided was formally condemned as one of the greatest
of modern errors.[11]

Despite the prominence customarily given to the struggle for
supremacy waged between church and state throughout the French
Revolution, the primary meaning of that new and acute phase of

---

[8] J. B. Bury, *The Idea of Progress* (London, 1920), 291.

[9] With critics such as Henry Thomas Buckle the fact that religious codes were fixed
and unchanging seemed a logical reason for denying them a share in the advancement
of mankind, since "a stationary agent can only produce a stationary effect." Buckle,
History of Civilization in England, 2 vols. (London, 1857-1861), I, 130-131.

[10] C. Mirbt, *Quellen zur Geschichte des Papsttums und des römischen Katholizismus*,
4th ed. (Tübingen, 1924), 450-454.

[11] Consult, in this connection, the volume in this series by R. C. Binkley, *Realism and
Nationalism* (New York, 1935). chap. IV.

the struggle is not always clearly brought out. The Revolution not only represented a renewal of the perennial warfare between rationalism and traditionalism, or between naturalism and supernaturalism, it represented the point in modern history at which that warfare assumed its contemporary form. For the first time in modern annals the *civitas humana* was set forth unequivocally as the ultimate reality in place of the *civitas Dei*; for the first time the authority of reason was unblushingly acknowledged as superior to the authority of revelation, and the doctrine of human perfectibility (shortly to be reformulated as the doctrine of progress) substituted for the doctrine of miraculous redemption. With the Revolution the warfare between science and theology in Christendom entered a more explicit, a definitive phase. The century which followed witnessed the practical completion of that process which Andrew Dickson White described as the transition from oracles to higher criticism, from miracles to medicine, from Genesis to geology and organic evolution.[12] Measured by positive or by negative indices the most persistent and perhaps the most pervasive social trend since 1789 has been the consecration of the secular society. The march of the secular spirit is attested by the relaxation of compulsory tithes, compulsory church attendance and compulsory baptism; the reduction of clerical influence especially in education; the restriction on ecclesiastical endowments; the declining percentage of books published on religious topics, and the transference of control over matters of public decency and morals largely to lay hands. Corresponding to these changes, but of a positive nature, may be noted the extension of compulsory lay schooling and compulsory vaccination; the introduction of civil marriage and divorce; the multiplication of popular works and lectures on scientific subjects; the legalization, in the face of clerical protests, of such practices as cremation and contraception. In many countries today the only indissoluble oath recognized by law is that of allegiance to the state, the only inescapable obligation the liability to military service. And civil jurisdiction, when it abdicates before the authority of a rival system, finds it no longer in the *jus canonicum* but in the imperious voice

[12] A. D. White, *A History of the Warfare of Science with Theology in Christendom*, 2 vols. (New York, 1904), especially I, chap. 5, and II, chap. 13.

of military law. For almost all these revaluations and practices a logical precedent can be found, and found often for the first time in modern history, in the legislation of revolutionary and imperial France.

III. THE CANONS OF PATRIOTISM

The fact has frequently been noted, since De Tocqueville called attention to it nearly a century ago, that the French Revolution was a political movement which proceeded with the fervor of a religious crusade. "Search all the annals of history," De Tocqueville challenged, "you will not find a single political revolution which had this specific character. You will discover it only in certain religious revolutions, and it is to these that you must compare the French Revolution if you wish to understand it by the aid of analogy."[13] In the field of history such broad generalizations as this are more often suggestive than positively helpful, but it is not unprofitable to trace here the evidence which can be adduced to support the comparison.

That a patriotic cult of *la patrie* matured rapidly in the perfervid atmosphere of the revolutionary struggle there can be little dispute. Within a generation the civic faith acquired a hagiology, a set of symbols, and the rudiments of a creed. Voltaire and Rousseau were its prophets, Marat and Lepeletier its martyrs, the veterans of Valmy, the gunners of the *Vengeur*, and other dauntless defenders of the Republic, its more or less mythical heroes. The tricolor cockade and the tricolor flag became its sacred symbols, the civic festivals celebrated before the altar to the fatherland were its ceremonies, and the national fêtes enumerated in the new revolutionary calendar replaced (and were intended to replace) the holy days of Catholic observance. Patriotic processions, mass demonstrations, civic oaths, even civic baptisms and civic marriages, were commonplaces in the early years of the Republic, and all were enlivened by the *Marseillaise* or other chants called forth by the popular impulse. And concurrently the more austere apostles of liberty turned their thoughts to the preservation and formalization of the new orthodoxy. The *Declaration of the Rights of Man and the Citizen* was posted in all

[13] A. de Tocqueville, *L'Ancien régime et la révolution*, 7th ed. (Paris, 1866), chap. III.

public buildings, the constitution of 1793 was sealed reverently in an ark and deposited in the hall of the national convention. "It is essential," Saint-Just recorded in 1794, "to define and establish all the principles of liberty by a specific declaration which may be for society what the rights of man are for government." It was essential not only for purposes of convenience and accuracy but because the young cult, like all nascent religions, had to hew an undeviating path through the thickets of heresy; Saint-Just had already warned the faithful to be forever on their guard against plausible perversions, because "nothing so nearly resembles virtue as a great crime."[14] The necessity of preserving the new evangel in all its purity provided the strongest argument for a national system of secular education, for the standardization of the French tongue throughout the territories of the Republic, for the regulation of public opinion in such a manner that sound principles would be propagated and subversive opinions checked. Herein is to be found the basis for the institution of the Napoleonic censorship. The truth was doubtless mighty and would prevail, but the character of its triumph could be controlled more satisfactorily by official methods. How these methods operated under Napoleon may be noted in the *Moniteur,* which listed Eylau and Aspern as French victories and neglected to discuss Trafalgar until after the fall of the empire.

Characteristically, as the civil cult crystallized, its emphasis tended to shift from altruism to acquisition and its leadership passed from the doctrinaires to the disciples of action. "They prate to you constantly of our victories, . . ." Robespierre had expostulated in 1794, in that final speech which he called his last will and testament. "It is not by rhetorical phrases, nor by military exploits, that we will conquer Europe, but by the wisdom of our laws, by the majesty of our deliberations, by the nobility of our characters."[15] But the constitutional cult, so vital in the first years of the revolutionary turmoil, declined steadily as successive charters failed to unlock the gates of Utopia, and with the postponement of these apocalyptic expectations the French people turned their gaze, half-fascinated, half-consoled, from the foresworn prophets of the legislature to the

[14] L. A. de Saint-Just, *Œuvres complètes,* ed. by C. Vellay, 2 vols. (Paris, 1908), II, 532.
[15] M. Robespierre, *Discours et rapports,* ed. by C. Vellay (Paris, 1908), 416.

achievements of the successful soldiers. Not the assembly-hall but the temple of victory became the shrine of the national cult.

The outward drive of those national energies generated and released by the Revolution made the era of French conquests possible. A conscription law, the first of its kind, established compulsory military service for all males between twenty and twenty-five (1798). Careers open to talent soon came to mean more particularly careers open to military talent; the most generous gratuities, the most coveted decorations, went to military men, and frequently the most important diplomatic missions or administrative posts were intrusted to army officers. As a logical consequence of the French expansion the creed of patriotism and the policy of militarization infected the other European powers. One by one they augmented their armies and exalted the dignity of the citizen soldier in order to withstand the French threat. By 1814 Prussia had adopted universal military service, Austria had created a *Landwehr*, and Great Britain and Russia were sustaining the largest and most expensive military forces in their history. The relatively tranquil decades which followed Waterloo naturally brought a reduction in armaments, but the lesson of numbers and of national propaganda had been learned. With the intensification of nationalism in the 'sixties and 'seventies, and the triumphs of power diplomacy and *Realpolitik*, the European governments demonstrated how well they had profited by the experience of the revolutionary wars. The modern concept of the nation in arms, a homogeneous population welded to a unit by a common patriotic faith, dedicated to a theory of militant defense that is scarcely distinguishable from a policy of military expansion— this concept took concrete shape between 1789 and 1814.

The economic foundations of the modern state, no less than the political and military, likewise took their enduring shape in this era. "Only a radical improvement in the means of transportation and communication and a revolutionary change in the social life of the masses could introduce the type of political democracy which would foster nationalism."[16] The increase in the food supply which resulted from improvements in agriculture, the increase in manufacturing activity consequent upon the mechanization of industry,

[16] C. J. H. Hayes, *Essays in Nationalism* (New York, 1926), 52.

and the growth of population which accompanied these movements, created the strong warp of the national society. The woof was provided by quickened transportation and communication which knit scattered provinces together, by the rise in literacy which sensitized the masses to the pervasive power of the press and of propaganda, by a sense of closer identity between a people and its government which developed with the representative system. The use of sea power, blockades, and embargoes in the battle for markets throughout the Napoleonic struggles impressed the advantages of economic self-sufficiency upon the popular consciousness for the first time with indelible effect. To bring a people to surrender through starvation was an ancient military device; but the continental system had invoked a new principle—that of bringing a nation to ruin by paralyzing its commerce. In Great Britain no one could view the economic war with indifference. The investor who had bought government bonds, the manufacturer who sought foreign markets for his product, the shipowner who pleaded for naval protection, down to the mill-hand or farmer, all must have suffered if Bonaparte had triumphed and subordinated British interests to the economic prosperity of France as he had those of Italy and Holland. British national life had already achieved an economic integration which matched the political integration imposed upon France, and for that reason the two states represented in the revolutionary epoch two distinctive aspects of emergent nationalism.

One further contribution to the growing spirit of nationalism, and that a less tangible influence, may be ascribed to the early decades of the nineteenth century. While the Napoleonic reforms were speeding the development of a bureaucracy adequate to direct the energies of a centralized territorial state, and the industrial revolution multiplied the *matériel* indispensable for a nation in arms, the romantic revival helped to gild the cult of patriotism with a mystic sentimentality. In these years a nostalgic preoccupation with remembered childhood scenes, with the contours of familiar hills, with local landmarks and ballads and all the quaint historical associations which invest ancestral acres acquired an astounding literary vogue. The instant popularity of Scott's *Waverly* (1814) and its successors provides the illustration of this trend most familiar, probably, to English readers. But other forms of literature yielded .. influence. The hero of the Byronic tradition, the "wandering outlaw of his own dark mind," reappeared more realistically in prose and verse as the proud and desolate exile from his native heath, and the suffering of political fugitives, Polish, Italian, Hungarian, German, Russian, who flocked to other lands after each abortive rising during the Restoration, advertised anew the indissoluble ties that bound every man to his *Vaterstadt.* The first generation of romanticists had turned, in their sentimental quest for a city of the soul, to the golden age of Greece; the second generation had sought it in an idealized picture of life in the high middle ages or among the gentle savages in the American wilds. With the third generation the quest found its most natural, homely, and democratic fulfillment in an exaltation of the native landscape and native character, in *genre* paintings and dialect novels, in the preservation of local antiquities and the collection of local ballads as the most authentic and enduring expressions of the *Volksgeist.*[17]

It remains one of the supreme ironies of the revolutionary drama that the philosophy which inspired the movement had envisaged as its ultimate goal the creation of a world society, subject to the harmonious rule of universal laws, and disciplined by institutions which would be the same for all men. Napoleon's grandiose attempt to realize this aim left the peoples of Europe more intractably divided than they had ever been, and in nothing did he show himself more unmistakably the heir of the *philosophes* than in his misconception of the national impulse. For he acted throughout his career as if the triumphs of the French were only in a secondary sense the triumphs of a nation of patriots; as if Frenchmen should be prepared to march and fight indefinitely for the vindication of a principle and a system which transcended national loyalties. In the same spirit, he treated the resistance of other national groups as the opposition of subordinate units which could have no permanent identity and no political meaning outside that system. Yet the most striking political consequence of his labors was to hasten the dissociation of European society into discrete nation-states, each

[17] For a more detailed discussion of the connection between nationalism and romanticism the reader may consult F. B. Artz, *Reaction and Revolution* (New York, 1934), 189-203.

destined to become for its inhabitants (in Hobbes's quaint and thoughtful phrase) "a Mortall God." Or as Mussolini has more recently defined it, with no discourtesy to metaphysics, "an absolute before which all else is relative."

IV. THE NAPOLEONIC LEGEND

The legend which grew up during the nineteenth century concerning Napoleon's career and character is a romantic creation which pays scant respect to the facts. Napoleon himself began the great work of apotheosis at St. Helena, and the classical bent of his mind and education did not blind him to the romantic possibilities which the drama had taken on with his fall from power. He was the great outlaw and the great exile for whom the whole of Europe had proved too narrow a stage, and the two thousand miles of water which separated him from the world of his exploits was in some sense a tribute to his demonic powers. By the rules of classical drama he should have sought the clue to the fate which had overtaken him in some ineradicable flaw of his own character, but such a conclusion was little to his taste. It was much more flattering to pose as a modern Prometheus, chained to that lonely rock in the ocean by those jealous Olympians, the leagued monarchs of Europe, who could not forgive the Titan who had stolen fire from heaven in a generous effort to inspire and liberate mankind. Ever the opportunist, Napoleon had caught up the banner of liberalism during the Hundred Days, and Waterloo had saved him from betraying that cause a second time as he had already done under the Consulate. While the reactionary despots of the Restoration era coped none too happily with the problem of governing a disillusioned generation, Napoleon had a chance to perfect his liberal pose in a realm of pure political abstractions, and as he was never vouchsafed a further chance to dishonor it in action the pose remained his by the unimpeachable accord of death.

That the liberals of the eighteen-twenties and eighteen-thirties should have endorsed the legend when many of them could still remember the facts is less surprising than its seems. Napoleon's name was still one to conjure with; he had fought and humiliated the despots whose Holy Alliance and complacent vogue of immobility so exasperated the progressives; and he had died, in one sense at least, a victim of monarchical malice. Politics can make strange bedfellows, and imperial Cæsar dead and turned to myth might serve the cause of freedom in a way the living Corsican could never have done. With a few adroit elisions, a little deft reëditing, the facts of Napoleon's rule might be adapted to the liberal program. Though his management of Italian affairs, for instance, had been arbitrary and selfish, he had recanted by prophesying ultimate unification for the peninsula; and he had never been so poor a press agent as to provide his enemies with such a slogan as Metternich did when he called Italy a geographical expression. Tsar Alexander's intentions towards the Poles were as liberal as Napoleon's had been, but Napoleon could still be lauded as the only ruler who had attempted to rescue Poland from her ravishers. French chauvinists, smarting under the events of 1814, and disgusted after 1830 with the "peace without honor" policy of the July Monarchy, found it pleasant to gild the imperial epic, and it was impossible to honor the epic without honoring the hero. To liberals and nationalists everywhere, groaning under the inconveniences of the Vienna settlement and the quadruple alliance which perpetuated it, there was something irresistibly attractive in remembering a man who had shaken thrones with his nod and rearranged the map of Europe after each campaign. Political malcontents, if they grow desperate enough, are likely to think of any force as friendly provided only that it is powerful enough to break the stalemate which they find it so difficult to endure.

The alliance between the growing spirit of democracy and the Napoleonic legend was fostered by quite other arguments. As the masses saw the bourgeoisie intrench themselves more firmly in power—in France after 1830, in Great Britain after 1832—they looked about for a champion, and the idea of Cæsarean democracy, under a despot of such prestige and authority that he could subordinate all selfish classes to the general welfare, seemed to them, if not the most ideal, at least the most prompt and practical solution to the problem of social justice. This line of thought was to bear fruit in the French elections of 1848, when Louis Napoleon Bonaparte, who had wooed the disinherited classes with proposals for *L'Ex-*

tinction du pauperisme, vanquished General Cavaignac who had wooed them (in a manner much more reminiscent of *le Général Vendémiaire*) with cannon. Nevertheless, the hope which in the eighteen-forties persuaded the forgotten man in France that he might fare better under the despotism of a dictator than under the despotism of a class suggests that the masses retained a more realistic image of Napoleon I than the liberals or the oppressed nationalists in other countries. They recalled his energy and efficiency as an administrator, his contempt for bankers and profiteers, his encouragement of industry and public works, and his solicitude for agriculture. He had exploited the working classes, but he had exploited other classes too in the name of national glory, and the workers, conceiving that exploitation to have been more impartial than it was, found the memory of it more attractive than the soulless, hypocritical extortion practiced upon them by so many bourgeois employers. Where they erred was in imagining that it would be easy to find two Napoleons. Louis Blanc warned against this fallacy as early as 1840. A Bonapartist restoration? he said. "It would be the despotism without the glory, the courtiers on our necks without Europe at our feet, a great name without a great man, in a word, the Empire without the Emperor."[18] But it was the prophecy of a Cassandra.

More than any other single impulse, it was the romantic movement which nourished the Napoleonic legend. The craving to find a hero larger than human turned the thoughts of many artists towards Napoleon while he was still living, and after 1821 the cult of the modern Prometheus became a recognized part of European literary tradition. Nor was the *rapport* which the romanticists divined between themselves and the Man of Destiny altogether an illusion. "The boundless yearning of the poets is but the negative aspect of the Will to Power unappeased. And the Will to Power, which was to find supreme literary expression in Nietzsche, had already found its most complete realization in Bonaparte."[19] The resultant myth, perfected almost within the memory of men yet living, deserves to take its place with other creations of folklore,

---

[18] "Louis Blanc," *La Grande Encyclopédie*, VI, 1004.
[19] A. L. Guérard, *Reflections on the Napoleonic Legend* (New York, 1924), 177.

amorphous, international, indestructible. Heine has recorded how, watching a great East Indiaman at the London docks, and feeling a sudden impulse to greet the strange turbaned faces which peered down at him, he shouted the name 'Mohammed,' whereupon with a gleam of happy apprehension their spokesman shouted back the word 'Bonaparte.' It is a good story, and none the worse for being a patent fabrication. For so shrewdly does the Napoleonic legend gratify the romantic mood that facts are transmuted in its presence. Napoleon's abdication and exile, like his errors, are accepted without criticism, as predestined by the dramatic exigencies of the plot. To suggest that he might better have come to terms with his opponents and rounded out his reign in peace seems an esthetic irreverence, and so great is the violence which hero-worship inflicts upon historic facts that few critics trouble to evaluate Napoleon's achievements by the only standard he himself respected, the standard of material success.

In the coronation oath to which he swore on December 2, 1804, the Emperor pledged himself first of all to maintain the territorial integrity of France; to preserve the concordat and religious freedom, equality of rights, political and civil liberty, and the irrevocability of the sale of the national lands; to levy no impost or tax except by virtue of the law, to preserve the Legion of Honor, and to rule with the sole aim of promoting the happiness, the prosperity and the glory of the French people.[20] It is scarcely an exaggeration to say that all these objects were within his power. Yet he fulfilled his promises so ill that in 1814 an exhausted France was saved from dismemberment chiefly through the good sense of her enemies, and the remainder of the program was guaranteed, in so far as it had not been already violated, by the generosity of the Bourbons. His final attempt to shed glory on French arms cost the nation three years of military occupation and an indemnity of 700,000,000 francs. It is pertinent to ask what judgment he would himself have passed on any other ruler who had enjoyed such unprecedented opportunities for improving the material welfare and ennobling the lives of the French people, and had obtained such results.

It is doubtful, however, if the citation of facts will ever deflate

[20] *Correspondance de Napoléon Ier*, X, 60. No. 8201.

Napoleon's reputation so long as he remains, in his energy and his thirst for the unattainable, the most perfect historical expression of a dynamic and Faustian culture. A century of historical criticism, largely devoted to the depersonification of myths, has made him the best-documented figure in history, but it has not yet reduced him to mortal stature. At one moment he appears as the Son of the Revolution corrupted by power, a fit subject for Greek tragedy. At another he is a fifteenth-century *condottiere* coloring a later age with the indelible tincture of his personality. As the despot whose ambition diverted the march of democracy he wears the dark halo which the theologians wove for Lucifer, and as the exile banished to the rock of St. Helena he is the modern Prometheus. Seldom does he appear as General Bonaparte, an inspired administrator who restored to the French people the energetic administration they remembered and desired, and then pursued the policies of Richelieu and Louis XIV until the coalitions which inevitably form against a dominant European power destroyed his hegemony. Legends have little need of logic. The Man of Destiny continues to gratify the human hunger for miracles by the success with which he seems to have defied destiny, and too frequently remains, even in sober narratives, an apostate to the historical rules of proportion and continuity.

BIBLIOGRAPHICAL ESSAY

(Revised as of November, 1957)

A NOTE ON HISTORIOGRAPHY

It has remained for the historians of the twentieth century to attempt a reconstruction of the Napoleonic era, based upon broad and exact documentation, and fortified by a profounder understanding of the economic forces at work behind the political façade. For a generation after the Congress of Vienna the historical works which purported to explain European developments in the years 1799-1814 seldom rose above the level of nationalist propaganda or pamphlet attacks upon the fallen emperor, to which were added slowly the more impressive self-justifications published by Napoleonic officials and the romantic version of the gospel according to St. Helena. After the exile of the Bourbons from France in 1830 the Napoleonic legend grew prolifically; the ashes of the emperor were brought back to Paris in 1840, and the cult of Bonapartism achieved its most spectacular triumph with the election of Louis Napoleon Bonaparte in 1848 and the *coup d'état* which introduced the Second Empire three years later. With this incarnation of the legend before their eyes, historians, perhaps naturally, became more critical of the great Napoleon's character and achievements. The first adequately documented treatments, Louis Adolphe Thiers' *Histoire du Consulat et de l'Empire* in twenty volumes (1845-1862) and Armand Lefebvre's *Histoire des cabinets de l'Europe pendant le Consulat et l'Empire* in three volumes (1845-1847) advertised the importance of archival resources, and the *Correspondance de Napoléon Ier* in thirty-two volumes (1858-1870), though edited with official discretion, made available the most revealing and most relevant body of documentary material on the period. The political discontent in France under the Second Empire produced a school of critics eager to utilize the increasing mass of source material to deflate the legend. Notable among their writings was Pierre Lanfrey's *Histoire de Napoléon Ier*, the first volume of which appeared in 1867. Few accounts more penetrating and more systematically cold to Napoleon's glamour have ever been written.

Across the Rhine in these years the Prussian school of historians, fighting the War of Liberation again on an intellectual plane, were devitalizing the legend with all the weight of their invincible prestige. Ludwig Häusser published his *Deutsche Geschichte vom Tode Friedrichs des Grossen bis zur Gründung des deutschen Bundes* between 1854 and 1857. Droysen (who praised Lanfrey's work as one that threw a bright light into a dark time), and Ranke, whose *Hardenberg und die Geschichte des preussischen Staates, 1793-1813,* was to appear between 1879 and 1881, to say nothing of Treitschke, already compiling his *Deutsche Geschichte im neunzehnten Jahrhundert,* taught Clio to speak with a Prussian accent while Bismarck was tarnishing the laurels of the First Empire by destroying the Second. For many sober-minded and disillusioned Frenchmen the verdict of 1870-1871 was a judgment on Cæsarism, and they endorsed Taine's censorious estimate of the Revolution and its fruits, an estimate which found expression in the later volumes of *Les Origines de la France contemporaine* (1875-1894).

The time had arrived when the conflicting interpretations of the Napoleonic era, reëxamined in the light of accumulating documents and memoirs, might yield to an objective and impartial synthesis. This was demonstrated by the publication of August Fournier's sanely conceived and brilliantly written study, *Napoleon I, eine Biographie,* in three volumes, 1886-1889. The two decades which followed brought a Napoleonic renascence. Albert Sorel was already at work on his monumental *L'Europe et la Révolution française.* Frédéric Masson issued the first of his intimate portraits, *Napoléon et les femmes,* in 1893. Arthur Chuquet completed the three volumes of *La Jeunesse de Napoléon* in 1899, and Albert Vandal the first part of *L'Avènement de Bonaparte* in 1903. In Russia, Serge Tatischeff had assembled his enlightening *Alexandre Ier et Napoléon* (1891), and in England Lord Rosebery rendered the belated amends of a generous nation in *Napoleon, The Last Phase* (1900), while John Holland Rose conceded the Corsican's greatness in *The Life of Napoleon I* (1901). As a fitting climax, volume IX of the *Cambridge Modern History,* which appeared in 1906 and embraced the period 1799-1815, bore the single eponymous title *Napoleon.*

One inevitable result of these multiple tributes was the realization that Napoleon had ceased to be a man and had become an epoch. It was growing difficult, if not impossible, to preserve a record of the inexhaustible list of memoirs, correspondence, documents, biographies, histories, and monographs which dealt with the eventful years 1799-1815, and Friedrich M. Kircheisen sounded the note for the next stage in Napoleonic historiography with the first volume of his *Bibliographie du temps de Napoléon* (1908). To organize and evaluate the vast body of literature already published, comb the archives for lacunæ, and settle the many disputed points by the methods of critical scholarship had become the program, and the *Revue des études napoléoniennes,* founded by Edouard Driault in 1912, provided an indispensable organ for directing the campaign. Despite the interruption of the war years, the progress towards a broader, saner, and more eclectic treatment of European history in the years 1799-1815 continued, and the post-war decades have demonstrated that the foundations thus laid will provide the twentieth-century historian with a vantage-ground from which he may attempt a truly comprehensive survey of the period. Evidence of this may be seen in the energetic exploration of the economic field, hitherto the most neglected sphere of Napoleonic history, which has been enriched by such timely studies as F. E. Melvin's *Napoleon's Navigation System* (1919), Eli Heckscher's *Continental System: an Economic Interpretation* (1922), and E. Tarlé's *Le Blocus continental et le Royaume d'Italie* (1928). If further proof were required that the time is ripe for a broader-visioned and more harmonious synthesis than was hitherto possible, it may be found in the progress of Kircheisen's erudite and inclusive biography, *Napoleon I, sein Leben und seine Zeit,* the ninth volume of which appeared in 1934; in Edouard Driault's panoramic survey, *Napoléon et l'Europe,* five volumes (1910-1927); and in the judicious and objective single volumes on the period composed by G. Pariset, *Le Consulat et l'Empire* (1921), G. Bourgin, *Napoleon und seine Zeit* (1925), G. Lefebvre, *Napoléon* (1935), H. C. Deutsch, *The Genesis of Napoleonic Imperialism* (Cambridge, Mass., 1938), and Willy Andreas, *Das Zeitalter Napoleons und die Erhebung der Völker* (Heidelberg, 1955). H. E. Friedrich, *Napoleon I, Idee und Staat* (Berlin, 1936) is a stimulating reconsideration of the basic ideas of Napoleon's domestic and foreign policy.

BIBLIOGRAPHICAL AIDS

Space forbids any attempt to indicate here the location and value of unpublished source material. For investigation into the printed literature the following guides are helpful. F. M. Kircheisen, *Bibliographie des napoleonischen Zeitalters* (Berlin, 1902), and *Bibliographie du temps de Napoléon comprenant l'histoire des États-Unis,* two volumes (Paris, 1908-1912); G. Davois, *Bibliographie napoléonienne française jusqu'en 1908,* three volumes (Paris, 1909-1911). The most convenient one-volume survey of books and articles on the period, terse, critical, and exhaustive, but Gallocentric in emphasis and selection, is L. Villat, *La*

Révolution et l'Empire, part II, *Napoléon, 1799-1815* (Paris, 1936, volume VIII in the series *Introduction aux études historiques.* J. H. Stewart, ed., *France, 1715-1815: a Guide to Materials in Cleveland* (Cleveland, 1942) is localized but valuable. P. Geyl, *Napoleon, For and Against* (New Haven, 1949), dissects the attitude of French historians toward Napoleon, and F. Stählin, *Napoleons Glanz und Fall im deutschen Urteil* (1952), is helpful for German opinion. *Revue des études napoléoniennes* (1912-1940), *Bulletin de l'Institut Napoléon* (1940-54), and *Revue de l'Institut Napoléon* (1954-   ) have current lists.

More general in scope are: *A Guide to Historical Literature,* ed. by W. H. Allison *et al.* (New York, 1931), a new edition of which is promised for 1958, and G. Franz *et al., Bücherkunde zur Weltgeschichte* (Munich, 1956). A. Grandin, ed., *Bibliographie générale des sciences juridiques, politiques, économiques et sociales de 1800 à 1925-26,* three volumes (Paris, 1926); and for contemporary publications, P. Caron, ed., *International Bibliography of the Historical Sciences* (1930-   ), which attempts to list current historical works and important articles in one volume to the year. For individual countries and regional studies reference may be had to P. Caron, ed., *Bibliographie des travaux publiés de 1866 à 1897 sur l'histoire de France depuis 1789* (Paris, 1907-1912) and supplements; B. Sánchez Alonzo, *Fuentes de la historia española* (Madrid, 1919); F. Lemmi, *Il Risorgimento, guide bibliografiche* (Rome, 1926), for the period 1748-1871; R. J. Kerner, *Slavic Europe, a selected bibliography in the western European languages* (Cambridge, Mass., 1918); F. C. Dahlmann and G. Waitz, *Quellenkunde der deutschen Geschichte,* 9th rev. ed. (Leipzig, 1931); and J. B. Williams, *Guide to Printed Materials for English Social and Economic History, 1750-1850,* two volumes (New York, 1926). G. M. Dutcher's "Napoleon and the Napoleonic Period," *Journal of Modern History,* IV (1932), 446-463, should be supplemented by J. H. Stewart *et al.,* "The Era of the French Revolution: Opportunities for Research and Writing," XXIX (1957), 85-98. See also the bibliographical article by G. Lefebvre, "La Révolution et l'Empire," *Revue historique* (Jan.-March and Apr.-June, 1951), and J. Leflon and A. Latreille, "Répertoire des fonds napoléoniens aux archives vaticanes," in the same journal (Jan.-Mar., 1950). On two somewhat neglected areas there are recent articles by J.-E. Goby, "Les travaux d'un siècle en Egypte sur l'expédition française de 1798-1801," and, by F. Boyer, "Les études napoléoniennes en Italie," in *Revue de l'Institut Napoléon* (Jan., 1955, and Jan., 1956, respectively).

GENERAL WORKS

The best single volumes treating Europe as a whole in the period 1799-1815 are to be found in the collaborative series now becoming common. Among the most notable are: E. Lavisse and A. Rambaud, ed., *Histoire générale du IVᵉ siècle à nos jours*, 3rd ed. rev., volume IX (Paris, 1925); *The Cambridge Modern History*, volume IX, *Napoleon* (Cambridge, 1906), popular edition omitting bibliographies (1934); L. M. Hartmann, ed., *Weltgeschichte in gemeinverständlicher Darstellung*, volume VII, part II, by G. Bourgin, *Napoleon und seine Zeit* (Gotha, 1925), brief and logical; W. Goetz, ed., *Propyläen Weltgeschichte*, volume VII, by A. Stern, *Die grosse Revolution, Napoleon und die Restauration, 1789-1848* (Berlin, 1929), competent, and beautifully illustrated; L. Halphen and Ph. Sagnac, ed., *Peuples et Civilisations*, volume IX, by G. Lefebvre (Paris, 1935), admirably objective. Text books with selected bibliographies, convenient for the American reader, are H. E. Bourne's logical survey, *Revolutionary Period in Europe, 1763-1815* (New York, 1914), L. R. Gottschalk, *The Era of the French Revolution, 1715-1815* (Boston, 1929), and L. Gershoy, *The French Revolution and Napoleon* (New York, 1932).

The monumental biography by F. M. Kircheisen, *Napoleon I, sein Leben und seine Zeit*, nine volumes completed (Munich, 1911-1934), is a virtual history of the period. Equally valuable are the five volumes of J. E. Driault, *Napoléon et l'Europe* (Paris, 1910-1927), with two peripheral studies, *Napoléon en Italie, 1800-1812* (Paris, 1906) and *La Politique orientale de Napoléon, 1806-1808* (Paris, 1904). Driault commenced his investigations with the Near Eastern issue and it has continued to shape his interpretation of Napoleon's policies. Louis Madelin has carried his lively *Histoire du Consulat et de l'Empire* to Waterloo in sixteen volumes (Paris, 1937-1954), and J. M. Thompson, *Napoleon Bonaparte* (New York, 1952), is history in the large rather than a biography. For the study of international affairs throughout the revolutionary era the outstanding work is still A. Sorel's *L'Europe et la Révolution française*, eight volumes (Paris, 1895-1904). To Sorel the preponderance of France in the revolutionary age appeared an abnormality contrary to historical trends and the genius of Napoleon could not prevent the predictable restoration of the balance of power.

POLITICAL HISTORY

Modern political histories are so firmly subordinated to the concept of the territorial state as the administrative unit that any attempt to arrange them under other than national captions would prove confusing.

1. Great Britain

A standard work in this class is W. Hunt and R. L. Poole, ed., *Political History of England,* twelve volumes (London, 1905-1910), volume XI, by G. C. Broderick and J. K. Fotheringham, covering the years 1801 to 1837. A. F. Freemantle, *England in the Nineteenth Century,* volumes I and II (London, 1929-1930), traces the story in greater detail for the years 1801-1810. For an analysis of English life during the years 1793-1822 Sir Arthur Bryant's trilogy, *Years of Endurance, Years of Victory,* and *The Age of Elegance* (London, 1942-1950), is lively and entertaining, and E. Halévy, *History of the English People,* volume I in English translation (London, 1924), is unsurpassed for charm and objectivity. The British war effort is discussed with J. H. Rose's usual clarity and penetration in *Pitt and the Great War* (London, 1911); for the earlier phase, O. Brandt, *England und die Napoleonische Weltpolitik* (Heidelberg, 1916) is an able interpretation of the divergent lines of the Anglo-French rivalry, but the broadest and sanest treatment of this issue is still P. Coquelle, *Napoléon et l'Angleterre* (Paris, 1904). Irish history in the early nineteenth century is handled with competence and reasonable detachment by J. O'Connor, *History of Ireland,* two volumes (London, 1925), volume I. For the British colonies there is *The Cambridge History of the British Empire,* volume II (New York, 1940).

2. France

L. A. Thiers, *Histoire du Consulat et de l'Empire,* twenty volumes (Paris, 1845-1862), English translation in twelve volumes (London, 1893-1894), still commands a deserved prestige and is particularly useful for details of administration. Of more recent works the most noteworthy are M. Deslandres, *Histoire constitutionelle de la France,* two volumes (Paris, 1932-1933), and J. Godechot, *Les institutions de la France sous la Révolution et l'Empire* (Paris, 1951); also L. de Lanzac de Laborie, *Paris sous Napoléon,* eight volumes (Paris, 1905-1913), of which the first two are the more specifically political in content; G. Pariset, *Le Consulat et l'Empire* (Paris, 1921), volume III of the *Histoire de France contemporaine,* edited by E. Lavisse, is well balanced, lucid, and carries excellent topical bibliographies; L. Madelin, *Le Consulat et l'Empire* (Paris, 1932-1934), two volumes comprising part VII of the series *Histoire de France racontée à tous,* edited by F. Funck-Brentano, is written with Madelin's customary brilliance, is somewhat pro-clerical in tone and over-respectful toward Napoleon. For the advent of Napoleon to power, A. Vandal's *L'Advènement de Bonaparte*, two volumes (Paris, 1902-1907), is unsurpassed, and the same problem has been reëxamined by J. B. Morton, *Brumaire, the Rise of Bonaparte* (London, 1948), and by J. Thiry, *Le coup d'état du 18 Brumaire* (Paris, 1947). On the events that account for his fall, H. Houssaye, *1814* (Paris, 1888) and *1815*, three volumes (Paris, 1898-1925) with many subsequent editions of both. Also J. Thiry, *La première abdication de Napoléon Ier*, 2nd ed. (Paris, 1948); F. Sieburg, *Napoleon: Die Hundert Tage* (Stuttgart, 1956); M. Lajusan, "La deuxieme et dernière phase de la catastrophe napoléonienne (1814-1815)," *Bulletin de la Société d'histoire moderne* (June-July, 1952); and J. M. Thompson, "Napoleon's Journey to Elba in 1814," *American Historical Review* (Oct., 1949, and Jan., 1950).

For the administration of the *départements,* J. Regnier, *Les Préfets du Consulat et de l'Empire* (Paris, 1913), and A. Aulard, "La Centralisation napoléonienne: les préfets" in his *Etudes et leçons*, VII (Paris, 1913), 113-195, are critical and suggestive, and may be checked now against the rising number of localized investigations, of which R. Durand's *Le Département des Côtes-du-nord sous le Consulat et l'Empire, 1800-1815,* two volumes (Paris, 1926), is an outstanding example.

A neglected topic, the resistance offered by the legislature to the encroachments of the executive, is the subject of a thesis by A. Gobert, *L'Opposition des assemblées pendant le Consulat, 1800-1804* (Paris, 1925); and the senate has been studied anew by J. de Soto, "La constitution sénatoriale de 6 avril 1814," *Revue internationale d'histoire politique et constutionelle* (Oct.-Dec., 1953), and by J. T. B. Bury, "The End of the Napoleonic Senate," *Cambridge Historical Journal*, IX, No. 2 (1948). The civil war in the western departments has been made the subject of a factual and dispassionate study by L. Dubreuil, *Histoire des insurrections de l'Ouest,* of which the second volume (Paris, 1930) takes its place beside the careful work of E. Gabory, *Napoléon et la Vendée,* three volumes (Paris, 1924-1928). More recent than either is G. Walter, *La guerre de Vendée, sociologie d'une contre-révolution* (Paris, 1953). Opposition to the imperial régime remained a persistent factor in French society, as L Madelin has indicated anew in his semi-popular lectures, *Le contrerévolution sous la Révolution, 1789-1815* (Paris, 1935). How efficiently the police watched political malcontents is clear from the records edited and compressed by E. d'Hauterive, *La Police secrète du premier empire: bulletins quotidiens adressés par Fouché à l'empereur,* three volumes (Paris, 1908-1922), and the earlier activities of the royalists are traced in his *Le Contre police royaliste en 1800* (Paris, 1931). The abortive plots against Napoleon's life had already been analyzed by E. Daudet, *La Police et les Chouans sous le Consulat et l'Empire, 1800-1815* (Paris, 2nd ed., 1895), and the victims of the secret warfare listed by J. Destrem, *Les Déportations du Consulat et l'Empire* (Paris, 1885).

3. The Germanies

F. Meinecke, *Das Zeitalter der deutschen Erhebung, 1795-1815*, 2nd ed. (Bielefeld, 1913), is an excellent survey of these difficult years. Of the older works, W. Oncken, *Das Zeitalter der Revolution, des Kaiserreiches und der Befreiungskriege*, two volumes (Berlin, 1884-1886), and A. Rambaud, *La Domination française en Allemagne*, two volumes, 4th ed. (Paris, 1897), are scholarly and still useful; and of the newer, J. Droz, *L'Allemagne et la Révolution française* (Paris, 1949), and F. Valjavic, *Die Entstehung der politischen Strömungen Deutschlands, 1770-1815* (1951). G. Servières, *L'Allemagne française sous Napoléon Ier* (Paris, 1904), covers the Hanse Towns during the period of French annexation; Ch. Schmidt, *Le Grand-duché de Berg, 1806-1818* (Paris, 1905), R. Göcke and T. Ilgen, *Das Königreich Westfalen* (Düsseldorf, 1888), and E. Hölzle, *Württemberg im Zeitalter Napoleons und der Deutsch Erhebung* (Stuttgart, 1939), do the same for the territories indicated. On the rôle of Prussia G. S. Ford has contributed two judicious and illuminating studies, *Hanover and Prussia, 1795-1803; A Study in Neutrality* (New York, 1903), and *Stein and the Era of Reforms in Prussia* (Princeton, 1922), and E. N. Anderson a thoughtful study on *Nationalism and the Cultural Crisis in Prussia, 1806-1815* (New York, 1939). J. M. E. G. Cavaignac, *La Formation de la Prusse contemporaine*, two volumes (Paris, 1897-1898), stresses the force of French examples in guiding the reforms after Jena. The pleasing and still valuable work of J. R. Seeley, *Life and Times of Stein*, three volumes (London, 1870), is better described by its subtitle, *Germany and Prussia in the Napoleonic Age*. New light has recently been thrown on Prussian politics in the critical years before Jena by K. Griewank, "Hardenberg und die preussische Politik 1804-1806," *Forschungen zur Brandenburgischen und Preussischen Geschichte*, XLVII (1935), 227-308, and indispensable source material from the Prussian archives is now appearing in the series, *Die Reorganisation des preussischen Staates unter Stein und Hardenberg*, of which volume I, part I, *Allegemeine Verwaltungs- und Behördereform*, has already appeared (Leipzig, 1931).

4. Austria

In contrast to Prussia, the Hapsburg lands have been somewhat neglected by the historians of the revolutionay era. L. Léger, *History of Austria-Hungary*, ed. by W. E. Lingelbach (Philadelphia, 1906), is an English translation of an authoritative work now a little outdated. J. Bryce, *The Holy Roman Empire*, rev. ed. (London, 1919), is the classic study of this venerable institution, but only the closing chapters are relevant here. For more specialized histories there are E. Wertheimer, *Geschichte Österreichs und Ungarns im ersten Jahrzehnt des XIX Jahrhunderts*, two volumes (Leipzig, 1884-1890), and A. Beer, *Zehn Jahre österreichischer Politik, 1801-1810* (Leipzig, 1877). The demise of the Holy Roman Empire has been made the subject of a short *post mortem* by H. von Srbik, *Das österreichische Kaisertum und das Ende des Heiligen Römischen Reiches, 1804-1806* (Berlin, 1927). For the ferment of the national spirit W. C. Langsam, *The Napoleonic Wars and German Nationalism in Austria* (New York, 1930), is stimulating and scholarly, with a well-selected bibliography; A. Robert, *L'Idée nationale autrichienne et les guerres de Napoléon* (Paris 1933), stresses particularly the renascent pride in the Austrian past. L. Lanyi touches a minor neglected topic in "Napoléon et les Hongrois," *Annales historiques de la Révolution française* (Oct.-Dec., 1955). On the plight of the defiant Tyrolese who were transferred to Bavarian sovereignty in 1805 consult J. Hirn, *Tirols Erhebung im Jahre 1809*, 2nd ed. (Innsbruck, 1909), and I. Caracciolo, *Andrea Hofer nella insurrezione anti-bavarese del 1809* (Bologna, 1927); for the Austrian share in the War of Liberation, H. Oncken, *Österreich und Preussen im Befreiungskriege, 1813-1815*, two volumes (Berlin, 1876-1879), and H. Rössler, *Osterreichs Kampf um Deutschlands Befreiung, 1805-1815*, two volumes, 2nd ed. (1947).

5. Russia

Of the longer histories of Russia available in English the most helpful for the reign of Alexander I are V. O. Kluchevsky, *A History of Russia*, translated by C. J. Hogarth, volume V (London, 1931), A. A. Kornilov, *Modern Russian History . . . from the Age of Catherine the Great to the Present*, English translation, rev. ed. (New York, 1924), and the old but still excellent work of A. N. Rambaud, *Popular History of Russia from the Earliest Times*, new ed., two volumes (New York, 1904). In French, the *Histoire de Russie*, volume II (Paris, 1933), published under the direction of Ch. Seignobos, P. Milioukov, and L. Eisenmann, is lucid and modern in tone; in German, K. Stählin, *Geschichte Russlands,* volume III, *Vom Kaiser Paul bis zum Ende des Krimkrieges,* is heavy and conventional, but sound. Equally authentic and much more readable are the historical biographies of K. Waliszewski, *Le Fils de la grande Catherine, Paul Ier, empereur de Russie* (Paris, 1912), English translation, *Paul I of Russia* (London, 1913), and *Le règne d'Alexandre Ier,* three volumes (Paris, 1923-1925). For political and military affairs a good recent study is A. A. Lobanov-Rostovsky, *Russia and Europe 1789-1825* (Durham, 1947).

6. *Italy*

Good general surveys of the period in Italian are G. de Castro, *Italia dal 1799 al 1814,* volume VII of the *Storia politica d'Italia scritta da una società di amici,* eight volumes, ed. by P. Villari (Milan, 1874-1882); F. Lemmi and V. Fiorni, *Storia d'Italia dal 1799 al 1814* (Milan, 1918); F. Lemmi, *L'età Napoleonica* (Milan, 1938); A. Fugier, *Napoléon et l'Italie* (Paris, 1947); and E. Driault, *Napoléon en Italie, 1800-1812* (Paris, 1912). A. Pingaud has supplemented his work *La Domination française dans l'Italie du nord, 1790-1805,* two volumes (Paris, 1914) by numerous monographs. G. B. McClellan, *Venice and Bonaparte* (Princeton, 1931); L. Madelin, *La Rome de Napoléon* (Paris, 1904); P. Marmottan, *Bonaparte et la république de Lucques: le royaume d'Etrurie* (Paris, 1896); J. Borel, *Gênes sous Napoléon* (Paris, 1929); and R. M. Johnston, *The Napoleonic Empire in Southern Italy and the Rise of the Secret Societies,* two volumes (London, 1904) cover the major individual states. A discursive treatment of the close of the period is provided in M. H. Weil, *Le Prince Eugène et Murat,* five volumes (Paris, 1902) and *Joachim Murat, roi de Naples,* five volumes (Paris, 1909-1919), and an excellent brief monograph by R. J. Rath, *The Fall of the Napoleonic Kingdom of Italy* (New York, 1941).

7. *Spain and Portugal*

An intelligent foundation for the period is furnished by J. Sarrailh, *L'Espagne éclairée de la seconde moitié di 18 siècle* (Paris, 1954). H. Baumgarten, *Geschichte Spaniens vom Ausbruch der französischen Revolution bis auf unsere Tage,* three volumes (Leipzig, 1865-1871), is still valuable for the years 1788-1839; volume IV of the work by R. Altamira y Crevea, *Historia de la nacion y de la civilizacion española,* four volumes, rev. ed. (Barcelona, 1913-1914), is broader in concept and modern in tone. From the French point of view, A. Fugier, *Napoléon et l'Espagne,* two volumes (Paris, 1930), is excellent, but stops at 1808. It should be supplemented by Geoffroy de Grandmaison, *L'Espagne et Napoléon,* three volumes (Paris, 1908-1931). For the closing episodes there is the monograph of P. Vidal de la Blache, *L'Evacuation de l'Espagne* (Paris, 1914), and the military histories cited below.

8. *Lesser States*

Few monographs on the Scandinavian countries in the era of Napoleon have appeared in English. Two recent studies of value are S. Carlsson and T. Höjer, *Den svenska utrikes politikens historia, 1792-1814* (Stockholm, 1954), and G. Nørregaard, *Denmark og Wienerkongressen 1814-1815* (Copenhagen, 1954). The most satisfactory general histories are K. Gjerset, *History of the Norwegian People,* two volumes (New York, 1915), and C. Hallendorff and A. Schück, *History of Sweden* (Stockholm, 1929). The relation of Sweden to the great events of 1810-1814 has been brilliantly analyzed by F. D. Scott, *Bernadotte and the Fall of Napoleon* (Cambridge, 1935), and the origins of Finnish nationalism in the nineteenth century are discussed by J. M. Wuorinen, *Nationalism in Modern Finland,* and E. K. Osmonsalo, *Suomen valloitus 1808* (Helsinki, 1947). For Belgium the standard history is that by H. Pirenne, *Histoire de Belgique,* six volumes (Brussels, 1900-1926), of which volume VI is relevant here, and Pirenne prepared a *Bibliographie de l'histoire de Belgique,* 3rd ed. (Brussels, 1931). A good *Guide to Dutch Bibliographies* has been issued by the Library of Congress (Washington, 1951). H. T. Colenbrander's studies, from *De Bataafsche Republiek* to *Vestigung van het Koninkrijk* (Amsterdam, 1908-1927), and H. Brugman's *Van Republiek tot Koninkrijk* (Amsterdam, 1939) are excellent. For Switzerland the account by W. Oechsli is available in English, *History of Switzerland, 1499-1914* (Cambridge, 1922). The years of the French supremacy have been presented by E. Guillon, *Napoléon et les suisses, 1803-1815* (Paris, 1910), and by W. Martin, *La Suisse en l'Europe, 1813-1814* (Lausanne, 1931). The destiny of Poland under the Napoleonic dispensation is discussed by M. Handelsmann, *Napoléon et la Pologne* (Paris, 1909), A. Mansuy, *Jérome Napoléon et la Pologne en 1812* (Paris, 1931), E. Kips, *Austria a sprawa polska 1809* (Warsaw, 1952), and E. Wawrzkowicz, *Anglia a sprawa polska 1813-1815* (Warsaw, 1919).

9. *The Balkans and the Near East*

R. Ettinghausen has prepared, with special emphasis on medieval and modern times, *A Selected Bibliography of Books and Periodicals in Western Languages, Dealing with the Near and Middle East,* 2nd ed. (Washington, 1954). W. Miller, *The Ottoman Empire and Its Successors, 1801-1936* (Cambridge, 1936), is good for general history and H. A. R. Gibb and H. Bowen, *Islamic Society and the West,* Volume One (London, 1950), is a valuable analysis. N. Iorga, *Geschichte des Osmanischen Reiches,* includes the revolutionary era in volume V (Gotha, 1913), but his treatment is detailed and well compressed rather than enlightening. O. von Schlechta-Wssehrd, *Die Revolutionen in Constantinopel, 1807, 1808* (Vienna, 1882), is still valuable for its use of Turkish materials, and the general problem of reform in the time of Selim III is well covered in Harold Temperley, *England and the Near East, the Crimea* (London, 1936), and by N. Mouschopoulos, "Le Despotisme éclairé en Turquie," *Bulletin of the International Committee of the Historical Sciences,* IX (1937), 147-181. Older works on the Serbian insurrection, like S. Novakovič, *Die Wiedergeburt des serbischen Staates* (Sarajevo, 1912), and Yakchič, *L'Europe et la résurrection de la Serbie, 1804-1834* (Paris, 1917), may be supplemented by E. Haumant, *La Formation de la Yougoslavie* (Paris, 1930). E. Driault, *La Politique orientale de Napoléon, 1806-1808* (Paris, 1904) is comprehensive and stimulating; P. F. Shupp, *The European Powers and the Near Eastern Question, 1806-1807* (New York, 1931), and Paul Rüter, *Die Türkei, England und das russisch-französische Bündnis, 1807-1812* (Emsdetten, 1935), cover much the same ground from a strictly international point of view. On the Anglo-French duel for control of Egypt the works of F. Charles-Roux should be consulted, notably *L'Angleterre et l'expédition française en Egypte,* two volumes (Paris, 1925), and also G. Douin, *L'Angleterre et l'Egypte: la politique mameluke, 1801-1807,* two volumes (Cairo, 1929-1930); and for Franco-Turkish relations V. J. Puryear, *Napoleon and the Dardanelles* (Berkeley, 1951).

10. The Colonial World

J. Saintoyant, *La Colonisation française pendant la période napoléonienne 1799-1815* (Paris, 1931), is the most recent study, by a leading authority. C. L. Lokke, *France and the Colonial Question: a study of contemporary French opinion, 1763-1801* (New York, 1932), is excellent. For a colonial dream, frustrated and all but forgotten today, see E. Scott, *Terre Napoleon: a History of French Explorations and Projects in Australia* (London, 1910). B. Moses has traced *Spain's Declining Power in South America, 1730-1806* (Berkeley, California, 1919), H. T. Manning has studied *British Colonial Government after the American Revolution, 1782-1820* (Oxford, 1934), and Charles Webster, *Britain and the Independence of Latin America 1812-1830,* two volumes (New York, 1938). Notable, in the extensive literature on the Louisiana question, are F. P. Renaut, *La Question de la Louisiane, 1796-1803* (Paris, 1919), E. W. Lyon, *Louisiana in French Diplomacy* (Norman, Okla., 1933), and *Bonaparte's Proposed Louisiana Expedition* (Chicago, 1934), A. P. Whitaker, *The Mississippi, 1795-1803, a study in trade, politics, and diplomacy* (New York, 1934), and from a broader angle but significant for its background, D. Echeverria, *Mirage in the West: A History of the French Image of America to 1815* (Princeton, 1957).

CONSTITUTIONAL AND LEGAL HISTORY

The political theories which inspired the constitutional experiments of the revolutionary age can be followed to advantage in W. A. Dunning, *History of Political Theories from Rousseau to Spencer* (New York, 1920). A. Lewkowitz has provided an acute and suggestive study in the same field, *Die klassische Rechts- und Staatsphilosophie, Montesquieu bis Hegel* (Breslau, 1914). For France the clearest and most objective treatment of constitutional issues is M. Deslandres, *Histoire constitutionelle de la France de 1789 à 1870,* volume I (Paris, 1932), covering the period 1789-1815. Ph. Sagnac's enlightening analysis, *La Législation civile de la Révolution française, 1789-1804* (Paris, 1898), J. van Kam, *Les Efforts de Codification en France* (Paris, 1929), and P. Viard, *Histoire générale du droit privé français de 1789 à 1830* (Paris, 1931), discuss the legal problems and experiments. The confused state of German constitutional ideals at this stage is well suggested by A. Berney, "Reichstradition und Nationalstaatsgedanke, 1789-1815," *Historische Zeitschrift,* CXL (1929), 57-86. The troublesome question of Napoleon's concept of international law was examined by E. Chevalley, *Essai sur le droit de gens napoléonien, 1800-1807* (Paris, 1912), and B. Mirkin-Gecevič, in "L'Influence de la Révolution française sur le developpement du droit international dans l'Europe orientale," *Recueil des cours de l'Académie de droit international,* XXII (1928), 295-456. For a list of the numerous constitutions promulgated in Europe during the revolutionary age, and a critical estimate of the most useful collections in which they may be found, see H. B. Hill, "The Constitutions of Continental Europe," *The Journal of Modern History,* VIII (1936), 82-94.

ECONOMIC HISTORY

E. Heckscher, *The Continental System, an economic interpretation* (Oxford, 1922), is the best one-volume study on the subject. A short monograph, excellent but not easily available, is G. Drottboom, *Wirtschaftsgeographische Betrachtungen über die Wirkungen der napoleonischen Kontinentalsperre auf Industrie und Handel* (Bonn, 1906). A study in perspective which surveys the modifications of the agrarian system, written by a master of the subject, is H. Sée's *Esquisse d'une histoire du régime agraire en Europe aux XVIIIe et XIXe siècles* (Paris, 1921). For the state of French finances, R. Stourm, *Les Finances du Consulat* (Paris, 1902), is lucid, critical, and somewhat hostile towards Napoleon; M. Marion, *Histoire financière de la France depuis 1715*, of which volume IV (Paris, 1921) covers the years 1797-1818, is also censorious, but lays the chief blame for the insecurity of French national credit on the mistakes of the revolutionary assemblies. C. P. Higby and C. B. Willis have analyzed economic conditions in "Industry and Labor under Napoleon," *American Historical Review*, LIII, No. 3 (Apr., 1948), and F. E. Melvin has done the same for *Napoleon's Navigation System* (New York, 1919) in a cool and judicious monograph. For French commerce and industry the outstanding authorities are E. Levasseur's *Histoire du commerce en France*, volume II (Paris, 1912), and *Histoire des classes ouvrières et de l'industrie en France depuis 1789 à 1870*, volume I, rev. ed. (Paris, 1903). Ch. Ballot, *L'Introduction du méchanisme dans l'industrie française* (Lille, 1923), and O. Viennet, *Napoléon et l'industrie française: La Crise de 1810-1811* (Paris, 1947), are good, especially the first. For northern Italy under the French domination consult E. Tarlé, *Le Blocus continental et le royaume d'Italie*, new ed. (Paris, 1931), and A. Pingaud, "Le Premier royaume d'Italie: l'œuvre financière," *Revue d'histoire diplomatique*, XLIV (1930), 269-287, 435-449, and for the Illyrian Provinces, M. Pivec-Stele, *La Vie économique des provinces illyriennes, 1809-1813* (Paris, 1930). For Great Britain, N. J. Silberling, "Financial and Monetary Policy of Great Britain during the Napoleonic Wars," *Quarterly Journal of Economics*, XXXVIII (1924), 214-233, 397-439, is a compendium of exact information lucidly presented; A. Cunningham, *British Credit in the last Napoleonic War* (Cambridge, 1910), a brief but useful monograph on the Anglo-French economic duel from 1803 to 1814; W. F. Galpin, *The grain supply of England during the Napoleonic Period* (Philadelphia, 1925), a careful examination of a debated topic which minimizes the risk Britain then ran of facing an acute food shortage. A. Hope-Jones uses newly found records in *Income Tax in the Napoleonic Wars* (Cambridge, 1939), and W. O. Henderson opens broad vistas in *Britain and Industrial Europe* (Liverpool, 1954). The British merchant marine and its organization is well portrayed by C. N. Parkinson, *Trade in the Eastern seas, 1793-1813* (Cambridge, 1937). For Russia and its economy G. F. Robinson, *Rural Russia under the Old Regime* (London, 1949), and J. Mavor, *Economic History of Russia,* 2nd rev. ed. (New York, 1926), may be consulted.

SOCIAL HISTORY

For France, the relevant volume of the *Histoire socialiste,* edited by J. Jaurès, VI, P. Brousse and H. Thurot, *Le Consulat et l'Empire* (Paris, 1905) is useful, though not up to the general standard for the series. The state of French society in the first years of the nineteenth century has been portrayed by G. Hanotaux, "La Transformation sociale à l'époque napoléonienne," *Revue des deux mondes,* XXIII (1926), 89-123, 562-597. A. Aulard has shed considerable light on the state of public opinion in *Paris sous le premier empire: recueil des documents pour l'histoire de l'esprit public à Paris,* three volumes (Paris, 1912-1923), and L. de Lanzac de Laborie, *Paris sous Napoléon,* eight volumes (Paris, 1905-1913), offers a wealth of detail on social life and the condition of the poor, particularly in volumes III and V. For the working class see E. Levasseur, *Histoire des classes ouvrières et de l'industrie française depuis 1789,* volume II, rev. ed. (Paris, 1904), already cited, and G. Mauco, *Les Migrations ouvrières in France au début du XIX⁰ siècle* (Paris, 1932). The abolition of serfdom in Prussia is discussed in the old but competent study of G. F. Knapp, *Die Landarbiter in Knechtschaft und Freiheit* (Leipzig, 1891). For popular discontent in England towards the close of the Napoleonic period there is a study by F. O. Darvall, *Popular Disturbances and Public Order in Regency England . . . 1811-1817* (New York, 1934), and for the harsh lot of the laboring classes the three well-documented monographic indictments by J. L. and B. Hammond, *Village Labourer, 1760-1832,* new ed. (London, 1920), *Town Labourer, 1780-1832* (London, 1917), and *Skilled Labourer, 1760-1832* (London, 1919).

DIPLOMATIC HISTORY AND INTERNATIONAL RELATIONS

The outstanding work on the foreign policies of the European states, large and small, in the revolutionary era is Albert Sorel's *L'Europe et la révolution française,* eight volumes (Paris, 1895-1904). The best one-volume studies of the period are E. Bourgeois, *Manuel historique de politique étrangère,* four volumes, new ed. (Paris, 1945-1949), the relevant volume here being II (1789-1930), and A. Fugier, *La Révolution française et l'Empire napoléonien* (Paris, 1954). For Great Britain there is A. W.

Ward and G. P. Gooch, *Cambridge History of British Foreign Policy,
1783-1919*, three volumes (Cambridge, 1922-1923), volume I; for Russia
the comprehensive studies of S. S. Tatischeff, *Alexandre Ier et Napoléon
d'après leur correspondance inédite, 1801-1812* (Paris, 1891), and A.
Vandal, *Napoléon et Alexandre Ier: l'alliance russe sous le premier
empire*, three volumes (Paris, 1891-1896); for Austria, C. S. Buckland,
Metternich and the British Government from 1807 to 1813 (London,
1932); for Prussia, K. A. von Hardenberg, *Denkwürdigkeiten*, five
volumes, ed. by L. von Ranke (Leipzig, 1877). The foundation for
Napoleon's policy in the Germanies was laid in the 1790's, and S. S.
Biro has analyzed this phase thoroughly in *The German Policy of
Revolutionary France*, two volumes (Cambridge, Mass., 1957). The
problems of the neutral state in this war-filled epoch can be studied in
W. A. Philips and A. H. Reede, *Neutrality, Its History, Economics and
Law*, volume II, *The Napoleonic Period* (New York, 1936). The attempts
to curb the abuses resulting from British maritime supremacy are set
forth in J. B. Scott, ed., *The Armed Neutralities of 1780 and 1800* (New
York, 1918), and F. Piggott and G. W. T. Ormond, *Documentary
History of the Armed Neutralities of 1780 and 1800* (London, 1919). On
the abduction and execution of the Duc d'Enghien, for a reasoned indict-
ment of Napoleon as responsible see H. Welschinger, *Le Duc d'Enghien:
l'enlèvement d'Ettenheim et l'exécution de Vincennes* (Paris, 1913);
for an extenuation, J. Dontenville, "La Catastrophe du duc d'Enghien,"
Revue des études napoléoniennes, XXV (1925), 43-69. Napoleon's diplomatic technique and its effects from Campoformio to his second abdication have been brilliantly analyzed by R. B. Mowat, *The Diplomacy
of Napoleon* (London, 1924); H. Butterfield has essayed the same task
for a shorter period with even greater penetration in *The Peace Tactics
of Napoleon, 1806-1808* (Cambridge, 1929) and the diplomatic developments of the critical years from 1800 to 1805 have been reëxamined
with scholarly care by H. C. Deutsch in *The Genesis of Napoleonic
Imperialism* (Cambridge, Mass., 1938). R. B. Holtman has assessed
Napoleonic Propaganda (Baton Rouge, 1950), C. L. Lokke has thrown
new light on a much debated rupture in "Secret Negotiations to Main-
tain the Peace of Amiens," in *American Historical Review*, XLIX, No. 1
(Oct., 1943), and J. H. Gleason in *The Genesis of Russophobia in Great
Britain* analyzes its early nineteenth-century origins (New York, 1951).
On the closing episodes of the era and the European concert W. A.
Phillips, *The Confederation of Europe* (London, 1920), and C. K.
Webster, *The Congress of Vienna, 1814-1815*, new ed. (London, 1934),

are lucid and informative, and have been more recently supplemented by H. Nicolson, *The Congress of Vienna* (New York, 1946), and H. A. Kissinger, *A World Restored* (Boston, 1957). For the chief crises in the foreign relations of the United States during these years see the works cited above on the Louisiana question; for the embargo acts, L. M. Sears, *Jefferson and the Embargo;* for the breach with Great Britain, F. A. Updyke, *The Diplomacy of the War of 1812* (Baltimore, 1915).

MILITARY AND NAVAL HISTORY

T. A. Dodge, *Napoleon, a History of the Art of War, from the beginnings of the French Revolution to the battle of Waterloo,* four volumes (Boston, 1904-1907), is still useful; later works in English are R. W. Phipps, *The Armies of the First French Republic and the Rise of the Marshals of Napoleon I,* five volumes (Oxford, 1926-1939), and A. G. Macdonell, *Napoleon and his Marshals* (New York, 1934). Sir Charles Oman's *Studies in Napoleonic Wars* (London, 1929) are charming and authoritative; H. Camon's *La Guerre napoléonienne: précis des campagnes* (Paris, 1903) is succinct, honest, and full of admiration. For individual phases of the Napoleonic struggle, A. Grasset, ed., *La Guerre d'Espagne, 1807-1813,* is a shapeless narrative on the Spanish conflict of which three volumes have appeared (Paris, 1914-1932) carrying the action to 1808. It seems doubtful if the historical section of the French general staff will overcome the Spanish obstacles even at this date, and English readers will prefer Sir Charles Oman, *History of the Peninsular War,* seven volumes (Oxford, 1902-1930). The standard history of the British military forces is that of J. W. Fortescue, *History of the British Army,* thirteen volumes in twenty (London, 1899-1930), of which volumes III to X are relevant for the period. *Napoleon's Invasion of Russia,* English translation (Oxford, 1942), by the noted Russian historian E. Tarlé, is prejudiced, but W. O. Shanahan has done an objective appraisal of a confused topic in *Prussian Military Reforms, 1786-1813* (New York, 1945). An official record of the Austrian military effort with the last coalition has been edited for the general reader by E. von Woinovich and A. Veltzé, *1813 bis 1815: Oesterreich in den Befreiungskriegen,* nine volumes (Vienna, 1911-1914). For the naval war the recognized authority is A. T. Mahan, *The Influence of Sea Power upon the French Revolution and Empire, 1793-1812,* 14th ed., two volumes (Boston, 1919). Mahan's thesis that mastery of the sea was the decisive factor in the struggle often led him to overrate it, as in his companion work, *Sea Power in its Relation to the War of 1812,* two volumes

(Boston, 1905). Two more recent works are R. Maine, *Trafalgar: Napoleon's Naval Waterloo* (New York, 1957), a careful and incisive study, and A. A. Thomazi, *Napoléon et ses marins* (Paris, 1950). For the controversial question of the Boulogne flotilla, the most thorough study is E. Desbrière, *Projects et tentatives de débarquement aux îles britanniques, 1793-1805,* four volumes in five (Paris, 1900-1912).

INTELLECTUAL AND CULTURAL HISTORY

On early nineteenth-century thought in England, France, and Germany T. Merz, *History of European Thought in the Nineteenth Century,* four volumes, 4th ed. (Edinburgh, 1923-1924), is philosophic in treatment and fluent in style. The leading history of philosophy as such is that by K. Fischer, *Geschichte der neueren Philosophie,* ten volumes in eleven (Heidelberg, 1897-1904), of which books IV-VIII are particularly applicable here. The brilliant work of H. Høffding, *Geschichte der neueren Philosophie,* 2nd ed., two volumes (Leipzig, 1921), is available in English translation (New York, 1950). E. Friedell, *Cultural History of the Modern Age,* three volumes (New York, 1930), contains eloquent sections on the period in volumes II and III. On art there are the popular work of E. Faure, *History of Art,* five volumes (New York and London, 1921-1930), volume IV, and A. Hauser, *The Social History of Art* (New York, 1950), volume II, both of which cover the subject since the seventeenth century in a suggestive and readable synthesis. In J. Jaurès, *Histoire socialiste de la Révolution française,* reëdited by A. Mathiez, eight volumes (Paris, 1922-1924), volume V, *La Révolution en Europe,* is a brilliant survey of the influences emanating from France, and E. Bourgeois has a volume on *Le style Empire, ses origines et ses caractères* (Paris, 1930). The force of scientific and materialistic doctrines in French thought after 1800 can be best studied in F. J. Picavet, *Les idéologues* (Paris, 1891). For practical results of the scientific bent see A. Fabre, *Les Origines du système métrique* (Paris, 1931), and K. Duane, "Telegraphs and Telegrams in Revolutionary France," *Scientific Monthly* (Dec., 1944); the same journal (Feb., 1955) also published the acute estimate by H. Guerlac on "Some Aspects of Science during the French Revolution." Equally relevant are the articles by F. B. Artz on "L'Enseignement technique en France pendant l'epoque revolutionnaire, 1789-1815," in *Revue historique* (July-Sept., 1946). Edward Dowden, *The French Revolution in English Literature* (London, 1897), relates the major British writers of the age to that complex of generalities which was then the French climate of opinion. In A. Cobban, *Edmund Burke and the Revolt against the Eighteenth Century* (New York, 1929), the anti-rationalist mood is analyzed in brief monographic fashion, and C. Brinton does the same for the *Political Ideas of the English Romanticists* (Oxford, 1926). For German thought there are a number of excellent studies. G. P. Gooch, *Germany and the French Revolution* (New York, 1920), is chiefly an appraisal of intellectual challenges and responses as these are reflected in the works of leading German writers at the close of the century. A. Stern, *Der Einfluss der französischen Revolution auf das deutsche Geistesleben* (Stuttgart, 1928), covers much the same field. On German political thought a recent and competent but uninspiring account is R. Aris, *History of Political Thought in Germany from 1789 to 1815* (London, 1936). F. Meinecke has integrated the anti-rationalist and particularly the anti-mechanistic trends of German thought in *Die Entstehung des Historismus,* two volumes (Munich, 1936); D. Baumgardt has emphasized the importance of the mystics in *Franz von Baader und die philosophische Romantik* (Halle, 1927); and R. Haym has written what is probably the best study of *Die Romantische Schule,* new ed. (Berlin, 1928). For the close connection between the revival of German literature, philosophy and nationalism there is the excellent study of R. R. Ergang, *Herder and the Foundations of German Nationalism* (New York, 1931). F. H. Taylor, *The Taste of Angels, a History of Art Collecting from Rameses to Napoleon* (Boston, 1948), has some pertinent chapters, and D. M. Quynn traced "The Art Confiscations of the Napoleonic Wars" in *American Historical Review,* L, No. 3 (Apr., 1945).

RELIGIOUS HISTORY

On the concordat there is a lucid and scholarly monograph in English by H. H. Walsh, *The Concordat of 1801: A study of the problem of nationalism in the relations of church and state* (New York, 1933). The standard French accounts are those of A. Boulay de la Meurthe, *Histoire de la négotiation du concordat de 1801* (Tours, 1920), *Histoire du rétablissement du culte en France, 1802-1805* (Tours, 1925), and G. L. M. J. Constant, *L'Eglise de France sous le Consulat et l'Empire, 1800-1814* (Paris, 1928). M. Lühr's brief discussion *Napoleons Stellung zu Religion und Kirche* (Berlin, 1939) and R. B. Holtman, "The Catholic Church in Napoleonic Propaganda," *Catholic Historical Review* (Apr., 1949), are interesting. The policies and problems of the papacy for the years 1800-1815 can be studied in the neglected but valuable collection, *La diplomazia pontificia nel secolo XIX,* five volumes (Rome, 1902-1906), edited by I. Rinieri. The situation of the Jews under the Consulate and the Empire has been carefully studied by R. Anchel, *Napoléon et les juifs* (Paris, 1928). For the contemporary religious developments in England a useful work is still J. Stoughton, *Religion in England from 1800 to 1850*, two volumes (London, 1884); for the condition of the Roman Catholics in that kingdom, B. N. Ward, *Eve of Catholic Emancipation, being the history of the English Catholics during the first thirty years of the nineteenth century*, three volumes (London and New York, 1911-1912). On the secularization of church lands in the Germanies, the difficulties of Pius VII, and the reëstablishment of the Society of Jesus in 1814, the best general histories are those of F. Nielsen, in English translation, *History of the Papacy in the Nineteenth Century*, two volumes (New York, 1906), and J. MacCaffrey, *History of the Catholic Church in the Nineteenth Century, 1789-1908*, 2nd rev. ed., two volumes (Dublin, 1910).

BIOGRAPHIES, MEMOIRS AND CORRESPONDENCE

The biographical and autobiographical material relating to the period is so extensive that this section can do no more than list a few dozen outstanding titles, reserving particular mention for publications of the past decade.

F. M. Kircheisen's monumental biography, *Napoleon I: sein Leben und seine Zeit*, reached the ninth volume (Munich, 1934), carrying the story to 1821. A two-volume abridgment, *Napoleon I, ein Lebensbild* (Stuttgart, 1927-1929), is available in an English tranlsation, *Napoleon* (New York, 1932). The excellent lives by Fournier and Rose, cited earlier, have also been supplemented in recent years by the thoughtful studies of J. Bainville, *Napoléon* (Paris, 1931), E. Tarlé, *Bonaparte* (New York, 1937), and L. Madelin, *Napoléon* (Paris, 1935), the first two available in English. E. Driault has sought to relate Napoleon to his age in *La Vraie figure de Napoléon* (Paris, 1929) and *Napoléon le grand*, three volumes (Paris, 1930). On the Bonaparte family a sane and detailed treatment is now available to English readers in W. Geer, *Napoleon and his family, the story of a Corsican clan*, three volumes (New York, 1927-1929), which surveys the field so exhaustively explored by F. Masson in *Napoléon et sa famille*, thirteen volumes (Paris, 1897-1919).

Space limits forbid a full citation of the published memoirs of Eugène de Beauharnais, Hortense de Beauharnais, Bertrand, Jerôme Bonaparte, Bourrienne, Brune, Caulaincourt, Chaptal, Fain, Fouché, Gaudin,

Gourgaud, Las Cases, Marbot, Maret, Méneval, Miot de Melito, Mollien, Norvins, Pasquier, Remusat, Roederer, Savary, Ségur, Talleyrand, Thibaudeau—to name the more important—and the student is referred to more ample bibliographies for titles and editions.

Several leading figures of the Napoleonic epoch have found new biographers. G. Lacour-Gayet, *Talleyrand, 1754-1838,* three volumes (Paris, 1928-1931), will probably remain the definitive life despite the author's hostility towards his subject; there are later lives by Saint-Aulaire, C. Brinton, and L. Madelin. For Stein there is the work of G. Ritter, *Stein, eine politische Biographie,* two volumes (Stuttgart, 1931). The ponderous life of Metternich by H. von Srbik, *Metternich, der Staatsmann und der Mensch,* two volumes (Munich, 1925), has been followed by the more readable volumes of A. Cecil, *Metternich, 1773-1859: a study of his period and personality* (New York, 1933), and H. du Coudray, *Metternich* (London, 1935). P. Guedalla, *Wellington* (New York, 1930), will probably remain the most entertaining account of the Iron Duke's long and illustrious career. For Pitt there is the admirable contribution of J. H. Rose, *Life of William Pitt* (London, 1923), and the popular portrait by P. Wilson, *William Pitt the Younger* (New York, 1934). Two secondary figures who have gained merited recognition are Gentz and Barbé-Marbois: P. R. Sweet published *Friedrich von Gentz, Defender of the Old Order* (Wisconsin, 1941) and G. Mann *Secretary of Europe: the Life of Friedrich Gentz* (New Haven, 1946), while E. W. Lyon did justice to *The Man Who Sold Louisiana: the Career of François Barbé-Marbois* (Norman, Okla., 1942).

The letters and papers of Baron vom Stein have at last been made conveniently accessible by E. Botzenhart, ed., *Freiherr vom Stein: Briefwechsel, Denkschriften und Aufzeichnungen,* two volumes (Berlin, 1931-1937). Other interesting source material includes the *Fürstenbriefe an Napoleon I,* ed. F. M. Kircheisen, two volumes (Stuttgart, 1929), and some not very significant *Manuscrits de Napoléon, 1793-1795, en Pologne,* ed. by S. Askenazy (Warsaw, 1929). Kircheisen found time amid his many labors to prepare an autobiographical record of Napoleon's career under the title *Memoiren Napoleons* (Dresden, 1927), translated as *Napoleon's Autobiography* (New York, 1931), which ranks with other collections of Napoleon's words, R. M. Johnston, *The Corsican* (Boston, 1930), Somerset de Chair, *Napoleon's Memoirs* (London, 1948), and the brilliant compilation prepared by J. Christopher Herold and entitled *The Mind of Napoleon* (New York, 1955). To feel the authentic impact of Napoleon's personality and thought, so skillfully projected in these mosaics, and contrast this net impression with the cloudy legends described by J. Dechamps, *Sur la légende de Napoléon* (Paris, 1931), and A. L. Guérard, *Reflections on the Napoleonic Legend* (New York, 1923), is the easiest way to comprehend the gulf that separates the man and the myth.

SUPPLEMENT, JANUARY 1963

For a recent assessment of Napoleon's place in history and a select bibliography of some five hundred titles, see *Napoléon et l'Europe* by Marcel Dunan and others (Paris, 1961). Some recent additions to the literature of the period include an exhaustive study by François Crouzet, *L'Économie britannique et le blocus continental (1806-1813)*, 2 volumes (Paris, 1958), and a second work on economic history, R. S. Fitton and A. P. Wadsworth, *The Strutts and the Arkwrights: A Study of the Early Factory System* (New York, 1958). In legal history, Marcel Garaud has supplemented the earlier work of P. Viard with an *Histoire générale du droit privé français (de 1789 à 1804)*, (Paris, 1958). In military history Carlo Zaghi throws new light on the first Italian campaign in *Bonaparte e il direttorio dopo Campoformio* (Naples, 1956); Comte Philippe de Ségur's account of the disaster of 1812 appeared in English translation as *Napoleon's Russian Campaign* (Boston, 1958), Godfrey Davis provided a new study of *Wellington and His Army* (Oxford, 1954) and C. N. Parkinson surveyed a neglected area in *War in the Eastern Seas, 1793-1815* (London, 1954). The relations of Spain and its colonies have been further clarified by Robert J. Shafer, *The Economic Societies in the Spanish World, 1763-1821* (Syracuse, 1958), and William W. Kaufman amplifies the work of Charles Webster in a more recent study, *British Foreign Policy and the Independence of Latin America, 1804-1828* (New Haven, 1951). For Napoleon's last years, Henri-Gatien Bertrand's *Cahiers de Sainte-Hélène*, three volumes (Paris, 1949-1959), are significant.

Several secondary characters of the Napoleonic drama have found new biographers: Marjan Kukiel, *Czartoryski and European Unity, 1770-1861* (Princeton, 1955); Robert T. Clark, *Herder: His Life and Thought* (Berkeley, 1955); Angelo Pereira, *D. João VI, principe e rei*, 2 volumes (Lisbon, 1953-1956); Torvald T. Höjer, *Karl XIV Johan*, three volumes (Stockholm, 1939-1960); Marc Raeff, *Michael Speransky: Statesman of Imperial Russia, 1772-1839* (The Hague, 1957).

INDEX

hARPER ✦ ԵORChBOOKS

HUMANITIES AND SOCIAL SCIENCES

American Studies: General

THOMAS C. COCHRAN: The Inner Revolution: *Essays on the Social Sciences in History*   TB/1140
EDWARD S. CORWIN: American Constitutional History. *Essays edited by Alpheus T. Mason and Gerald Garvey*   TB/1136
CARL N. DEGLER, Ed.: Pivotal Interpretations of American History   TB/1240, TB/1241
A. HUNTER DUPREE: Science in the Federal Government: *A History of Policies and Activities to 1940*   TB/573
OSCAR HANDLIN, Ed.: This Was America: *As Recorded by European Travelers in the Eighteenth, Nineteenth and Twentieth Centuries. Illus.*   TB/1119
MARCUS LEE HANSEN: The Atlantic Migration: 1607-1860. *Edited by Arthur M. Schlesinger. Introduction by Oscar Handlin*   TB/1052
MARCUS LEE HANSEN: The Immigrant in American History. *Edited with a Foreword by Arthur M. Schlesinger*   TB/1120
JOHN HIGHAM, Ed.: The Reconstruction of American History   TB/1068
ROBERT H. JACKSON: The Supreme Court in the American System of Government   TB/1106
JOHN F. KENNEDY: A Nation of Immigrants. *Illus. Revised and Enlarged. Introduction by Robert F. Kennedy*   TB/1118
RALPH BARTON PERRY: Puritanism and Democracy   TB/1138
ARNOLD ROSE: The Negro in America: *The Condensed Version of Gunnar Myrdal's An American Dilemma*   TB/3048
MAURICE R. STEIN: The Eclipse of Community: *An Interpretation of American Studies*   TB/1128
W. LLOYD WARNER and Associates: Democracy in Jonesville: *A Study in Quality and Inequality* ‖   TB/1129
W. LLOYD WARNER: Social Class in America: *The Evaluation of Status*   TB/1013

American Studies: Colonial

BERNARD BAILYN, Ed.: The Apologia of Robert Keayne: *Self-Portrait of a Puritan Merchant*   TB/1201
BERNARD BAILYN: The New England Merchants in the Seventeenth Century   TB/1149
JOSEPH CHARLES: The Origins of the American Party System   TB/1049
LAWRENCE HENRY GIPSON: The Coming of the Revolution: 1763-1775. † *Illus.*   TB/3007
LEONARD W. LEVY: Freedom of Speech and Press in Early American History: *Legacy of Suppression*   TB/1109

PERRY MILLER: Errand Into the Wilderness   TB/1139
PERRY MILLER & T. H. JOHNSON, Eds.: The Puritans: *A Sourcebook of Their Writings*
   Vol. I TB/1093;   Vol. II TB/1094
EDMUND S. MORGAN, Ed.: The Diary of Michael Wigglesworth, 1653-1657: *The Conscience of a Puritan*
EDMUND S. MORGAN: The Puritan Family: *Religion and Domestic Relations in Seventeenth-Century New England*   TB/1227
RICHARD B. MORRIS: Government and Labor in Early America   TB/1244
KENNETH B. MURDOCK: Literature and Theology in Colonial New England   TB/99
WALLACE NOTESTEIN: The English People on the Eve of Colonization: 1603-1630. † *Illus.*   TB/3006
LOUIS B. WRIGHT: The Cultural Life of the American Colonies: 1607-1763. † *Illus.*   TB/3005

American Studies: From the Revolution to 1860

JOHN R. ALDEN: The American Revolution: 1775-1783. † *Illus.*   TB/3011
MAX BELOFF, Ed.: The Debate on the American Revolution, 1761-1783: *A Sourcebook*   TB/1225
RAY A. BILLINGTON: The Far Western Frontier: 1830-1860. † *Illus.*   TB/3012
EDMUND BURKE: On the American Revolution: *Selected Speeches and Letters.* ‡ *Edited by Elliott Robert Barkan*   TB/3068
WHITNEY R. CROSS: The Burned-Over District: *The Social and Intellectual History of Enthusiastic Religion in Western New York, 1800-1850*   TB/1242
GEORGE DANGERFIELD: The Awakening of American Nationalism: 1815-1828. † *Illus.*   TB/3061
CLEMENT EATON: The Freedom-of-Thought Struggle in the Old South. *Revised and Enlarged. Illus.*   TB/1150
CLEMENT EATON: The Growth of Southern Civilization: 1790-1860. † *Illus.*   TB/3040
LOUIS FILLER: The Crusade Against Slavery: 1830-1860. † *Illus.*   TB/3029
DIXON RYAN FOX: The Decline of Aristocracy in the Politics of New York: 1801-1840. ‡ *Edited by Robert V. Remini*   TB/3064
FELIX GILBERT: The Beginnings of American Foreign Policy: *To the Farewell Address*   TB/1200
FRANCIS J. GRUND: Aristocracy in America: *Social Class in the Formative Years of the New Nation*   TB/1001
ALEXANDER HAMILTON: The Reports of Alexander Hamilton. ‡ *Edited by Jacob E. Cooke*   TB/3060
THOMAS JEFFERSON: Notes on the State of Virginia. ‡ *Edited by Thomas P. Abernethy*   TB/3052
JAMES MADISON: The Forging of American Federalism: *Selected Writings of James Madison. Edited by Saul K. Padover*   TB/1226

† The New American Nation Series, edited by Henry Steele Commager and Richard B. Morris.
‡ American Perspectives series, edited by Bernard Wishy and William E. Leuchtenburg.
* The Rise of Modern Europe series, edited by William L. Langer.
‖ Researches in the Social, Cultural, and Behavioral Sciences, edited by Benjamin Nelson.
§ The Library of Religion and Culture, edited by Benjamin Nelson.
Z Harper Modern Science Series, edited by James R. Newman.
o Not for sale in Canada.

1

4

B. NAMIER: Vanished Supremacies: Essays on European History, 1812-1918 ° TB/1088
JHN U. NEF: Western Civilization Since the Renaissance: Peace, War, Industry, and the Arts TB/1113
REDERICK L. NUSSBAUM: The Triumph of Science and Reason, 1660-1685. * Illus. TB/3009
JHN PLAMENATZ: German Marxism and Russian Communism. ° New Preface by the Author TB/1189
RAYMOND W. POSTGATE, Ed.: Revolution from 1789 to 1906: Selected Documents TB/1063
ENFIELD ROBERTS: The Quest for Security, 1715-1740. * Illus. TB/3016
RISCILLA ROBERTSON: Revolutions of 1848: A Social History TB/1025
LBERT SOREL: Europe Under the Old Regime. Translated by Francis H. Herrick TB/1121
N. SUKHANOV: The Russian Revolution, 1917: Eyewitness Account. Edited by Joel Carmichael
Vol. I TB/1066; Vol. II TB/1067
J. P. TAYLOR: The Habsburg Monarchy, 1809-1918: A History of the Austrian Empire and Austria-Hungary ° TB/1187
JHN B. WOLF: The Emergence of the Great Powers, 1685-1715. * Illus. TB/3010
JHN B. WOLF: France: 1814-1919: The Rise of a Liberal-Democratic Society TB/3019

Intellectual History & History of Ideas

ERSCHEL BAKER: The Image of Man: A Study of the Idea of Human Dignity in Classical Antiquity, the Middle Ages, and the Renaissance TB/1047
R. BOLGAR: The Classical Heritage and Its Beneficiaries: From the Carolingian Age to the End of the Renaissance TB/1125
ANDOLPH S. BOURNE: War and the Intellectuals: Collected Essays, 1915-1919. ‡ Edited by Carl Resek TB/3043
BRONOWSKI & BRUCE MAZLISH: The Western Intellectual Tradition: From Leonardo to Hegel TB/3001
RNST CASSIRER: The Individual and the Cosmos in Renaissance Philosophy. Translated with an Introduction by Mario Domandi TB/1097
ORMAN COHN: The Pursuit of the Millennium: Revolutionary Messianism in Medieval and Reformation Europe TB/1037
C. GILLISPIE: Genesis and Geology: The Decades before Darwin § TB/51
RACHEL LEVY: Religious Conceptions of the Stone Age and Their Influence upon European Thought. Illus. Introduction by Henri Frankfort TB/106
RTHUR O. LOVEJOY: The Great Chain of Being: A Study of the History of an Idea TB/1009
RANK E. MANUEL: The Prophets of Paris: Turgot, Condorcet, Saint-Simon, Fourier, and Comte TB/1218
ERRY MILLER & T. H. JOHNSON, Editors: The Puritans: A Sourcebook of Their Writings
Vol. I TB/1093; Vol. II TB/1094
ILTON C. NAHM: Genius and Creativity: An Essay in the History of Ideas TB/1196
OBERT PAYNE: Hubris: A Study of Pride. Foreword by Sir Herbert Read TB/1031
ALPH BARTON PERRY: The Thought and Character of William James: Briefer Version TB/1156
EORG SIMMEL et al.: Essays on Sociology, Philosophy, and Aesthetics. ‖ Edited by Kurt H. Wolff TB/1234
RUNO SNELL: The Discovery of the Mind: The Greek Origins of European Thought TB/1018
AGET TOYNBEE: Dante Alighieri: His Life and Works. Edited with Intro. by Charles S. Singleton TB/1206
RNEST LEE TUVESON: Millennium and Utopia: A Study in the Background of the Idea of Progress. ‖ New Preface by the Author TB/1134
AUL VALÉRY: The Outlook for Intelligence TB/2016
HILIP P. WIENER: Evolution and the Founders of Pragmatism. Foreword by John Dewey TB/1212

Literature, Poetry, The Novel & Criticism

JAMES BAIRD: Ishmael: The Art of Melville in the Contexts of International Primitivism TB/1023
JACQUES BARZUN: The House of Intellect TB/1051
W. J. BATE: From Classic to Romantic: Premises of Taste in Eighteenth Century England TB/1036
RACHEL BESPALOFF: On the Iliad TB/2006
R. P. BLACKMUR et al.: Lectures in Criticism. Introduction by Huntington Cairns TB/2003
ABRAHAM CAHAN: The Rise of David Levinsky: a documentary novel of social mobility in early twentieth century America. Intro. by John Higham TB/1028
ERNST R. CURTIUS: European Literature and the Latin Middle Ages TB/2015
GEORGE ELIOT: Daniel Deronda: a novel. Introduction by F. R. Leavis TB/1039
ADOLF ERMAN, Ed.: The Ancient Egyptians: A Sourcebook of Their Writings. New Material and Introduction by William Kelly Simpson TB/1233
ÉTIENNE GILSON: Dante and Philosophy TB/1089
ALFRED HARBAGE: As They Liked It: A Study of Shakespeare's Moral Artistry TB/1035
STANLEY R. HOPPER, Ed.: Spiritual Problems in Contemporary Literature § TB/21
A. R. HUMPHREYS: The Augustan World: Society, Thought and Letters in 18th Century England ° TB/1105
ALDOUS HUXLEY: Antic Hay & The Giaconda Smile. ° Introduction by Martin Green TB/3503
ALDOUS HUXLEY: Brave New World & Brave New World Revisited. ° Introduction by Martin Green TB/3501
HENRY JAMES: Roderick Hudson: a novel. Introduction by Leon Edel TB/1016
HENRY JAMES: The Tragic Muse: a novel. Introduction by Leon Edel TB/1017
ARNOLD KETTLE: An Introduction to the English Novel.
Volume I: Defoe to George Eliot TB/1011
Volume II: Henry James to the Present TB/1012
ROGER SHERMAN LOOMIS: The Development of Arthurian Romance TB/1167
JOHN STUART MILL: On Bentham and Coleridge. Introduction by F. R. Leavis TB/1070
KENNETH B. MURDOCK: Literature and Theology in Colonial New England TB/99
SAMUEL PEPYS: The Diary of Samuel Pepys. ° Edited by O. F. Morshead. Illus. by Ernest Shepard TB/1007
ST.-JOHN PERSE: Seamarks TB/2002
GEORGE SANTAYANA: Interpretations of Poetry and Religion § TB/9
HEINRICH STRAUMANN: American Literature in the Twentieth Century. Third Edition, Revised TB/1168
PAGET TOYNBEE: Dante Alighieri: His Life and Works. Edited with Intro. by Charles S. Singleton TB/1206
DOROTHY VAN GHENT: The English Novel: Form and Function TB/1050
E. B. WHITE: One Man's Meat. Introduction by Walter Blair TB/3505
MORTON DAUWEN ZABEL, Editor: Literary Opinion in America Vol. I TB/3013; Vol. II TB/3014

Myth, Symbol & Folklore

JOSEPH CAMPBELL, Editor: Pagan and Christian Mysteries. Illus. TB/2013
MIRCEA ELIADE: Cosmos and History: The Myth of the Eternal Return § TB/2050
MIRCEA ELIADE: Rites and Symbols of Initiation: The Mysteries of Birth and Rebirth § TB/1236
C. G. JUNG & C. KERÉNYI: Essays on a Science of Mythology: The Myths of the Divine Child and the Divine Maiden TB/2014
DORA & ERWIN PANOFSKY: Pandora's Box: The Changing Aspects of a Mythical Symbol. Revised Edition. Illus. TB/2021

7

JOHN GRAY: Archaeology and the Old Testament World. Illus.   TB/127

JAMES MUILENBURG: The Way of Israel: *Biblical Faith and Ethics*   TB/133

H. H. ROWLEY: The Growth of the Old Testament   TB/107

D. WINTON THOMAS, Ed.: Documents from Old Testament Times   TB/85

The Judaic Tradition

LEO BAECK: Judaism and Christianity. *Trans. with Intro. by Walter Kaufmann*   JP/23

SALO W. BARON: Modern Nationalism and Religion   JP/18

MARTIN BUBER: Eclipse of God: *Studies in the Relation Between Religion and Philosophy*   TB/12

MARTIN BUBER: The Knowledge of Man: *Selected Essays. Edited with an Introduction by Maurice Friedman. Translated by Maurice Friedman and Ronald Gregor Smith*   TB/135

MARTIN BUBER: Moses: *The Revelation and the Covenant*   TB/27

MARTIN BUBER: Pointing the Way. *Introduction by Maurice S. Friedman*   TB/103

MARTIN BUBER: The Prophetic Faith   TB/73

MARTIN BUBER: Two Types of Faith: *the interpenetration of Judaism and Christianity* °   TB/75

ERNST LUDWIG EHRLICH: A Concise History of Israel: *From the Earliest Times to the Destruction of the Temple in A.D. 70* °   TB/128

MAURICE S. FRIEDMAN: Martin Buber: *The Life of Dialogue*   TB/64

LOUIS GINZBERG: Students, Scholars and Saints   JP/2

SOLOMON GRAYZEL: A History of the Contemporary Jews   TB/816

WILL HERBERG: Judaism and Modern Man   TB/810

ABRAHAM J. HESCHEL: God in Search of Man: *A Philosophy of Judaism*   JP/7

ISAAC HUSIK: A History of Medieval Jewish Philosophy   JP/3

FLAVIUS JOSEPHUS: The Great Roman-Jewish War, *with The Life of Josephus. Introduction by William R. Farmer*   TB/74

JACOB R. MARCUS The Jew in the Medieval World   TB/814

MAX L. MARGOLIS & ALEXANDER MARX: A History of the Jewish People   TB/806

T. J. MEEK: Hebrew Origins   TB/69

C. G. MONTEFIORE & H. LOEWE, Eds.: A Rabbinic Anthology.   JP/32

JAMES PARKES: The Conflict of the Church and the Synagogue: *The Jews and Early Christianity*   JP/21

PHILO, SAADYA GAON, & JEHUDA HALEVI: Three Jewish Philosophers. *Ed. by Hans Lewey, Alexander Altmann, & Isaak Heinemann*   TB/813

HERMAN L. STRACK: Introduction to the Talmud and Midrash   TB/808

JOSHUA TRACHTENBERG: The Devil and the Jews: *The Medieval Conception of the Jew and its Relation to Modern Anti-Semitism*   JP/22

Christianity: General

ROLAND H. BAINTON: Christendom: *A Short History of Christianity and its Impact on Western Civilization. Illus.*   Vol. I TB/131; Vol. II TB/132

Christianity: Origins & Early Development

AUGUSTINE: An Augustine Synthesis. *Edited by Erich Przywara*   TB/335

ADOLF DEISSMANN: Paul: *A Study in Social and Religious History*   TB/15

EDWARD GIBBON: The Triumph of Christendom in the Roman Empire (*Chaps. XV-XX of "Decline and Fall," J. B. Bury edition*). § Illus.   TB/46

MAURICE GOGUEL: Jesus and the Origins of Christianity.° *Introduction by C. Leslie Mitton*
Volume I: *Prologomena to the Life of Jesus*   TB/65
Volume II: *The Life of Jesus*   TB/66

EDGAR J. GOODSPEED: A Life of Jesus   TB/1

ADOLF HARNACK: The Mission and Expansion of Christianity in the First Three Centuries. *Introduction by Jaroslav Pelikan*   TB/92

R. K. HARRISON: The Dead Sea Scrolls: *An Introduction* °   TB/84

EDWIN HATCH: The Influence of Greek Ideas on Christianity. § *Introduction and Bibliography by Frederick C. Grant*   TB/18

ARTHUR DARBY NOCK: Early Gentile Christianity and Its Hellenistic Background   TB/111

ARTHUR DARBY NOCK: St. Paul °   TB/104

ORIGEN: On First Principles. *Edited by G. W. Butterworth. Introduction by Henri de Lubac*   TB/310

JAMES PARKES: The Conflict of the Church and the Synagogue: *The Jews and Early Christianity*   JP/21

SULPICIUS SEVERUS et al.: The Western Fathers: *Being the Lives of Martin of Tours, Ambrose, Augustine of Hippo, Honoratus of Arles and Germanus of Auxerre. Edited and translated by F. R. Hoare*   TB/309

F. VAN DER MEER: Augustine the Bishop: *Church and Society at the Dawn of the Middle Ages*   TB/304

JOHANNES WEISS: Earliest Christianity: *A History of the Period A.D. 30-150. Introduction and Bibliography by Frederick C. Grant*   Volume I TB/53
Volume II TB/54

Christianity: The Middle Ages and The Reformation

JOHN CALVIN & JACOPO SADOLETO: A Reformation Debate. *Edited by John C. Olin*   TB/1239

JOHANNES ECKHART: Meister Eckhart: *A Modern Translation by R. B. Blakney*   TB/8

DESIDERIUS ERASMUS: Christian Humanism and the Reformation: *Selected Writings. Edited and translated by John C. Olin*   TB/1166

ÉTIENNE GILSON: Dante and Philosophy   TB/1089

WILLIAM HALLER: The Rise of Puritanism   TB/22

HAJO HOLBORN: Ulrich von Hutten and the German Reformation   TB/1238

JOHAN HUIZINGA: Erasmus and the Age of Reformation. Illus.   TB/19

A. C. MCGIFFERT: Protestant Thought Before Kant. *Preface by Jaroslav Pelikan*   TB/93

JOHN T. MCNEILL: Makers of the Christian Tradition: *From Alfred the Great to Schleiermacher*   TB/121

G. MOLLAT: The Popes at Avignon, 1305-1378   TB/308

GORDON RUPP: Luther's Progress to the Diet of Worms °   TB/120

Christianity: The Protestant Tradition

KARL BARTH: Church Dogmatics: *A Selection*   TB/95

KARL BARTH: Dogmatics in Outline   TB/56

KARL BARTH: The Word of God and the Word of Man   TB/13

RUDOLF BULTMANN et al.: Translating Theology into the Modern Age: *Historical, Systematic and Pastoral Reflections on Theology and the Church in the Contemporary Situation. Volume 2 of Journal for Theology and the Church, edited by Robert W. Funk in association with Gerhard Ebeling*   TB/252

WINTHROP HUDSON: The Great Tradition of the American Churches   TB/98

SOREN KIERKEGAARD: Edifying Discourses. *Edited with an Introduction by Paul Holmer*   TB/32

SOREN KIERKEGAARD: The Journals of Kierkegaard. ° *Edited with an Introduction by Alexander Dru*   TB/52

SOREN KIERKEGAARD: The Point of View for My Work as an Author: *A Report to History.* § *Preface by Benjamin Nelson*   TB/88